New England Warplanes

Maine, New Hampshire, Vermont, Massachusetts, Rhode Island, Connecticut

Harold A. Skaarup

iUniverse, Inc.
Bloomington

New England Warplanes

Maine, New Hampshire, Vermont, Massachusetts, Rhode Island, Connecticut

iUniverse books may be ordered through booksellers or by contacting:

iUniverse
1663 Liberty Drive
Bloomington, IN 47403
www.iuniverse.com
1-800-Authors (1-800-288-4677)

Many significant elements of the aviation history of New England have not yet been told. The information that is found within this collection of technical data, historical reports and aviation photos may not be complete or fully accurate. The story will continue to unfold as additional research turns up the missing data. This is only an interim part of the story.

ISBN: 978-1-4502-7386-2 (pbk)
ISBN: 978-1-4502-7387-9 (ebk)

Printed in the United States of America

iUniverse rev. date: 12/06/10

Dedication

This book is dedicated to the highly professional men and women of the United States Armed Services and the Canadian Forces of Northern Command (NORTHCOM), and North American Aerospace Defence Command (NORAD). Many of them have flown or serviced the military aircraft described in this handbook.

Because of their service, you and I can sleep soundly at night.

Epigraph

To control the air, aircraft bring certain characteristics which are not shared by land or sea forces – the ability to carry weapons over long ranges at great speed, the ability to concentrate rapidly large forces over a distant point, the ability to switch targets and to surprise and deceive – in a word, flexibility. John Pimlot, Strategy & Tactics of Air Warfare, Chartwell Books, Secaucus, New Jersey, 1979, p. 80.

Table of Contents

Dedication   v

Epigraph   vi

Table of Contents   vii

List of Illustrations   viii

Preface   xiii

Acknowledgements   xiv

List of Abbreviations   xv

Epigraph   xvii

Introduction   xix

Aircraft Museums and Displays in New England   1

Annex A - Technical Data on Warplanes on Display in New England   29

Annex B – New England Air National Guard and USAF Units   179

Annex C – The Collings Foundation   185

Epilogue   187

Afterword   188

Appendix A - New England Warplanes Checklist   189

Appendix B - New England Aviation Historical Societies   194

Bibliography   197

About the Author   201

Index   203

List of Illustrations

1. Alenia C-27J Spartan   29

2. Beechcraft UC-45H Expeditor   30

3. Bell UH-1N Iroquois Helicopter   31

4. Bell AH-1G Cobra Helicopter New England Air Museum   32

5. Bell OH-58D Kiowa Helicopter   34

6. Blériot XI Monoplane   35

7. Boeing-Stearman PT-17 Kaydet, New England Air Museum   36

8. Boeing B-17G Flying Fortress   37

9. Boeing B-29 Superfortress   39

10. Boeing B-29 Superfortress, New England Air Museum   39

11. Boeing KC-135R Stratotanker, New Hampshire Air National Guard   41

12. Bunce-Curtiss Pusher New England Air Museum   42

13. Burnelli CBY-3 Loadmaster, New England Air Museum   42

14. Cessna AT-17 Bobcat   44

15. Cessna T-37B Tweet   45

16. Chance Vought F4U Corsairs on deck   46

17. Chance Vought XF4U-4 Corsair, New England Air Museum   46

18. Classic Fighters Industries Inc Me 262 B-1c   48

19. Consolidated B-24J Liberator, Collings Foundation   50

20. Convair F-102A Delta Dagger   52

21. Convair F-106A Delta Dart, Massachusetts ANG   53

22. Convair C-131D Samaritan   54

23.	Curtiss JN-4D Jenny,	55
24.	Curtiss XF15C-1, Quonset Air Museum	57
25.	Dassault HU-25A Guardian, USCG	58
26.	DeHavilland D.H.100 Vampire	59
27.	DeHavilland Canada U6A Beaver, New England Air Museum	60
28.	DeHavilland Canada C7A Caribou, New England Air Museum	61
29.	Douglas C-47 Skytrain	62
30.	Douglas C-54D Skymaster	63
31.	Douglas A-26C Invader	64
32.	Douglas F4D-1 Skyray, New England Air Museum	65
33.	Douglas A4D-1 Skyhawk, New England Air Museum	66
34.	Douglas F3D-2 Skyknight	68
35.	Douglas A-3B Skywarrior, New England Air Museum	70
36.	Etrich Taube	71
37.	(Owls Head Transportation Museum photo)	71
38.	Fairchild A-10A Thunderbolt II, Massachusetts Air National Guard	72
39.	Fieseler Fi-156 Storch, Collings Foundation	73
40.	Fokker Dr.I replica, New England Air Museum	74
41.	Fokker C.IVA, Owls Head Transportation Museum	75
42.	Fouga CM 170R Magister	76
43.	Gee Bee Model A, New England Air Museum	77
44.	Gee Bee R1 Supersportster Racer, New England Air Museum	78
45.	Goodyear ZNP-K Airship car	79
46.	General Dynamics F-16A Fighting Falcon, Vermont ANG	81
47.	Grumman TBF-1 Avenger	82
48.	Grumman F6F-3 Hellcats	84
49.	Grumman HU-16E Albatross	86
50.	Grumman S2F-3 Tracker	87
51.	Grumman C-1A Trader	88
52.	Grumman E-1B Tracer, New England Air Museum	89

53.	Grumman OV-1A Mohawk	90
54.	Grumman A-6B Intruder	92
55.	Grumman F-14A Tomcat, New England Air Museum	93
56.	Gyrodyne QH-50 DASH	95
57.	Hiller OH-23G Raven Helicopter, New England Air Museum	96
58.	Hughes OH-6A Cayuse	98
59.	Kaman HH-43A Huskie Helicopter	99
60.	Kaman K-16B V-STOL	100
61.	Learjet C-21A	102
62.	Ling-Tempco-Vought A-7D Corsair II	103
63.	Lockheed L-10A Electra, New England Air Museum	104
64.	Lockheed L-1649A-98 Starliner	105
65.	Lockheed T-33A Shooting Star, New England Air Museum	106
66.	Lockheed F-94C Starfire, New England Air Museum	107
67.	Lockheed F-104A Starfighter	108
68.	Lockheed P2V-7 Neptune	109
69.	Lockheed P-3C Orion	110
70.	Lockheed Martin C-130J Super Hercules, Rhode Island Air National Guard	112
71.	Lockheed Martin F-35 Lightning II	113
72.	Martin RB-57A Canberra, New England Air Museum	116
73.	McDonnell F-101B Voodoo	117
74.	McDonnell F-4D Phantom II, Collings Foundation	118
75.	McDonnell Douglas F-15A Eagle	122
76.	McDonnell Douglas AV-8B Harriers, USMC	123
77.	MiG-15 Fagot, New England Air Museum	126
78.	MiG-17 Fresco	127
79.	Nieuport 28	128
80.	North American AT-6 Texan	129
81.	North American A-36A Apache	131

82.   North American P-51C Mustang "Betty Jane"   132

83.   North American P-51D Mustang   133

84.   North American B-25H Mitchell   134

85.   North American B-25J Mitchell, New England Air Museum   135

86.   North American F-86H Sabre, Hanscom AFB   137

87.   North American F-86H Sabre, New England Air Museum   138

88.   North American F-100D Super Sabre, Connecticut ANG   140

89.   North American F-100D Super Sabre, New England Air Museum   140

90.   North American T-28B Trojan   141

91.   North American AGM-28 Hound Dog Missile   143

92.   Northrop F-89J Scorpion   144

93.   Northrop T-38A Talon   145

94.   Piasecki/Vertol CH-21C Shawnee Helicopter   146

95.   Piper J-3 Cub   147

96.   Republic JB-2 Loon   148

97.   Republic P-47D Thunderbolt, New England Air Museum   149

98.   Republic F-84F Thunderstreak   150

99.   Republic F-105B Thunderchief   151

100. Republic RC-3 Seabee   152

101. Royal Aircraft Factory F.E.8   153

102. Royal Aircraft Factory S.E.5E   155

103. Sikorsky S-16, New England Air Museum   156

104. Sikorsky S-39B, New England Air Museum   157

105. Sikorsky VS-44-A Flying Boat, New England Air Museum   158

106. Sikorsky R-4B Hoverfly Helicopter, New England Air Museum   159

107. Sikorsky R-6 Helicopter, New England Air Museum   160

108. Sikorsky S-51 Executive Transport Helicopter   161

109. Sikorsky UH-34D Seabat Helicopter   162

110. Sikorsky SH-3H Sea King Helicopter   164

111. Sikorsky HH-52A Sea Guard Helicopter   165

112.	Sikorsky CH-54A Tarhe Helicopter, New England Air Museum	166
113.	Sikorsky UH-60 Blackhawk Helicopter	166
114.	Sikorsky HH-60J Jayhawk Helicopter	168
115.	Sopwith Pup	169
116.	SPAD XIII, with Eddie Rickenbacker	171
117.	Standard J-1	172
118.	SUD Aviation SE 210 Caravelle VIR Airliner, New England Air Museum	173
119.	Vought-Sikorsky OS2U-3 Kingfisher	174
120.	Waco YKC-S	175
121.	Wright Flyer	176
122.	Wright Model B Vin Fiz	177

The cover photo shows the Collings Foundation Consolidated B-24J Liberator "Witchcraft" banking in flight.

Preface

Military aircraft have held a special fascination for me for most of my life. My father served in the Royal Canadian Air Force (RCAF) for many years, retiring as a Warrant Officer in 1974. As a dependent member of his family, we lived at a number of bases and stations including overseas in Germany and at home in Canada during his service. As both a dependent back then, and in my current service as an Army Intelligence Officer, I have had the chance to see NATO airpower when its list of combat ready aircraft numbered in the thousands. Today, to have hundreds available at any given time would be unusual.

As a member of the Skyhawks Canadian Army Parachute Team, I've participated in a good number of air shows where a handful of former front-line warplanes may still be seen aloft. Many have been retired to museums, or they are now standing as gate guardians outside their former airbases. This is particularly true for the State of New England. These warplanes are a significant part of our military history, and they deserve to be remarked upon and remembered. For this reason, I felt there was a need for handbooks that could be used as a guide for aviation enthusiasts to point the way to where you can find surviving warplanes and perhaps take the opportunity to visit the museums and display sites where you can view them. This edition is devoted to those historic aircraft that can be found in the state of New England.

Many examples of aircraft that saw service with the United States Army Air Corps (USAAC), the United States Army Air Force (USAAF), the United States Navy (USN), the United States Marine Corps (USMC), the United States Coast Guard (USCG) and the present day United States Army have been or are currently being salvaged and preserved in New England, particularly where they are of significant historical interest.

There are unfortunate numbers of former military aircraft that saw service in the skies over the New England landscape and waters where no examples exist. Many others have been lost, but a wonderful collection of historic survivors can still be found and viewed in New England.

The purpose of this handbook is to provide a simple checklist of where the surviving military aircraft in New England are now, and to provide a photograph of each of the major types mentioned. This list is also appended with a brief summary of the aircraft presently on display within the state by location, and a bit of the warplane's history in the US military. Due to space limitations, the details contained in this handbook are limited to a selection of only those warplanes that can be found in or have a connection with the state of New England. If you are interested in other aviation books like this one, they can be found in online bookstores in the Warplane Survivor series. It is my sincere hope that the list of "New England Warplanes" will continue to grow as more of them are recovered and restored. Grant that you find this handbook useful.

Harold A. Skaarup

Acknowledgements

I would like to acknowledge and thank each and every member of the museum staffs, particularly the volunteers of the Air Museums throughout the New England states of Maine, Vermont, New Hampshire, Massachusetts, Rhode Island and Connecticut, for their patience and assistance in helping me to ensure that the data that has gone into the compilation of this handbook is as complete as it can be to the time of printing. Each and every visitor to your museums and aviation displays owes you that same appreciation, and to all of you, thank you for preserving our aviation heritage.

I extend special thanks to the archival staffs in the Library at the United States Air Force Academy in Colorado Springs, Colorado; the historians and staff of the National Museum of the United States Air Force in Dayton, Ohio; the National Museum of Naval Aviation historians and staffs in Pensacola, Florida; the National Museum of the Marine Corps, Triangle, Virginia; The Army Historical Foundation, Arlington, Virginia; The United States Coast Guard Museum, New London, Connecticut; Hunter Chaney, Collings Foundation Director of Marketing; Mike Speciale and Ron Lindlauf with the New England Air Museum; Dave Payne with the Quonset Air Museum; Aviation Photographer Tom Hildreth of Vermont, and Les Shaw with the Maine Air Museum.

Their patience and assistance has been invaluable in helping me to ensure that the data that has gone into the compilation of this handbook is as complete and accurate as it can be at the time of printing. Their support and assistance in tracking down the information pertaining to each of the individual aircraft listed here is greatly appreciated. I would like to acknowledge and thank Bob McKellar for his incredible list of "Preserved US Military Aircraft" (www.coastcomp.com/av/pres/index.html); and Michael A. Blaugher for his invaluable "Guides to Aircraft Museums in Canada and the USA." Again, I would like to extend my thanks to each and every one of you.

List of Abbreviations

AB   afterburner

AFB   Air Force Base

AGL   above ground level

AWAC   Airborne Warning and Control

BuAer   US Navy Bureau of Aeronautics

BuNo.   US Navy Bureau Number

CF   Canadian Forces

CAF   Commemorative Air Force

CoC   Chain of Command

COS   Chief of Staff

DFC   Distinguished Flying Cross

FL ANG   Florida Air National Guard

FIW   Fighter Interceptor Wing

GPS   Global Positioning System

HOTAS   hands-on throttle and stick

HUD   Heads Up Display

IFF   Identification Friend or Foe

ILS   Instrument Landing System

IRST   infrared search and track

LRDT   Long-Range Detection Team

MISREP   Mission Report

NAS   Naval Air Station

NMNA	National Museum of Naval Aviation
NMUSAF	National Museum of the United States Air Force
NORAD	North American Aerospace Command
NORTHCOM	Northern Command
RCAF	Royal Canadian Air Force
RIO	Radio Interception Officer
ROE	Rules of Engagement
RTB	Return to Base
SAC	Strategic Air Command
UAV	Unmanned Aerial Vehicle
USAAC	United States Army Air Corps
USAAF	United States Army Air Force
USAF	United States Air Force
USAFA	United States Air Force Academy
USCG	United States Coast Guard
USMC	United States Marine Corps
USN	United States Navy
USSPACECOM	United States Space Command

Epigraph

New England is a region in the north-eastern corner of the United States, bordered by the Atlantic Ocean, Canada and the state of New York, consisting of the states of Maine, New Hampshire, Vermont, Massachusetts, Rhode Island, and Connecticut. In one of the earliest European settlements in North America, Pilgrims from England first settled in New England in 1620, to form Plymouth Colony. Ten years later, the Puritans settled north of Plymouth Colony in Boston, thus forming the Massachusetts Bay Colony in 1630. In the late 18th century, the New England colonies were among the first North American British colonies to demonstrate ambitions of independence from the British Crown through the American Revolution, although they would later oppose the War of 1812 between the United States and United Kingdom of Great Britain and Ireland.

New England produced the first pieces of American literature and philosophy and was home to the beginnings of free public education. In the 19th century, it played a prominent role in the movement to abolish slavery in the United States. It was the first region of the United States to be transformed by the Industrial Revolution. Today, New England is a major center of education, high technology, insurance, medicine, and tourism. It is one of the most liberal regions in the United States, known for its universities, historic cities and landmarks, and natural beauty.

New England has the only non-geographic regional name recognized by the US federal government. It maintains a strong sense of cultural identity set apart from the rest of the country, although the terms of this identity are often contested, paradoxically combining Puritanism with liberalism, agrarian life with industry, and isolation with immigration. Wikipedia.

There are a number of outstanding military aviators who trained or served in New England, and this story is intended as a continuing record of the military heritage that needs to be remembered and preserved for all of those who have served or continue to serve in the Armed Forces on our behalf.

Introduction

For those of you who are familiar with the airspace over New England and its environs, the weather and colors of the landscape can be incredibly beautiful, particularly in the fall when the leaves change color and the foam covered waves rise up along the North East coastline's stormy shores. I live "across the line" from the state of Maine in the province of New Brunswick and have many relatives in various New England states. My ancestors first set foot in Massachusetts in 1632 and from there, a number of them came to the Saint John River in 1760. (Back then it was part of Nova Scotia until it was partitioned and the colony of New Brunswick was created on 16 August 1784). My first grandson Cole was born in Attleboro, Massachusetts on 29 November 2009, so I have good reason to visit New England often.

As an Army Officer in the Canadian Forces, it has been my privilege to serve alongside a good number of the highly professional military men and women of both our nations while serving with them at NORAD on Cheyenne Mountain in Colorado Springs and alongside them in Germany, Cyprus, Bosnia-Herzegovina and in Afghanistan. I have learned much about our common history, and this fascination has led me to write about it and to seek out the stories about the military airmen and women and the aircraft they flew that helped preserve our security when warclouds darkened our skies.

As an aviation enthusiast, I have learned over the years that a lot of other people like me have an interest in military aircraft and aviation history. Unfortunately, many retired warplanes which helped to make this history happen have completely disappeared, particularly those from the early years. Fortunately, a good number of retired warplanes continue to exist, preserved in aviation museums and in some cases as gate-guardians in a wide variety of locations throughout the New England states.

Volunteers working in many of New England's museums have been successful in preserving a good number of retired military aircraft, and many are still being sought and in some cases, being restored to flying condition again. As an aviation artist, photographer and enthusiast, I have attempted to keep track of where these warplane survivors are presently located and to make that information available to others with the same interest. For those of like mind, the purpose of this handbook is to provide a simple checklist of the classic military heritage aircraft that have been preserved in New England. The book includes a number of photographs to illustrate an example of each warplane preserved in New England wherever possible, and to list the locations in each of the six states where one can find these surviving aircraft now.

It is exciting to see the actual numbers of restored warplanes increasing as a few rare examples are being recovered from their crash sites in the wildlands, traded for, or bought back from owners who have been flying them in other countries. In a few outstanding cases, accurate replicas have been constructed and are making a welcome return appearance. One of the aims of this book is to help an enthusiast track down New England's retired warplanes and to have on hand for reference more detailed information about them such as a serial number and a museum location which might be helpful in learning the history of a particular aviator and the aircraft he or she flew. The aircraft detailed in this handbook are listed alphabetically by manufacturer, number and type. The data is also appended with a list of most of the current aircraft found in the various collections and air museums in New England.

No list can ever be completely up to date, and therefore, if a reader has additional information to add an update would be most welcome. It is my sincere hope that more of the aircraft like those listed here will one day be added to the list of survivors that have been recovered and restored. Grant that you find this checklist useful.

Major Harold A. Skaarup
Fredericton, New Brunswick

Aircraft Museums and Displays in New England

MAINE

Auburn

Auburn-Lewiston Municipal.

Lockheed L-1649A-98 Starliner (Serial No. 1018), Reg. No. N7316C, being restored at LEW for Lufthansa, with first post restoration flight planned for late 2011. Registered in Salt Lake City, Utah.

Lockheed L-1649A-98 Starliner (Serial No. 1038), Reg. No. N8083H, also being restored at LEW, with first flight planned for 2011. Registered in Salt Lake City, Utah.

Augusta, Camp Keyes

The Maine Army National Guard headquarters is located at Camp Keyes in Augusta, as is the Maine Military Historical Museum. Named for General Erasmus Darwin Keyes, a notable Civil War Union Army Corps Commander, Camp Keyes has been an integral part of Maine's rich military heritage since the 1860's and before. Camp Keyes, up to WWII, was also unofficially known to local central Maine residents as "the Muster Ground".

Bell UH-1H Iroquois (Serial No.), 112th Medical Company, Camp Keyes.

Bangor

The 112th Medical Company (Air Ambulance), Maine Army National Guard (ME ARNG), is based in Bangor, Maine. The 112th is supported with the Sikorsky UH-60 Black Hawk helicopter.

Cole Land Transportation Museum, 405 Perry Road, Bangor, ME 04401. Telephone: (207) 990-3600, (207) 990-3600, Fax: (207) 990-2653. The Cole Land Transportation Museum collects, preserves, and displays a cross section of Maine's land transportation equipment from which this and future generations will gain knowledge of the past. The Museum records and displays American military memorabilia with the aim of inspiring and challenging the young people of today to continue on in the footsteps of pioneers who have built this state and country. Website: http://www.colemuseum.org.

Bell UH-1D Iroquois (Serial No.), Vietnam Memorial. This Huey Helicopter was found at Patrick Air Force Base in Florida and served in Vietnam during the war. At one time it suffered a crash landing but was recovered and placed back into service. It was placed on 12 September 2003.

Bangor, Maine Air Museum, Maine Aviation Historical Society, PO Box 2641, 98 Maine Ave., Bangor, ME 04402. Phone: (207) 941-6757, (207) 941-6757. Website: http://www.maineairmuseum.org; Email: mam@maineairmuseum.org

The Maine Aviation Historical Society was founded to collect, document and preserve the rich aviation history of the State of Maine. Civil, commercial, military and recreational flying have always been an important part of Maine history. The Societies goal is to preserve the history of the people and events of the past. From the earliest balloon flights, to barn storming pilots to space travel, Maine has been an active player. The society's collection of artifacts and memorabilia are displayed at the Maine Air Museum at 98 Maine Avenue, Bangor, Maine. The museum is located at Bangor International Airport and as a point of interest, the museum building is a former cold war era missile assembly and maintenance facility.

Link Trainer

J-57 Jet Engine

Scorpion homebuilt helicopter

Luscombe 8A

Aircraft models

Aircraft artifacts

Bangor, Maine Air National Guard, Bangor International Airport), Bangor, ME 04401-3099. The base is the home of the 101st Air Refueling Wing (101st ARW), providing air refueling and airlift under Air Mobility Command. Since 1994, the 101st has operated the Northeast Tanker Task Force together with Pease AFB. The wing currently flies the Boeing KC-135R Stratotanker.

Bell UH-1 Iroquois (Serial No.), mounted on a pylon.

McDonnell F-101B Voodoo (Serial No. 57-0374), ex-CF-101B (Serial No. 101041), painted as 57-0377, 04, mounted on a pylon.

Northrop F-89J Scorpion (Serial No. 52-1856)

Brunswick

Naval Air Station Brunswick, 1251 Orion Street, Brunswick, ME 04011. Phone: (207) 921-2000, (207) 921-2000.

Naval Air Station Brunswick is the last, active-duty Department of Defense airfield remaining in the northeast, and is home to five active duty and two reserve squadrons. Flying Lockheed P-3C Orion long-range maritime patrol aircraft tasked by Patrol and Reconnaissance Wing Five. NAS Brunswick has 29 tenant commands, including a Reserve Lockheed P-3 Orion Squadron and a Reserve Fleet Logistics Support Squadron flying Lockheed C-130 Hercules transports. In addition, over 1,600 Naval Reservists travel from throughout New England to drill at Naval Air Reserve Brunswick, SeaBee Battalion and numerous other reserve commands.

Lockheed P2V-7 Neptune (BuNo. 131427), VP-21, located near the Main Gate.

Lockheed P-3A Orion (BuNo. 152156), located near the Main Gate.

Eliot

Curtiss Wright Jr CW1 (Serial No. 1225), Reg. No. N11818, John E. Hardy, Littlebrook Airport, Eliot, ME 03903.

Greenville

Douglas DC-3 (Serial No. 11761), Reg. No. N130Q, HBF Inc, PO Box 507, Greenville, ME 04441-0507.

Limestone

On 22 September 1950, the first nonstop transatlantic jet flight was carried out by Colonel David C. Schilling (USAF), when he flew 3,300 miles from England to Limestone, Maine, in 10 hr., 1 min.

Mars Hill

North American AGM-28B Hound Dog Missile (Serial No. 61-2213), Mars Hill Town Park.

Millinocket

Bell UH-1H Iroquois (Serial No. 64-13678), mounted on a pylon near the airport.

Owls Head

Owls Head Transportation Museum, Knox County Airport, Route 73, PO Box 277, Owls Head, ME 04854. Phone: (207) 594-4418, (207) 594-4418, Fax: (207) 594-4410.

The Owls Head Transportation Museum has one of the finest collections of pioneer-era aircraft and automobiles in the world. More than 100 historic aircraft, automobiles, bicycles, carriages and engines are on permanent display. The Aircraft Collection contains replicas and originals representing the first century of flight, from Cayley's unmanned glider (1804) to the legendary Curtiss Jenny of the barnstorming era. An outstanding collection of automobiles spans the late 19th Century and early 20th century, and includes the 1963 Prototype Mustang and a 1935 Stout Scarab (called the world's first mini-van, one of only six ever made). Website: http://www.ohtm.org. Email: info@ohtm.org.

Antoinette replica

Bellanca replica (Serial No. 2), Reg. No. N1911G

Blériot XI replica

Boeing-Stearman A75N1/PT-17 Kaydet Biplane (Serial No. 75-1795), Reg. No. N55361

Burgess-Wright F replica

Cayley Glider replica

Chanute Glider ½-scale model

Clark Biwing Ornithopter

Curtiss JN-4D Jenny (Serial No. 34094), Reg. No. N94JN

Curtiss Model D replica (Serial No. M-4), Reg. No. N1GJ

Deperdussin Gordon Bennett Racer replica (Serial No. 01), Reg. No. N78TJ

Domenjoz Glider

Etrich Taube replica

Fokker C.IVA (Serial No. 4127), Reg. No. N439FK, restoration

Fokker Dr.I Triplane replica (Serial No. 2001), Reg. No. N425FK

Henri Farman III Biplane replica

Lilienthal Glider ½-scale model

Milliken M-1 Special

Nieuport 28 replica (Serial No. C-1), Reg. No. N27226

Penaud Planaphore replica

Piper J-3C Cub (Serial No.)

Piper PA-18-150 (Serial No. 18-7809185), Reg. No. N703ES

Rhon Ranger (Serial No. 1), Reg. No. N306V

Royal Aircraft Factory F.E.8 replica (Serial No. 298), Reg. No. N928

Royal Aircraft Factory S.E.5a replica (Serial No.)

Sopwith Pup replica (Serial No. 83213), Reg. No. N5139

SPAD XIII replica (Serial No. C-1), Reg. No. N14574

Standard J-1 (Serial No. 581), Reg. No. N22581

Waco UBF-2 Biplane (Serial No. 3766), Reg. No. N13442.

Wright Flyer replica

Presque Isle

North American AGM-28 Hound Dog Missile (Serial No.), Veterans Memorial Park, Presque Isle, ME 04769.

Sugarloaf Mountain

The first transatlantic hot-air balloon flight was accomplished by Richard Branson and Per Lindstrand. They flew 2,789.6 miles from Sugarloaf Mountain, Maine, to Ireland in the hot-air balloon Virgin Atlantic Flyer from 2-4 July 1987.

NEW HAMPSHIRE

Concord

Bell UH-1 Iroquois (Serial No.), New Hampshire Army National Guard Aviation Support Facility, Medevac version mounted on a pylon.

Concord

Christa McAuliffe, a schoolteacher from Concord, was to have been the first ordinary citizen in space. She died in the horrifying space shuttle Challenger explosion on 28 January 1986, watched by her family, friends, students, and the world. McAuliffe had been selected from over 11,000 candidates for the honor of fulfilling President Reagan's plan to send a teacher into space.

McAuliffe taught social studies at a grade school in Bow, New Hampshire, before moving to Concord High School. T he personable social science teacher wore the honor of her selection with grace and dignity and applied herself to the six-month training schedule for the mission. She was fulfilling a fantasy she had harbored since the day Alan Shepard became the first American in space.

McAuliffe's genuine enthusiasm for the undertaking attracted a big following and fostered much enthusiasm for the mission. She had planned to conduct two lessons while orbiting in space and they were to be broadcast to schools across the country. As a fitting tribute to her memory, a planetarium was built in Concord following the tragedy.

East Derry

The 1957 news of Russia's Sputnik I spurred a national urgency to keep pace in the space race. The Mercury Project was being developed and in early 1959 one hundred candidates, including East Derry, New Hampshire's Alan Shepard, were chosen for astronaut training. After carefully screening the candidates, the United States' seven original astronauts were selected.

Shepard was chosen for the first manned sub-orbital flight, which took place on 5 May 1961, from Cape Canaveral, Florida. The tiny Mercury capsule was mounted on top of a Redstone rocket, which produced 78,000 pounds of thrust. The capsule was shot in an arc over the Atlantic reaching an altitude of 116 miles and speeds up to 5,180 mph. Shepard's flight of

15 minutes and 28 seconds ended when he splashed down in the Atlantic 297 miles from the launch site.

In 1986, Shepard was inducted into the National Aviation Hall of Fame at ceremonies held in Dayton, Ohio, and given the Hall of Fame's Spirit of Flight Award. Shepard retired from the Navy and wrote a book, Moon Shot, with his close friend, the late Mercury astronaut Donald "Deke" Slayton. Alan Shepard died at the age of 74 on 21 July 1998.

Holderness

North American P-51D Mustang (Serial No. 44-84753), "The Vorpel Sword", RJ-P, Reg. No. N251BP, Cielos LLC, PO Box 683, Holderness, NH 03245-0683.

Jefferson Mills

Aerial Reconnaissance in the Civil War: Thaddeus Lowe, also known as Professor T. S. C. Lowe, was an American Civil War aeronaut, scientist and inventor. He was born in 1832 in Jefferson Mills and was mostly self-educated in the fields of chemistry, meteorology, and aeronautics. With the onset of the American Civil War, Lowe offered his services as an aeronaut for the purposes of performing aerial reconnaissance on the Confederate troops on behalf of the Union Army.

Lowe's first outing was performed at First Bull Run. His performance was impressive though he had the misfortune of having to land behind enemy lines. Fortunately members of the 31st New York Volunteers found him before the enemy could discover him, but after the landing he had twisted his ankle and was not able to walk out with them. They returned to Fort Corcoran to report his position. Eventually his wife, disguised as an old hag, came to his rescue with a buckboard and canvas covers and was able to extract him and his equipment safely. In July 1861 Lowe was appointed Chief Aeronaut of the Union Army Balloon Corps by President Abraham Lincoln. Learn more about aeronauts in the Civil War. Wikipedia.

Londerry

The **New Hampshire Aviation Museum** is located at 13 East Perimeter Road in Londonderry, NH. It is housed in Manchester Airport's historic 1937 terminal building and is open Friday, Saturday and Sunday. Museum exhibits cover persons, places, events and artifacts related to the aviation history of New Hampshire. There are no full size aircraft on exhibit at this time. The Museum does present live programs covering aeronautical history and aviation related science and publishes a monthly newsletter.

Loudon

Curtiss-Robertson Robin (Serial No. 55), Reg. No. N3115L, Fred H. Dexter, PO Box 7009, Loudon, NH 03307-7009.

Manchester

Grumman C-1A Trader (BuNo. 136788), Reg. No. N6788, Martha C. MacGoldrick, 555 Canal Street, Ste 1613, Manchester, NH 03101.

North American T-28B Trojan (Serial No. 138140), Reg. No. N504GH, Tan Air Ltd, 321 Lincoln Street, Manchester, NH 03103.

Manchester, Grenier Army Air Field

Some would suggest the history of aviation in New Hampshire began with the first balloon ascension over Manchester. In the 1850's balloonist Eugene Goddard ascended over Manchester on the back of a horse.

But it was the success of Charles A. Lindbergh in crossing the Atlantic Ocean in his single-engine "Spirit of St. Louis" in 1927 that truly sparked great interest in aviation. Manchester, like most American cities, embraced the aviation phenomenon with enthusiasm.

On 25 August of that year, a loan was approved to establish an airport in the Queen City. Construction of two 1800-ft. runways began on 25 October, at what became known as Smith Field. In 1933 Amelia Earhart landed here. The airport saw gradual improvement during the 1930s, including construction of a hangar and administration building. During this time the runways were paved with asphalt. A Civilian Pilot Training program was begun in 1939 under the auspices of the Civil Aeronautics Administration. This led to a tremendous increase in flying activity at Smith Field.

On 3 October 1940, the War Department announced that the Manchester Airport would be developed as the Manchester Army Air Base (later renamed Grenier Army Air Field). Expansion efforts began immediately. The Works Project Administration (WPA) broke ground in October. During December, work began around the clock on the strengthening and expansion of the airfield's runway and tarmac areas. The rapid construction of the base was a remarkable feat. By June the empty field had been transformed into an airbase capable of housing more than 2,000 people.

During a crucial part of World War II, this airport was the primary staging base for heavy bombers en route to the war in Germany. The hospital, occupying fifteen different buildings, was designated as an Air Evacuation Center for war casualties returning from combat in Europe. Training of combat aircrew required access to a practice bomb range, and in 1941 the government acquired a plot of land near Joe English Mountain in New Boston, New Hampshire.

German submarines had begun to take their toll on Allied shipping, and Manchester-based aircraft armed with depth bombs participated in the search for the U-boats. The 13th Anti-Submarine Squadron began operating from Grenier during the summer of 1942 with bombers and a number of Lockheed aircraft.

An uncertain future lay ahead for many of the nation's wartime facilities after the war. Beginning as early as 1943, military leaders had discussed the need for the formation of National Guard and Reserve flying units following the termination of hostilities. Manchester eventually became home to units of the Air National Guard and Air Force Reserve until 1966.

The sharp-eyed traveler today can still catch a glimpse of the airport's wartime history. A group of wooden two-story barracks exists in the southwest corner of the property, not far from the UPS and FedEx facilities. Located among the tall pines in this area, these remnants of

Grenier Army Air Field house a number of small businesses. (Excerpts from Grenier Army Air Field in WWII by Tom Hildreth and the NH Aviation Museum's timeline.)

Mason

Douglas DC-3C (Serial No. 20215), Reg. No. N33623, Dakota Aviation Museum Inc, 492 Old Ashby Road, Mason, NH 03048. NORTHEAST colors.

Merrimack

Grumman OV-1A Mohawk (Serial No. 63-13128), Reg. No. N87864, Transupport Inc, 53 Turbine Way, Merrimack, NH 03054-4129.

Milton

Aviation history buffs will quickly recognize the name Alberto Santos-Dumont as Europe's premier aviator when they drive by the Santos Dumont Coffee and Ice Cream Parlor. In 1906 Dumont achieved Europe's first manned, powered, and controlled flight. He is recognized as one of the great pioneers of aviation with an array of recognizable aircraft. Fewer may realize that he funded his endeavors through his thriving coffee bean trade.

Nashua

North American P-51D Mustang (Serial No. 44-84745), Reg. No. N851D, "Crazy Horse", Doug Shultz, Stallion 51 Corp, 47 Factory Street, Nashua, NH 03061-0388. Flown out of Kissimmee, Florida.

Plaistow

Douglas C-47 Skytrain (Serial No. 45-0972), Atlantic Warbirds.

Douglas C-54D-1 Skymaster (Serial No. 42-72525), 056498, Atlantic Warbirds, "June's Behind".

Portsmouth

The Portsmouth Municipal Airport had a role to play in the Granite State's development. Airline passenger service was inaugurated on the Boston-Bangor Civil Airway in 1933, with Portsmouth designated as an auxiliary landing field on the route. During part of World War II, the airfield came under Army Air Force jurisdiction, but was not used as a military airbase.

During the 1950s, the US Air Force grew from a fledgling branch of the military to a global force. The backdrop of this growth was the arms race. The Air Force's Stratojet program produced more than 2,100 of the medium jet bombers, and SAC officials looked hard to find real estate from which to operate this burgeoning fleet. Nearness to Europe and the North Atlantic air routes made New England a prime choice for new base construction.

On 7 October 1954, the Air Force opened a liaison office in the Portsmouth area. Their sights were set on a large, sparsely populated tract of land situated between Great Bay to the west, the Piscataqua River to the north, and Portsmouth to the east. This acreage was easily reached by rail, highway and water. In December 1954 the initial phase of base construction began.

Land clearing and construction gained momentum with base activation early in 1956. The 100th Bomb Wing (BW) was activated at Portsmouth AFB. Then the 100th Air Refueling Squadron (ARS), which operated 18 tankers, was assigned to the 100th BW. Construction of a badly needed 1,100-unit housing project was begun in 1957. The importance of these and other expansions to Pease AFB became obvious on 1 July 1958, when the 509th BW arrived on permanent assignment from Roswell, New Mexico. The 100th Bomb Wing operated from Pease AFB for ten years. They performed global strategic bombardment training and air refueling missions. On 1 April 1991, after 36 years as a bomber base, Pease was closed as an active Air Force installation. (Excerpts from an article by Tom Hildreth).

Wentworth

Douglas B-26B Invader (Serial No. 44-35696N), Reg. No. N8036E, Clarke L. Hill, 1 Pond Brook Road, Wentworth, NH 03282.

Grumman/General Motors TBM-3E Avenger (Serial No. 91733), C/N 4638, Reg. No. N9590Z, Clarke L. Hill, 1 Pond Brook Road, Wentworth, NH 03282.

North American AT-6F Texan (Serial No. 121-42583), Reg. No. N4503B, Clarke L. Hill, 1 Pond Brook Road, Wentworth, NH 03282.

North American P-51C Mustang (Serial No. 42-103740), Reg. No. N309PV, Clarke L. Hill, 1 Pond Brook Road, Wentworth, NH 03282.

West Lebanon

North American T-28B Trojan (Serial No. 140020), Reg. No. N8046D, Alton Aviation LLC, PO Box 5398, West Lebanon, NH 03784-5398.

Wolfeboro

The Wright Museum of WWII History, P.O. Box 1212, 77 Center Street, Wolfeboro, NH 03894. Phone: 603/569-1212, 603/569-1212, Fax: 603/569-6326. Email: info@ wrightmuseum.org. The museum's mission is to preserve and share the stories of America's Greatest Generation for the benefit of generations to come. To fulfill this mission, the Wright Museum collects, cares for, and exhibits artifacts illustrating the heroic efforts of ordinary people living during extraordinary times.

VERMONT

Burlington

Curtiss-Wright C-46A Commando (Serial No. 32699), Reg. No. N75296, Webair Inc, Box 883, Burlington, VT 05401.

Burlington International Airport, Vermont Air National Guard

The USAF 158th Fighter Wing is based in Burlington. In July 2010, the Secretary of the Air Force announced the selection of the Vermont Air National Guard to be the first Air Guard unit to base the Lockheed Martin F-35 Lightning II. Burlington is one of two preferred choices for F-35 operations, along with Hill Air Force Base in northern Utah, while Luke Air Force Base in Arizona is the top pick for training. Final basing decisions will be made later in the ongoing selection process. Under the current production schedule, the planes could begin arriving in Vermont in the 2018 federal fiscal year. The F-35 Joint Strike Fighter is the next generation multi-purpose joint service aircraft that the Defense Department is testing for procurement for the Air Force, Navy and Marines. The Air Force version of the F-35 will serve multiple roles and will be the primary replacement for the F-16s and A-10s. Wikipedia.

Beechcraft C-45H Expeditor (Serial No. 52-10841), Reg. No. N128V

Convair F-102A Delta Dagger (Serial No. 55-3462)

Convair C-131D Samaritan (Serial No. 58-2810)

Douglas C-47B Skytrain (Serial No. 43-161141)

General Dynamics F-16A Fighting Falcon (Serial No. 78-0025)

General Dynamics F-16A Fighting Falcon (Serial No. 79-0357)

Lockheed T-33A Shooting Star (Serial No. 58-0592)

Lockheed F-94A Starfire (Serial No. 49-2517)

Martin EB-57B Night Intruder (Serial No. 52-1500)

McDonnell F-4D Phantom II (Serial No. 65-0793), 65-0712, marked with a MiG kill.

McDonnell F-4D Phantom II (Serial No. 66-0240)

Northrop F-89D Scorpion (Serial No. 53-2494), painted as 0-21883.

Camp Johnson, Vermont Militia Museum. Website: http://www.vtguard.com/museum.

The Vermont Militia Museum is dedicated to the accumulation, preservation and display of military artifacts and memorabilia spanning the history of the state of Vermont in particular and of America in general. Museum staff strive to research and present as much of the Vermont and National military history as possible. Current displays range from the Revolutionary War through the Iraqi conflict. Aircraft on display include:

Bell H-13E Sioux (Serial No.)

Bell UH-1V Iroquois (Serial No. 65-09613), Vermont ANG

Hughes OH-6A Cayuse (Serial No. 66-14390), Vermont ANG.

McDonnell F-4D Phantom II (Serial No. 65-0712), Vermont ANG.

Royal Aircraft Factory S.E.5a 7/8-scale replica (Serial No. C1096). Painted in the colors of Lt. H. J. Hank" Burden of 56 Squadron in April 1918.

Ferrisburg

Grace Hall Pugh, a native of Ferrisburg, Vermont, and Vermont's "First Lady of Aviation," took out a student permit to fly in 1932 and on 13 March 1938, she became the first licensed woman pilot in Vermont. "When I got my first license," she said, "there wasn't an Aeronautics Board. I got my license from the Motor Vehicle Department." Grace later explained, "We had to take at least ten hours of dual training and accumulate fifty hours of solo time. And there weren't the means of aerial navigation we have now. We had maps but no radios. We used the railroads and we called them our 'iron compass.' We had to stick our nose out of the cockpit to watch."

Grace summed up this early period of aviation history by saying, "The pilots were as free as birds. They landed where they dared; they took off where they could; and they flew as high or low as they pleased. There were only a few rules. Only the pilots knew what they were and they didn't always abide by them. Pilots flew by common sense and by the seats of their pants. They had few instruments, no radio, no tail wheel or brakes, and they often used automobile gas. They had to be good to survive. Recognized by their helmets and goggles, they were the daredevils of the sky and often the subjects of hero worship." Grace Pugh was one of these daredevils. Well after surviving the risk and excitement of her youth, she died in 1996. Internet: http://www.dot.state.mn.us/aero/aved/museum/aviation_firsts/vermont.html.

Hawks Mountain

On 14 June 1947, Boeing B-29A Superfortress (Serial No. 44-62228) of the 64th Bomb Squadron, Very Heavy (BVH), flown by 1st Lieutenant Robert G. Fessler crashed in bad weather while en route from Greater Pittsburgh Airport to Boston. None of the 12-man crew survived. The casualties were: 1st Lt Robert G. Fessler, Pilot; 2Lt Wilfred E. Gassett, Copilot; 2Lt Ceasare P. Fontana, Observer; MSgt D.D. Jack, Crew Chief; TSgt Paul H. Fetterhoff; TSgt Clayton K. Knight; SSgt Oliver W. Hartwell; SSgt Sylvester S. Machalac; SSgt John J. O'Toole; Cpl Harry Humphrey; Cpl Robert Clark; and PFC Robert M. Stewart.

Hyde Park

Hughes OH-6A Cayuse (Serial No. 68-17197), Veterans of Foreign Wars Post No. 7779.

Rutland

North American AT-6D Texan (Serial No. 41-34702-2), Reg. No. N80938, Nathaniel T. Natoli, 12 Green Knolls Lane, Rutland, VT 05701-3312.

North American T-6G Texan (Serial No. 51-14318-1), Reg. No. N1384Z, Nathaniel T. Natoli, 12 Green Knolls Lane, Rutland, VT 05701-3312.

Shelburne

Fouga CM 170R Magister (Serial No. FM30), Reg. No. N101TD, Dennis R. Demers, 958 Webster Road, Shelburne, VT 05482-6521.

MASSACHUSSETTS

Becket

North American AT-6 Texan (Serial No. 59-1938), Reg. No. N6665Y, Charles F. Andrews, PO Box 145, Becket, MA 01223-0145.

Bedford

North American AT-6G Texan (Serial No. 44-81687-A), Reg. No. N164US, T64 US Inc, c/o Dilltec Inc Civil Air Terminal, 200 Hanscom Drive, Bedford, MA 01730.

Bedford, Hanscom AFB, located 17-miles northwest of Boston.

North American F-86H Sabre (Serial No. 53-1328), mounted on a pylon.

Beverly

Bell UH-1M Iroquois (Serial No. 65-09560), Veterans of Foreign Wars Post No. 545.

North American SNJ-5 Texan (Serial No. 8819555), Reg. No. N6410D, Deschenes Construction Co Ltd, 163 Cabot Street, Beverly, MA 01915.

Boston

Museum of Science, Science Park, Boston, MA 02114-1099. Phone: (617) 723-2500, (617) 723-2500. The Museum of Science is a Boston, Massachusetts landmark, located in Science Park, a plot of land spanning the Charles River. Along with over 500 interactive exhibits, the Museum features a number of live presentations throughout the building everyday, along with shows at the Charles Hayden Planetarium and the Mugar Omni IMAX theater, the only domed IMAX screen in New England. Various space exhibits are on display.

The MIT Daedalus human-powered aircraft hangs in the entry lobby of the museum as does Decavitator, MIT's human-powered high-speed boat. The MIT Aeronautics and Astronautics Department's Daedalus was a human-powered aircraft that, on 23 April 1988, flew a distance of 71.5 mi (115.11 km) in 3 hours, 54 minutes, from Iraklion on the island of Crete to the island of Santorini. The flight holds official FAI world records for distance and duration for human-powered aircraft. The craft was named after the mythological inventor of aviation, Daedalus.

Boxford

North American SNJ-5 Texan (Serial No. 84979), Reg. No. N7296C, James M. Baker, 9 Inverness Circle, Boxford, MA 01921-1931.

Cape Cod

USCG Air Station, Race Point Beach, Cape Cod, MA.

U.S. Coast Guard Air Station Cape Cod (ASCC), with its four helicopters and four jets, is the only Coast Guard Aviation facility in the northeast. As such, ASCC is responsible for the waters from New Jersey to the Canadian border. Centrally located at the Massachusetts Military Reservation on Cape Cod, ASCC maintains the ability to launch a helicopter and/or jet within

30 minutes of a call, 365 days-a-year, 24 hours-a-day, and in nearly any weather conditions. U.S. Coast Guard Air Station Cape Cod is located at Otis Air Force Base in Cape Cod, Massachusetts.

Dassault HU-25A Guardian (Serial No.)

Grumman HU-16E Albatross (Serial No.)

Sikorsky HH-60J Jayhawk Helicopter (Serial No.)

Headquarters MassachusettsMilitary Reservation (MMR), Cape Cod, MA.

The MRR is a military training facility located on the upper western portion of Cape Cod, immediately south of the Cape Cod Canal in Barnstable County, MA.

Lockheed T-33A Shooting Star (Serial No.)

Fall River

Battleship Cove Heritage Park, Fall River, MA 02721. Phone: (508) 678-1100, (508) 678-1100. Fax: (508) 674-5597. Website: http://www.battleshipcove.org. Email: battleship@ battleshipcove.org .

Battleship Cove, located in Fall River, Massachusetts, is a nonprofit maritime museum and war memorial that traces its origins to the wartime crew of the World War II battleship USS *Massachusetts*. This dedicated veterans group was responsible for the donation of the decommissioned vessel from the Navy and its subsequent public display in Fall River, Massachusetts. The site is located at the confluence of the Taunton River and Mount Hope Bay, an arm of Narragansett Bay. Battleship Cove lies partially beneath the Braga Bridge and adjacent to Fall River Heritage State Park, at the heart of Fall River's waterfront. The battleship forms a small cove which serves as a protected harbor for pleasure craft during the summer months. The Fall River Yacht Club maintains a dock nearby. Wikipedia.

An Aircraft Model Collection is on display as well as the following aircraft:

Bell UH-1M Iroquois (Serial No. 66-60609), mounted on a pylon.

Bell AH-1S Cobra (Serial No. 70-16038)

North American T-28C Trojan (Serial No. 140454), 765.

Vought OS2U-2 Kingfisher (Serial No. 5909), was on loan from the NASM and placed on display on the USS Massachusetts for many years (1960s to 1980s) until it was returned to the NASM. It is now on display in the Udvar-Hazy Museum, Dulles Airport, Virginia.

Falmouth

Massachusetts Air National Guard, 102nd Fighter Wing, **Otis ANGB**, 158 Reilly Street,

Otis Air National Guard Base, Falmouth, MA 02542-5001. Phone: (508) 968-4667 begin_of_the_skype_highlighting, (508) 968-4667.

Lockheed T-33A Shooting Star (Serial No. 53-5960)

McDonnell Douglas F-15A Eagle (Serial No. 76-0040)

North American F-86H Sabre (Serial No. 53-1377)

North American F-100D Super Sabre (Serial No. 56-2995), mounted on a pylon.

Republic F-84F Thunderstreak (Serial No. 52-6382)

Fitchburg

Douglas C-47B Skytrain (Serial No. 45-972), New England Escadrille, Fitchburg Municipal Airport.

Freetown

Bell AH-1 Cobra (Serial No. 79-23240), Veterans of Foreign Wars, Post No. 6643.

Nantucket

North American SNJ-5 Texan (Serial No. 88-16388), Reg. No. N6436D, William F. McGrath Jr, 10 Sheep Commons Lane, Nantucket, MA 02554-2908.

Plymouth

Curtiss Wright Jr CW1 (Serial No. 1146), Reg. No. N10968, KEF Enterprises, PO Box 929, Plymouth MA 02362-0929.

Somerville

Boeing-Stearman PT-17 Kaydet (Serial No. 75-8438), Reg. No. N727A, Stearman Associates Inc., 13 Kingston Street, Somerville, MA 02144.

South Weymouth

North American SNJ-5 Texan (Serial No. 8814025), Reg. No. N64260D, Thomas F. Twomey, 1106 Main Street, South Weymouth, MA 02190.

Springfield

Science Museum, 236 State Street, Springfield, MA 01103. Phone: (413) 263-6800, (413) 263-6800. Miller Zeta (Serial No. 1), Reg. No. NX1331, 1937 Racing aircraft.

Stow

The Collings Foundation, 137 Barton Road, Riverhill Farm, Stow, MA 01775-1529. Phone: (978) 562-9182, (978) 568-8924. Mail: The Collings Foundation, P.O. Box 248, Stow, MA 01775. Email: info@collingsfoundation.org; hchaney@collingsfoundation.org. Website: http://www.collingsfoundation.org/menu.htm.

The Collings Foundation was founded in 1979 "to organize and support 'living history' events that enable Americans to learn more about their heritage through direct participation" and adopted aviation-related events, such as air shows and barnstorming, in the mid-eighties. It has since recovered and restored 20 historically-significant aircraft from the Early-Aviation, World War II, Korean War, and Vietnam War eras--from a 1909 Bleriot XI to a McDonnell-Douglas F-4D Phantom. The following aircraft are currently held in the collection, although not all are on site in Stow. The aircraft may only be viewed on designated open house days as advertised and at airshows.

Bell UH-1E Iroquois Helicopter (Serial No. 153762), Reg. No. N911KK, Houston, Texas.

Blériot XI (1909), Stow.

Boeing-Stearman A75N1/PT-17 Kaydet (Serial No. 75-3745), Reg. No. N55171, Stow.

Boeing B-17G Flying Fortress (Serial No. 44-83575), Reg, No. N93012, (Serial No. 32264), painted as 42-31909, "Nine-O-Nine", New Smyrna Beach, Florida.

Chance Vought F4U-5NL Corsair (Serial No. 124692C), Reg. No. N45NL, New Smyrna Beach, Florida.

Cessna AT-17 Bobcat (Serial No. 3696), Reg. No. N6HS, Stow.

Classic Fighters Industries Inc Messerschmitt Me 262 B-1c reproduction (Serial No. 501241), Reg. No. N262AZ, New Smyrna Beach, Florida.

Consolidated B-24J Liberator (Serial No. 44-44052), Reg. No. N224J, "Witchcraft", painted as 440973, New Smyrna Beach, Florida.

Douglas A-26C Invader (Serial No. 44-35696), "My Mary Lou", Uvalde, Texas (being restored).

Douglas F4D-1 Skyray (Serial No. 65-0749), Reg. No. N749CF, Stow.

Fieseler Fi-156-C1 Storch (Serial No. 4621), Reg. No. N156FC, Stow.

Fokker Dr.I Triplane replica (Serial No. DR1HB), Reg. No. N14TJ, Stow.

Grumman/General Motors/Eastern TBM Avenger (Serial No.), Stow.

Grumman S2F-1 Tracker (Serial No. 133242), Reg. No. N31957, Houston, Texas.

Lockheed T-33A Shooting Star (Serial No. 51-9129), Reg. No. N648, Stow.

Lockheed T-33A Shooting Star (Serial No. 51-6953), Houston, Texas.

McDonnell Douglas TA-4J Skyhawk (Serial No. 153524), Reg. No. N524CF, Houston, Texas.

McDonnell Douglas F-4D Phantom (Serial No. 67-463), Houston, Texas, painted as the fighter flown by Steve Ritchie and Chuck DeBellevue fighter during the Vietnam War.

North American AT-6F Texan (Serial No.), Stow.

North American A-36A Apache (Serial No. 15956), Reg. No. N4607V, New Smyrna Beach, Florida, being restored.

North American TP-51C Mustang (Serial No. 42-103293), Reg. No. N251MX, "Betty Jane", New Smyrna Beach, Florida.

North American B-25N Mitchell (Serial No. 44-28932), Reg. No. N3476G, "Tondelayo", painted as 02168, New Smyrna Beach, Florida.

Wright Model B Vin Fiz (1911 Replica), Stow.

Westfield

Massachusetts Air National Guard, Barnes Air National Guard Base, 175 Falcon Drive, Westfield, MA 01085-1482. Phone: (508) 968-4667, (508) 968-4667. 104th Fighter Wing.

Fairchild Republic A-10A Thunderbolt II (Serial No. 79-0100), painted as 78-648, mounted on a pylon.

Lockheed T-33A Shooting Star (Serial No.)

North American F-100D Super Sabre (Serial No. 56-3008), mounted on a pylon in a Memorial Park.

Republic F-84F Thunderstreak (Serial No. 51-19480)

Westover

The first transatlantic helicopter flight was carried out by Captain Vincent H. McGovern and 1st Lieutenant Harold W. Moore when they piloted two Sikorsky H-19s from Westover to Prestwick, Scotland (3,410 mi). The trip was made in five stops, with a flying time of 42 hr., 25 min, from 15-31 July 1952.

Worcester

Bell AH-1 Cobra (Serial No. 70-16096), Veterans of Foreign Wars, Chapter No. 554.

RHODE ISLAND

Bristol

North American SNJ-5 Texan (Serial No. 43936), Reg. No. N241F, Frank J. Govednik III, 2 Chester Ave, Bristol, RI 02809-1416.

North Kingstown, Quonset Air Museum, 488 Eccleston Ave., North Kingstown, RI 02852. Tel: 401-294-9540, Fax: 401-294-9887. Open May through September daily 10 AM to 5 PM, October through April Thursday through Monday 10 AM to 3 PM or by appointment. Directions: From the south: Route 95 north to RI exit 8A. Immediately go all the way across Route 2 and then go left on Route 401. Go ¼ mile to Route 4 south. Take Route 4 south exit 7, and stay to the left towards Route 403 to Quonset/Davisville (Devil's Foot Road). Go one mile, and then go through the underpass. Bear right and follow Roger Williams Way 2 miles (5 traffic lights) past General Dynamics on the right. Eccleston Road will be on the left. From the north: Route 95 south to RI exit 9 Route 4 south (left hand exit). Follow the directions from exit 7 above.

Website: http://www.theqam.org. Email: Quonsetairmuseum@gmail.com.

Founded in September 1992, the Quonset Air Museum was dedicated as an educational facility whose current mission is to preserve and interpret Rhode Island's aviation Heritage. The museum's collection includes military vehicles, missiles, aircraft and over 5000 smaller aviation artifacts. An extensive archive of books, magazines, manuals, photos, documents and blueprints is preserved within the Quonset Air Museum. The collection represents Rhode Island's achievement in private, commercial, and military aviation.

The museum occupies Painting Hangar No. 488 located at what was once the Quonset Naval Air Station. This 50,000 sq. ft. facility is one of only three existing specialized wood and brick hangars built during WWII. Current restoration projects the Walt Schiebe Restoration Area include a TBM Avenger, F6F Hellcat, and an F3D Skyknight. Other notable aircraft in the collection are the last surviving Curtis XF15C mixed propulsion prototype and a twin tail C1A COD. This one of a kind aircraft was the precursor to the E-1 Electronic Counter Measure aircraft and has the distinction of being the last aircraft to fly from Quonset Naval Air Station upon its closure in 1974. The museum houses several Vietnam era combat aircraft as well as the legendary F-14 Tomcat. Aircraft in the museum's collection:

Aero Commander 680 (Serial No. 680-432-105), Reg. No. N2100M

Aero L-29 Delphin (Serial No. 490925)

Antonov AN-2TD Colt (Serial No. 1G2619)

Bell UH-1B Iroquois (Serial No. 64-14021)

Bell UH-1H Iroquois (Serial No. 64-13492)

Bell UH-1H Iroquois (Serial No. 65-09560)

Bell UH-1H Iroquois (Serial No. 65-09996)

Bell UH-1M Iroquois (Serial No. 66-15083), served with the 57th Aviation Company in Vietnam as a gunship.

Bell AH-1S Cobra (Serial No. 66-15317), donated by the Rhode Island Army National Guard.

Bell OH-58A Kiowa (Serial No.)

Cessna T-37B Tweet (Serial No. 66-7983)

Curtiss XF15C-1 (BuNo. 01215)

DeHavilland D.H.100 Vampire (Serial No.), ex-Swiss Air Force

Douglas F3D-2Q Skyknight (BuNo. 124620)

Douglas A-4C Skyhawk (BuNo. 147790)

Douglas A-4F Skyhawk (BuNo. 155027), Blue Angels colors.

McDonnell Douglas A-4M Skyhawk (BuNo. 158148), SD-8, 1st A-4M built

Eaglet (Serial No.)

Fouga CM 170R Magister (Serial No.)

General Motors TBM-3E Avenger (BuNo. 53914)

Grumman F6F-5 Hellcat (Serial No. 70185), being restored.

Grumman F6F ¾-scale Hellcat (Serial No. 1), Reg. No. N6FN, 3, built by Al Sparling.

Grumman A-6B Intruder (BuNo. 155629), AG-501

Grumman C-1A Trader (BuNo. 136780), cockpit only

Grumman C-1A Trader (BuNo. 136792), converted to prototype E-1

Grumman F-14B Tomcat (BuNo. 162591), AD-260, C/N 513

Hughes OH-6A Cayuse (Serial No. 67-16265)

Hughes OH-6A Cayuse (Serial No. 67-16279)

Hughes OH-6A Cayuse (Serial No. 67-16570)

Ling-Tempco-Vought A-7D Corsair II (Serial No. 75-0408)

Lockheed T-33A Shooting Star (Serial No. 53-6091)

Lockheed TV-2 Shooting Star (BuNo. 137936)

Lockheed P-2E Neptune (BuNo. 131403), C/N 426-5272

McDonnell F-4A Phantom II (BuNo. 148252)

McDonnell F-4B Phantom II (BuNo. 148371)

McDonnell Douglas AV-8C Harrier (BuNo. 158710)

North American T-28S Fennec (Serial No. 51-3529)

Northrop T-38A Talon (Serial No. 63-8197)

Mikoyan-Gurevich MiG-15 Fagot (Serial No.)

Mikoyan-Gurevich MiG-17F/LIM 6bis Fresco C (Serial No. 1FO326)

Piasecki/Vertol CH-21C Shawnee (Serial No. 51-15892)

Sikorsky SH-3H Sea King Helicopter (Serial No. 149738)

Stinson L-9B Voyager (Serial No.)

Providence

Roy Knabenshue was a builder and exhibitor of dirigibles of his own design. His outstanding contributions to aviation include making balloon flights and being the first to pilot a steerable balloon. He also piloted the first successful American dirigible. In addition, he also became well-known by building US Army observation balloons during World War I.

Roy turned to ballooning to supplement his income because wages for a telephone man were not enough to support his large family. Because of his family's standing in the community and their embarrassment with his ballooning venture, he changed his name to "Professor Don Carlos" during the early days of his flying.

His first successful dirigible with constructed with an engine designed and built by Glenn Curtiss, in 1904. The second was built in August of 1905. He flew it over New York's Central Park, and stopped all traffic with the unusual sight.

In 1907 Knabenshue's third dirigible was completed and flown in exhibitions at Providence, Rhode Island; Hartford, Connecticut; Worchester, Massachusetts and London, Ontario. In the latter part of the year Knabenshue began building a three-man airship designed to carry passengers, and also for exhibition work.

By late 1909, public interest began to turn to airplanes and the Wright Brothers decided to put on flight exhibitions. They employed Knabenshue to plan exhibitions for the Wright Fliers being trained at a flying school in Montgomery, Alabama opened in March 1910, now known as Maxwell Field.

Knabenshue arranged for the first exhibition at the Indianapolis Speedway in June 1910. In July, the team performed at Atlantic City and in August the team made exhibition flights along the Chicago Lake Front. In October the team also participated in the Belmont Park International Air Meet.

CONNECTICUT
Brookfield

North American SNJ-5 Texan (Serial No. 43958), Reg. No. N3958, Aries Aviation and Development Co., 26 Obtuse Road South, Brookfield, CT 06804-3626.

Canton Center

North American T-6G Texan (Serial No. 49-3210), Reg. No. N8335H, Paul L Guilmette, PO Box 13, Canton Center, CT 06020-0013.

Chester

Chance Vought F4U-4 Corsair (Serial No. 9484), Reg. No. N5222V, Craig M. McBurney, PO Box 569, Chester, CT 06412-0569.

Bridgeport, Igor Sikorsky Memorial Airport

Goodyear FG-1D Corsair (Serial No. 92460)

Danbury

Grumman/General Motors TBM-3E Avenger (Serial No. 91388), Reg. No. N9564Z, Missionair Inc, 81 Kenosia Ave, Danbury, CT 06810-7361.

East Hampton

Bell AH-1 Cobra (Serial No. 66-15325), Veterans of Foreign Wars Post No. 5095.

Fairfield

The first civilian helicopter rescue took place in November 1945, off Fairfield, Connecticut. An Army Sikorsky R-5 was flown by Sikorsky pilot Dimitry "Jimmy" Viner to rescue two men from an oil barge that was breaking up on Penfield Reef during a storm.

Farmington

Douglas DC-3 (Serial No. 13321), Reg. No. N96BF, Turbo Power and Marine Systems Inc, 308 Farmington Ave, Farmington, CT 06032.

Greenwich

Douglas DC-3C-S1C3G (Serial No. 19677), Reg. No. N1944A, Wings Venture Ltd, c/o Gilbride Tusa Last and Spellane, 31 Brookside Drive, PO Box 658, Greenwich, CT 06836.

Groton

The US Navy **Submarine Force Library and Museum**, located on the Thames River near Groton, Connecticut, is the only submarine museum managed exclusively by the US Navy, which makes it a repository for many special submarine items of national significance, including USS *Nautilus* (SSN-571). Visitors may take a 30-minute self-guided audio tour of the submarine. Website: http://www.ussnautilus.org.

Established in 1955, the museum was originally operated by the Electric Boat Division of General Dynamics and was known solely as the Submarine Library. In 1964, it was donated to the US Navy and moved to its current location along the Thames. It received its official title in 1969. Hoping to convince the U.S. Navy to donate the Nautilus to the museum, in 1984 the "Connecticut Nautilus Committee" was formed to raise funds for an improved museum. A new, 14,000-square-foot facility was built with funding from the state, individuals and businesses, opening in 1986. In late 1997 the Committee decided to start planning and raising funds for a 13,465-square-foot addition to the museum building. Fundraising started the next year, and construction project ran from 1998 to early 2000. The new addition was officially opened to the public on 28 April 2000 "in conjunction with the Centennial Celebration of the United States Submarine Force", according to the museum.

The museum has 33,000 artifacts, including the first nuclear-powered submarine in the world, the USS *Nautilus*. Launched in 1955 and decommissioned in the 1980s, the submarine had travelled under the polar ice cap and reached the North Pole during the Cold War. Also at the museum is a replica of David Bushnell's *Turtle*, built in 1775 and the first submarine used in combat; midget submarines from World War II; working periscopes, a submarine control room, models of submarines, and the Explorer, an early U.S. research submarine.

In addition to its large collection of submarines and related objects, the museum also has a library with around 20,000 documents and 30,000 photos related to the history of submarine development. The library also includes 6,000 books related to the field of submarine history, including a 1551 text on submarine retrieval, and an original 1870 copy of Jules Verne's 20,000

Leagues Under the Sea (the museum also has a model of the fictional ship). Documents in the collection include notes and calculations by John Holland for the Navy's first submarine, "one-of-a-kind artifacts from World War I and World War II", and the submarine library collections of both Electric Boat Corporation and the U.S. Navy. Wikipedia.

New Milford

North American AT-6G Texan (Serial No. 49-3391A), Reg. No. N2878G, Stewart Nicolson, 16 Crescent Lane RR 3, New Milford, CT 06776.

North Brantford

North American SNJ-5 Texan (Serial No. 121-42110), Reg. No. N8218E, Richard S. Pollock, 17 Marjorie Drive, North Brantford, CT 06471-1014.

Pawcatuck

Grumman TBM-3E Avenger (Serial No. 85650), C/N 2469, Reg. No. N452HA, Simmons Aviation Services Ltd., 353 Greenhaven Road, Pawcatuck, CT 06379-2093.

North American AT-6A Texan (Serial No. 44-786199), Reg. No. N7649S, Mark A. Simmons, 353 Greenhaven Road, Pawcatuck, CT 06379-2093.

Prospect

Bell TAH-1F Cobra (Serial No. 67-15809), C/N 20473, Veterans of Foreign Wars Post No. 8075.

Stamford

Douglas A-26B Invader (Serial No. 28048), Reg. No. N500MR, ex USAF (Serial No. 44-34769), K, Sealink Aviation Ltd., 300 First Stamford Place 2E, Stamford, CT 06902-6765.

Stratford

National Helicopter Museum. The Museum is located at the Stratford, Connecticut Eastbound Railroad Station, at 2480 Main Street. Hours: The Museum is seasonal, and is open from Memorial Day weekend until the middle of October. Regular hours are Wednesday thru Sunday from 1 PM until 4 PM. Special tours can also be arranged by contacting the Museum at 203-375-8857/-375-8857, or 203-767-1123203-767-1123.

Directions to the Museum: Traveling on Interstate I-95 from the south (New York), take Stratford Exit 32, continue 2 blocks to Main Street, then left onto Main Street for 3 blocks. The Museum is on the right at the train station. Traveling on Interstate I-95 from the north (New Haven), take Stratford Exit 32, then left at the light for 2 blocks to Main Street. Then left onto Main Street for 3 blocks. The Museum is on the right at the train station. If traveling via the Merritt Parkway, take Exit 53 and go south on Main Street for about 4 miles to the train station.

The National Helicopter Museum is a non-profit museum focused on the history of the helicopter and aviation industry around Stratford, Connecticut. The museum was founded in 1983 by Dr. Raymond Jankowich and Robert McCloud. The museum is housed in the eastbound railroad station building of the Stratford station of the Metro-North Railroad. The National Helicopter Museum collects and exhibits images and objects related to the long history of the aviation and helicopter industry in Stratford, the home of Sikorsky Aircraft Company. Sikorsky Aircraft built the experimental helicopters developed by inventor Igor Sikorsky. The National Helicopter Museum traces the evolution of the rotary wing from early predecessors like the boomerang and Chinese tops to designs by Leonardo da Vinci and George Cayley to early motorized experiments to modern helicopters of today.

The Museum contains hundreds of photographs and models tracing the history of the helicopter both in the United States and around the world. An airport and seaplane base built in Stratford in the 1920's brought Igor Sikorsky to the area to build his flying boats. Then Sikorsky flew his US300 Helicopter on 14 September 1939 in Stratford and produced many helicopters and rotary wing aircraft from that time. Stratford is the birthplace of the American helicopter industry.

Igor Sikorsky's first helicopter success in Stratford is documented as well as his subsequent productions. Also displayed are the small gas turbine engines developed locally by Dr. Anselm Franz at Avco Lycoming which power such helicopters as the Bell Helicopter UH-1 Iroquois or "Huey" and the Boeing CH-47 Chinook. Other exhibits include information on tilt rotor development; current photos and models of aircraft by Bell, Boeing, Kaman Aircraft, Robinson Helicopter, and Sikorsky; and a working cockpit of the Sikorsky S-76 helicopter. Wikipedia.

Another exhibit features Stratford's other helicopter: the Bendix helicopter. It was the creation of Vincent Bendix, the inventor of the auto self-starter, four-wheel brakes, and carburetors. He was the developer of the Bendix air races and trophy. His helicopter models were based on the coaxial design as demonstrated in films of the 1940s. Bendix's sudden death stymied further development. The firm was purchased by Gyrodyne of Long Island who continued development and created Navy helicopter drones and mini rotary craft for individuals. *(Information courtesy of the National Helicopter Museum).*

Waterbury

Bell AH-1G Cobra (Serial No. 70-15986)

Windsor Locks

Douglas DC-3 (Serial No. 26458), Reg. No. N74844, New England Propeller Service Inc, Bldg 213, Bradley International Airport, Windsor Locks, CT 06096.

Douglas DC-3-G202A (Serial No. 6314), Reg. No. N165LG, Connecticut Aeronautical Historical Association Inc, Bradley International Airport, Windsor Locks, CT 06096.

Windsor Locks, Bradley International Airport

Bradley International Airport in Windsor Locks, Connecticut, was named in honor of the late Lt. Eugene M. Bradley of the 57th Fighter Group. In commemoration, the field on which he lost his life was officially designated, on 20 January 1942, "Army Air Base, Bradley Field, Connecticut." Lt. Bradley's name has remained on the airport in spite of attempts in the past to change it. Today it is known as Bradley International Airport, the principal airport in Connecticut.

Windsor Locks, **New England Air Museum**, Bradley International Airport, Windsor Locks, CT 06096. Phone: (860) 623-3305, Fax: (860) 627-2820. Email: staff@neam.org.

Open 7 days a week year round, 10 AM to 5 PM. Closed on Thanksgiving, Christmas and New Year's Day. The New England Air Museum is situated at Bradley International Airport in Windsor Locks, Connecticut midway between Hartford, Connecticut and Springfield, Massachusetts. Take I-91 North or South to Exit 40 (Rte 20). Take the second right exit off Route 20 and turn right onto Route 75 North. Continue for 2.8 miles. Take left at Museum sign onto Perimeter Road for approximately 1.5 miles. The Museum will be on the right.

The Museum is situated in three large display buildings consisting of more than 75,000 square feet of exhibit space. In fair weather, the outside storage yard is available for touring as well. It is recommended that you allow at least 1 1/2 hours for your visit, though hard-core aviation and history enthusiasts will want to spend several hours viewing not only our aircraft and engine displays, but our many fascinating exhibits on such diverse topics as the Lafayette Escadrille, WWII Combat Gliders, the History of Sikorsky Aircraft, Early French Aviation, a History of Air Mail, the Tuskegee Airmen, Airships, and many others. Exhibits include the following aircraft and equipment:

Aircraft

Aeronca 50 Chief (Serial No. C1018), Reg. No. NC21070

Bell 47D Sioux Helicopter (Serial No.)

Bell AH-1G Cobra Helicopter (Serial No. 70-15981)

Bell UH-1B Iroquois Helicopter (Serial No. 62-12550)

Benson B-8M Gyrocopter (Serial No. JC-1), Reg. No. N3112

Blanchard Balloon Basket

Blériot XI Monoplane (Serial No.), original

Boeing-Stearman PT-17 Kaydet (Serial No.)

Boeing B-29A Superfortress (Serial No. 44-61975)

Bunce-Curtiss Pusher (Serial No. 1)

Burnelli CBY-3 Loadmaster (Serial No.)

Chalais-Meudon Dirigible Nacelle (Serial No.)

Chance Vought XF4U-4 Corsair (Serial No. 80759)

Chanute Herring Glider (Serial No.)

Curtis XFC15-1 (Serial No. 01215)

DeHavilland Canada C-7A Caribou (Serial No. 62-4188)

DeHavilland Canada DHC-2/U-6A Beaver (Serial No. 57-2570)

Douglas A-26C Invader (Serial No. 43-22499), Reg. No. N86481

Douglas A-3B Skywarrior (BuNo. 142246)

Douglas A4D-1 Skyhawk (BuNo. 142219)

Douglas DC-3 (Serial No. 6314), Reg. No. N165LG

Douglas F-6 Skyray (BuNo. 134836)

Fairchild-Republic A-10A Thunderbolt II (Serial No. 79-0173)

Fokker Dr.I Triplane replica (Serial No. 1)

Gee Bee Model A (Serial No.), Reg. No. N901K

Gee Bee Model E (Serial No. 4), Reg. No. N856Y

Gee Bee R-1 Super Sportster Racer, replica (Serial No. R-1), Reg. No. N2100

Goodyear ZNP-K Airship car

Great Lakes 2T-1A Sportster replica (Serial No. 6931K-420), Reg. No. N107C

Grumman E-1B Cockpit Simulator

Grumman E-1B Tracer (Serial No. 147217)

Grumman F6F-5 Hellcat (Serial No. 79192)

Grumman HU-16E Albatross (Serial No. 51-7228), USCG 7228

Grumman F-14B Tomcat (BuNo. 162926)

Gyrodyne QH-50 DASH (Serial No. DS1258)

Heath Parasol (Serial No.)

Hiller OH-23G Raven (Serial No. 62-23812)

Hughes OH-6A Cayuse (Serial No. 67-16127)

Kaman HH-43A Huskie (Serial No. 60-0289)

Kaman K-16B V-STOL (Serial No.)

Kaman K-225 (Serial No.), Reg. No. N401A, the oldest surviving Kaman-built aircraft.

Laird LC-RW300 Solution racer (Serial No. 192), Reg. No. N10538

Ling-Tempco-Vought A-7D Corsair II (Serial No. 69-6201)

Link ANT-18 Flight Trainer w/Console

Lockheed L-10A Electra (Serial No. 1052), Reg. No. NC14262

Lockheed TV-2 Shooting Star (Serial No. 138048)

Lockheed F-94C Starfire (Serial No. 51-13575)

Lockheed F-104A Starfighter (Serial No. 56-0901)

Marcoux-Bromberg R-3 Special (Serial No. A-1), Reg. No. N14215

Martin RB-57A Canberra (Serial No. 52-1488)

MB-22 F-100 Cockpit Simulator

McDonnell-Douglas F-4D Phantom II (Serial No. 66-0269)

Mead Rhone Ranger replica (Serial No. 1)

Mikoyan-Gurevich MiG-15 Fagot (Serial No. 83277)

Monett Monerai S sailplane (Serial No. 22), Reg. No. N32WS

Mosquito 166 Hang Glider (Serial No.)

Nicks Special LR-1A (Serial No. 11), Reg. No. L11ZZ

Nixon Special (1918 homebuilt)

North American AGM-28 Hound Dog Missile (Serial No.)

North American B-25H Mitchell (Serial No. 43-04999)

North American F-86F Sabre (Serial No. 113371)

North American F-100A Super Sabre (Serial No. 52-5761)

Northrop F-89J Scorpion (Serial No. 52-1896)

Pioneer International Aircraft Flightstar MC (Serial No. MC 658), Reg. No. N54209

Piper J3L-65 Cub (Serial No. 5374), Reg. No. N31091

Pratt-Read PR-G1 glider (Serial No. 31561), Reg. No. N5346G

Rearwin 8135 Cloudster (Serial No. 825), Reg. No. N25549

Republic F-105B Thunderchief (Serial No. 57-5778)

Republic JB-2 Loon

Republic P-47D Thunderbolt (Serial No. 45-49458)

Republic RC-3 Seabee (Serial No.)

Rutan Quickie (Serial No. 175), Reg. No. N175HM

Rutan VARI EZE (Serial No. 0003), Reg. No. N477CM

Sikorsky S-16 replica (Serial No. 1)

Sikorsky S-39B (Serial No.), Reg. No. NC803W, the oldest surviving Sikorsky aircraft.

Sikorsky VS-44-A Flying Boat (Serial No. 4402), Reg. No. N41881

Sikorsky R-4B Hoverfly Helicopter (Serial No. 43-46503)

Sikorsky LH-34D Seabat Helicopter (Serial No. 145717)

Sikorsky S-51 Executive Transport Helicopter (Serial No. N-5519), Reg. No. N5219

Sikorsky HH-52A Sea Guard Helicopter (Serial No. USCG1428)

Sikorsky CH-54B Tarhe (Skycrane) Helicopter (Serial No. 69-18465)

Sikorsky R-6 Doman conversion YH-31 Helicopter (Serial No.), Reg. No. N74146

Silas Brooks Balloon Basket, the oldest surviving aircraft in the USA.

Stinson 10A (Serial No. 8045), Reg. No. N34645

SUD Aviation SE 210 Caravelle VIR (Serial No. 88), Reg. No. N902MW

Viking Kittyhawk B-8 (Serial No. 30), Reg. No. N13250

Waco YKC-S (Serial No.4236), Reg. No. N14614

Aircraft previously displayed at the New England Air Museum included the following:

Boeing WB-47E Stratojet. Moved to the Hill AF Museum in Utah.

Convair F-102 Delta Darts. There were two and both have been scrapped.

Fairey Gannet AEW3. Moved to the Pima Aerospace Museum in Tucson, Arizona.

Lockheed P2V Neptune. Moved to the Quonset Air Museum in Rhode Island.

Vought F8-K Crusader. Transferred to the USS Midway Aircraft Carrier and Museum in San Diego, California. (Information courtesy of Ron Lindlauf, NEAM).

Engines

Allison V-1710-81 12-cylinder (1940's); Anzani B Radial (1914); Armstrong Siddeley Genet (1926); BMW 801C (1940's); Boeing 502 Gas Turbine cutaway (1940's); Bradley V-8 Air-cooled (1911); Chrysler VIX-2220-1 V-16 (1942); Continental A-65 4-cyl opposed (1939); Curtiss OX-5 (V-8) Engine (1917); Curtiss-Wright RC2-60 Rotary (1988); Detroit Aero 2-cyl Opposed (1910); Elbridge 4-cyl in-line (1910); General Electric J47-GE-13 (1948); General Electric TF-34-GE-100 Turbofan (1970's); General Electric YT-58-GE-2A (1958); Gnome B-2 Monosoupape (1916); Gnome Omega (1914); Hall Scott A-2 (1910 - V-8 water cooled); Harriman 4-cyl in-line (1910); Heath Henderson B-4 in-line (1928 - with Propeller); Hispano Suiza V-8 (1910's); Isotta Fraschini Asso 750 (1927); Junkers Jumo 004B Turbojet (1942); Lycoming T-53-L11B (1957); Nakajima NK-9H Homare (1940's); Packard A-1551-1 Airship Engine (1923); Pratt & Whitney R-4360 Wasp Major (1944); Pratt & Whitney J42 (1950); Pratt & Whitney J58 (JT11D-20) Turbojet (1960's); Pratt & Whitney PT-6 Turboprop (1960's); Pratt & Whitney R-1535-96 Twin Wasp Jr. (1936); Pratt & Whitney R-1830-86 Twin Wasp Jr. (1942); Pratt & Whitney R-2800-39 (1940's); Pratt & Whitney RL-10 liquid rocket (1961); Pratt & Whitney T-34 Turboprop (1950's); Pratt & Whitney Wasp A (1926); Pratt

& Whitney Wasp C (1929); Rolls Royce Nene II (1947); Rolls Royce V-1650-1 Merlin V-16 (1940's); Smith 2-cyl opposed (1910); Wright R-1820-45 Cyclone (1936)

Exhibits

1979 Tornado; 57th Fighter Group (1940's); Airborne Optical Devices; Andrew V.D. Willgoos - Aero Industry; British Airship R-100 Model (1930's); Cdr. Victor Motarella - Skyhawk Pilot; Come Fly With Me (airliner seats); Cooley Aircraft Wind Tunnel Model (1931); Douglas DC-3 Story; Early Aircraft Engines 1908-1911; Early French Aviation; Early Helicopters; Evolution of the Airliner; Evolution of US Aircraft National Insignia; Fokker Aircraft - Model Exhibit; History of Air Mails; Joseph Sawicki, Conn. W.W.II Aviator; Kaman Aerospace Display; Lifestar Air Ambulance Display; Lockheed SR-71 Blackbird photos; Man's First Flight/ Montgolfier Brothers; Masters of Flight; Matthew Batson and Dream of Transatlantic Flight; Milestones of Flight; NAI - Tuskegee Airmen; Percival Spencer - Conn. Aviation Pioneer; Robert Powers - W.W.II Aviator; Sikorsky - Recollections of a Pioneer; The Flying Mollisons; Thompson Trophy Winners model exhibit; United States Air Force Insignia; World War I Memorabilia; World's First Scheduled Airline; Wright Brothers Story

Artifacts

20mm Mark 12 Mod O Gun (1970's); 750-lb. General Purpose Bomb (1953); 75-mm Cannon (B-25) & misc. bombs (1940's); Airways Beacon & Tower (1930); Assorted Beacons and Landing Lights; Champion Chemical Fire Engine (1800's); Charavay Propeller (1910); Crocker-Wheeler Training Turret (1940's); Gallaudet Seaplane Model (1910); General Electric GAU-8 30-mm Gatling Gun (1970's); Grumman 150 SE-2 Turret (1943); Hamilton Prop for Racing P-51 (1940's); Hamilton Standard 23E50 Propeller (1940's); Hindenburg Water Tank & Tools (1937); Kaman Fire Suppression Unit (1960's); M-39 20mm Aircraft Cannon (1950's); Mk. 141 16" Battleship Shells (1940's); Norden Bombsight; Turbo Supercharger; USAF Ejection Seat (1960's); W.W.II Battle-Damaged Propellers from RAF A-20 (1940's); W.W.II Navy Practice Bombs (1940's); World War II Aerial Torpedo Cart; and, World War II Bomb Cart (1940's)

Vehicles

Cord 810 Phaeton (1936); Crosley Gas Porter (1940's); Ford Model T (1918);

Indian '4' Motorcycle (1936); Indian Motorcycle with sidecar (1928 - airmail);

Midget Race Car (1940); Military Jeep (1942 - three examples); World War II era Aircraft Tug (1940's)

Windsor Locks

Connecticut Air National Guard - 103rd Airlift Wing, Bradley Air National Guard Base, East Grandby, 100 Nicholson Road, Bradley International Airport, Windsor Locks, CT 06026-9309. Phone: (203) 292-2526.

There are three aircraft are located at the entrance of the Bradley Air National Guard Base in a memorial park for all past and present CTANG members. The exhibits are only open to the public during the airport open house (usually in June) although they are easily viewed from outside the main gate.

Harold Skaarup

Convair GF-102A Delta Dagger (Serial No. 56-1264)

Fairchild-Republic A-10A Thunderbolt II (Serial No. 79-0103), mounted on a pylon

North American F-100D Super Sabre (Serial No. 55-3805), mounted on a pylon

Annex A - Technical Data on Warplanes on Display in New England

Alenia C-27J Spartan
(photo courtesy of Wikipedia)

Alenia C-27J Spartan

The Alenia C-27J Spartan is a medium-sized military transport aircraft. The C-27J is an advanced derivative of Alenia Aeronautica's G.222 (C-27A Spartan in US service), with the engines and systems of the Lockheed Martin C-130J Super Hercules. The aircraft was selected as the Joint Cargo Aircraft (JCA) for the United States military. The C-27J has also been ordered by the militaries of Italy, Greece, Bulgaria, Lithuania, Morocco, and Romania.

In 1995, Alenia and Lockheed Martin began discussions to improve Alenia's G.222 using C-130J's glass cockpit with a more powerful version of the G.222's T64G engine and four-blade propellers. The companies began a program for the improved G.222, named C-27J in 1996. This was a US military type designation based on the G.222's C-27A US designation. Then the design was changed to use the C-130J Super Hercules's Rolls-Royce AE 2100 engine and six-blade propeller. Alenia and Lockheed Martin formed *Lockheed Martin Alenia Tactical Transport Systems* (LMATTS) for the development of C-27J in 1997. The C-27J has a 35% increase in range and a 15% faster cruise speed than the G.222.

The United States received its first C-27J on 25 September 2008. In September 2008 the C-27J Schoolhouse, operated by L-3 Link, officially began classes at Robins Air Force Base, Georgia. By April 2009, the Army had accepted deliveries of two aircraft and had 11 more on order. A proposal in May 2009 that the US Army/Army National Guard relinquish all of its aircraft to the US Air Force, primarily the Air National Guard, with a reduction of the total buy to 38 aircraft, led the DoD to give total control of the US's C-27Js to the USAF in December. It will be entirely operated to the Air National Guard for direct support of the United States Army. The US Air National Guard has received 4 C-27Js and began using them for testing and training. Purchase of 38 Spartans is anticipated, with initial operational capability to be reached in October 2010 and its first combat deployment planned for March 2011.

The 103rd Airlift Wing, Connecticut ANG is expected to be equipped with the Spartan in 2014. Wikipedia.

Beechcraft UC-45H Expeditor
(photo courtesy of Wikipedia)

Beechcraft C-45H Expeditor

The Beech Model 18 is a twin-engine light transport powered by a pair of 450-hp Pratt & Whitney R-985-AN-14B radial piston engines. The aircraft had a maximum speed of 220 mph, a service ceiling of 21,400', and a range of 1,530 miles. *The Complete Encyclopedia of World Aircraft.*

One of the most famous twin engine aircraft ever built, the Beech was used during WWII for communications work and instrument flying training. After the war, the Expeditor was used as a basic multi-engine trainer. First flown in 1937, the aircraft was used to train pilots and radio officers, transport VIPs, and as a general transport aircraft. Later in its career, the aircraft was often used in search and rescue (SAR) missions.

The C-45 was the WW II military version of the popular Beechcraft Model 18 commercial light transport. Beech built a total of 4,526 of these aircraft for the Army Air Forces between 1939 and 1945 in four versions, the AT-7 Navigator navigation trainer, the AT-11 Kansan bombing-gunnery trainer, the C-45 Expeditor utility transport and the F-2 for aerial photography and mapping. The AT-7 and AT-11 versions were well-known to WW II navigators and bombardiers, for most of these men received their training in these aircraft. Thousands of AAF pilot cadets also were given advanced training in twin-engine Beech airplanes. *(Information courtesy of the National Museum of the United States Air Force).*

Bell UH-1N Iroquois Helicopter
(photo courtesy of the USAF)

Bell UH-1 Iroquois (Huey) Helicopter

The Bell UH-1H is a general-purpose utility helicopter powered by one 1,400-hp Avco Lycoming T5313B turboshaft. This helicopter had a maximum speed of 127 mph, a service ceiling of 12,600' and a range of 318 miles. *The Complete Encyclopedia of World Aircraft.* There are many UH-1B, UH-1E, UH-1H and UH-1M Iroquois helicopters on display in the New England states.

The HU-1 evolved from a 1955 Army competition for a new utility helicopter. The Army employed it in various roles, later including that of an armed escort or attack gunship in Vietnam. The USAF, USN, and USMC eventually adopted the model as did Canada, Brazil, and West Germany. The initial Army designation was HU-1, which led to the common unofficial nickname of Huey. It was redesignated in 1962 as the UH-1 under a tri-service agreement. USAF orders for the Huey began in 1963 for UH-1Fs, intended for support duties at missile sites, and for TH-1Fs for instrument and hoist training and medical evacuation. The HH-1 H incorporated a longer fuselage and larger cabin for a crew of two and up to eleven passengers or six litters. The USAF ordered these in 1970 as local base rescue helicopters to replace the HH-43 Huskie. The first of the USAF's UH-1Ns, a twin-engine utility version capable of cruising on one engine, was obtained in 1970. *(Information courtesy of the National Museum of the United States Air Force).*

Bell AH-1G Cobra Helicopter New England Air Museum
(Author photo)

Bell AH-1G/AH-1S Cobra Helicopter

The Cobra is an attack/close support helicopter powered by one 1,800-hp Pratt & Whitney Aircraft of Canada T400-CP400 twin-engined turboshaft or by a PT6T Twin Pac engine. It has a maximum speed of 207 mph, a service ceiling of 12,450', and a range of 359 miles. It is armed with one M-197 three-barrel 20mm cannon in a chin turret, and can carry up to 2,200-lb of weapons including the XM-157 seven-tube or XM-159 19-tube 2.75in rocket pods on four underwing racks. *The Complete Encyclopedia of World Aircraft.*

Bell initiated production of an armed derivative of the UH-1E Iroquois (Huey) for the Army under the designation of AH-1G Huey Cobra, and in 1968 set about the development of a modified version for the Marine Corps, designated the AH-1J Seacobra. The first model produced incorporated a new nose turret with Navalized avionics and airframe. In 1972, a Marine Corps squadron (HMA-369) operated its AH-1Js at night from the deck of the USS Cleveland off the coast of North Vietnam in support of blockade operations.

Later versions of the Seacobra, designated the AH-1T, were developed initially for Iran and used by the Marines, with provision for the Hughes BGM-71A TOW guided anti-tank missiles. Seacobras were combat-christened during the 1983 invasion of Grenada.

In 1986, deliveries of the Supercobra version commenced, designated the AH-1W, with two 1,690hp GE engines. In addition to the triple-barrel 20mm cannon in the nose turret, it could carry a variety of armament in four mount pods on the stub-wings. This included TOW or Hellfire anti-armor missiles, AIM-9L Sidewinder missiles, rocket pods, 20mm gun pods and flare or grenade dispensers.

The Supercobra was effectively used in combat against Iraq during the Gulf War as well as for surveillance and protection of US forces in Somalia. The Museum's aircraft (BuNo. 70280) was received from the United States Marine Corps. *Information courtesy of the National Museum of Naval Aviation.*

Bell OH-58D Kiowa Helicopter
(photo courtesy of Wikipedia)

Bell OH-58A/D Kiowa

The OH-58 Kiowa is a family of single-engine, single-rotor, military helicopters used for observation, utility, and direct fire support. The four-place Kiowa is powered by one Allison T63-A-700 turboshaft with 317-shp. It has a maximum speed of 212 mph, a range of 299 miles, and a service ceiling of 19,000'. It can be armed with one M134 7.62 mm Minigun mounted on the M27 Armament Subsystem, *or* one M129 40 mm Grenade Launcher mounted on the XM8 Armament Subsystem.

Bell Helicopter manufactured the OH-58 for the United States Army based on the 206A Jet Ranger helicopter. The OH-58 has been in continuous use by the U.S. Army since 1969. During its Vietnam development, it was fitted with the 7.62 mm M134 Minigun, an electrically operated machine gun. A total of 74 OH-58A helicopters were delivered to the Canadian Armed Forces as *COH-58A* and later redesignated as *CH-136 Kiowa* helicopters.

The latest model, the OH-58D Kiowa Warrior, is primarily operated in an armed reconnaissance role in support of ground troops. The OH-58 has been exported to Austria, Canada, Dominican Republic, Taiwan, and Saudi Arabia; as well as having been produced under license in Australia. Internet: Wikipedia.

Blériot XI Monoplane
(photo courtesy of Wikipedia)

Blériot XI

The Bleriot monoplane is one of the most significant of pre-WW I aircraft. It first achieved fame in 1909 when its designer, Louis Bleriot of France, flew one to Dover, England on the first flight across the English Channel. It is powered by one 20-hp Anzani three-cylinder piston engine and has a maximum speed of 45 mph.

During the early days of WW I, both the British and French used two-seat Bleriots for reconnaissance behind German lines. By 1915, Bleriots were outclassed by more advanced airplanes and they were relegated to training Allied aviators including many Americans who joined the British and French flying services prior to US Air Service entry into the war. By 1917, Bleriots were being used only as ground trainers.

Many members of the US Air Service sent to France for flight training received their first instructions in Bleriots with "clipped" wings, which prevented them from taking off. At full throttle, the fledgling pilots bounced across the airfield, learning to control the rudder with their feet; once they could keep the Bleriot on a fairly straight course, they advanced to an airplane, which could leave the ground. *(Information courtesy of the National Museum of the USAF).*

The Collings Foundation two-seat model was a type that was built in kit form in the US in the early part of the century. It currently has an 80-hp Continental engine in place of the 35-hp Anzani engine it originally carried. *Information courtesy of the Collings Foundation).*

Boeing-Stearman PT-17 Kaydet, New England Air Museum
(Author photo)

Boeing-Stearman PT-17 Kaydet

The Stearman PT-17 was a two-seat biplane trainer used during WWII powered by one Avco Lycoming R-680-17 radial piston engine. The aircraft had a maximum speed of 124 mph, a service ceiling of 11,200', and a range of 505 miles.

The Kaydet was a conventional biplane of rugged construction with large, fixed tailwheel undercarriage, and accommodation for the student and instructor in open cockpits in tandem. The radial engine was usually uncowled. After World War II, the thousands of PT-17 Stearmans were auctioned off to civilians and former pilots. Many were modified for crop-dusting use, with a hopper for pesticide or fertilizer fitted in place of the front cockpit. Additional equipment included pumps, spray bars, and nozzles mounted below the lower wings. A popular approved modification to increase the maximum takeoff weight and climb performance involved fitting a larger Pratt & Whitney R-985 engine and a constant speed propeller. Wikipedia.

At least 9,783 were built in the United States during the 1930s and 1940s for use as a military trainer aircraft. Stearman Aircraft became a subsidiary of Boeing in 1934. Widely known as the Stearman, Boeing-Stearman or Kaydet, it served as a primary trainer for the USAAF, as a basic trainer for the USN (as the NS & N2S), and with the RCAF as the Kaydet throughout World War II. *The Complete Encyclopedia of World Aircraft.*

Boeing B-17G Flying Fortress
(photo courtesy of the Collings Foundation)

Boeing B-17G Flying Fortress

The B-17G model of the Flying Fortress was a nine to ten-seat long-range medium bomber and reconnaissance aircraft powered by four 1,200-hp Wright R-1820-97 Cyclone turbo-charged radial piston engines. These aircraft had a maximum speed of 287 mph, a service ceiling of 35,800', and a range with full bombload of 2,000 miles. *The Complete Encyclopedia of World Aircraft.*

One of the most famous airplanes ever built, the B-17 prototype first flew on 28 July 1935. The G variants had redesigned and enlarged tail surfaces compared to their predecessors, and were easily recognizable by their large dorsal fin. The B-17 Gs had a chin turret housing an additional two .50 cal machine-guns, which gave the aircraft a total of 13 .50 cal machine-guns. 8,680 G models were built. The aircraft served in every WW II combat zone, but is best known for daylight strategic bombing of German industrial targets. Production of all versions of the B-17 ended in May 1945 and totaled 12,726. ((*Information courtesy of the National Museum of the United States Air Force*).

The B-17 four-engine heavy bomber was developed for the United States Army Air Corps (USAAC) introduced in the 1930s. Competing against Douglas and Martin for a contract to build 200 bombers, the Boeing entry outperformed both competitors and more than met the Air Corps' expectations. Although Boeing lost the contract because the prototype crashed, the Air Corps was so impressed with Boeing's design that they ordered 13 B-17s. The B-17 Flying Fortress evolved through numerous design advances.

The B-17 was primarily employed by the United States Army Air Forces (USAAF) in the daylight precision strategic bombing campaign of World War II against German industrial, civilian, and military targets. The United States Eighth Air Force based in England and the

Fifteenth Air Force based in Italy complemented the RAF Bomber Command's nighttime area bombing in Operation Pointblank to help secure air superiority over the cities, factories and battlefields of Western Europe in preparation for Operation Overlord. The B-17 also participated to a lesser extent in the War in the Pacific where it conducted raids against Japanese shipping and airfields.

From its pre-war inception, the USAAC (later USAAF) touted the aircraft as a strategic weapon; it was a potent, high-flying, long-ranging bomber capable of unleashing great destruction, able to defend itself, and having the ability to return home despite extensive battle damage. It quickly took on mythic proportions. Stories and photos of B-17s surviving battle damage widely circulated, increasing its iconic status. With a service ceiling greater than any of its Allied contemporaries, the B-17 established itself as a superb weapons system, dropping more bombs than any other US aircraft in World War II. Of the 1.5 million metric tons of bombs dropped on Germany by US aircraft, 640,000 tons were dropped from B-17s. Wikipedia.

The Collings Foundation B-17G with production Serial No. 44-83575, was built under contract from Boeing by the Douglas Aircraft Company in Long Beach, California, and was accepted on 7 April 1945. Too late to see combat in WWII, the airframe served as part of the Air/Sea 1st Rescue Squadron and the Military Air Transport Command. Seven years later, in April of 1952, it was used to test the effects of three nuclear explosions and was ultimately sold as part of an 800-ton scrap pile after a 13-year cool-down period.

Envisioning further airworthy application, the Aircraft Specialties Company purchased the B-17s remains and began the task of restoration, fabricating and replacing the damaged skin on site, and stripping, cleaning, repairing, and testing the engines. Instrumentation and electrical wiring were replaced, while 4,000 feet of control cable was installed. Remarkably, the aircraft ultimately took off from the desert under its own power. Following its restoration, the B-17G served as a fire bomber, dropping water and borate on forest fires for the next 20 years, before being sold to the Collings Foundation in January of 1986.

Reconfigured to full World War II bomber status by Tom Reilly Vintage Aircraft, it was given the current registration and designated "Nine-o-Nine" in honor of the original aircraft with production serial number 42-31909 which had served the 91st Bomb Group in the 323rd Squadron. Having operated 140 missions without crew loss or abort, it had made 18 trips to Berlin and flown 1,129 hours in the 13-month period between 25 February 1944 and April 1945, dropping 562,000 pounds of bombs and incurring 21 engine changes and the replacement of four wing panels and 15 main gas tanks. It returned to the United States at the end of the war with 600 holes, but was scrapped like almost all others of the type. Robert G. Waldvogel, Internet: http://www.collingsfoundation.org/newsdb.

Boeing B-29 Superfortress
(photo courtesy of the USAF)

Boeing B-29 Superfortress, New England Air Museum
(Author photo)

Boeing B-29 Superfortress

The Superfortress was a long-range strategic bomber and reconnaissance aircraft. The B-29 was introduced in June 1944, and at the time represented a tremendous leap forward in technology. With four powerful 3,500-hp Pratt & Whitney R-4360-35 Wasp Major or four Wright R-3350-23-23A/-41 Cyclone 18 turbo-charged radial piston engines, it had the speed of many fighters (358 mph). The aircraft had a service ceiling of 31,850' and a range of 3,250 miles. The B-29 was heavily armed with two .50 cal machine-guns in each of four remotely-controlled power-operated gun turrets and three .50 cal machine-guns and one 20mm cannon in the tail turret. It could carry a bomb-load of 20,000 lbs. *The Complete Encyclopedia of World Aircraft.*

The B-29 was the largest and most sophisticated bomber to enter combat in WWII. First flown in 1942 with initial production models revealed in 1943. Although plagued by engine problems early on it was an extremely strong, stable and efficient ac. A favorite with crews, due to pressurized and heated crew compartments. It had sophisticated RADAR and defensive armament. It served well in the Pacific during WWII, in Korea and then in the Strategic Air Command. Several versions were produced including an aerial re-fueling tanker. It was used as a launch platform for experimental supersonic aircraft. A total of 3979 aircraft were built.

The Superfortress primarily operated in the Pacific battle area, where it played a central role in the strategic campaign against Japan, which culminated in the dropping of Atomic bombs on Hiroshima (by the B-29 Enola Gay) and Nagasaki (by the B-29 Bocks Car). The Boeing B-29 was designed in 1940 as an eventual replacement for the B-17 and B-24. The first one built made its maiden flight on 21 September 1942. In December 1943 it was decided not to use the B-29 in the European Theater, thereby permitting the airplane to be sent to the Pacific area where its great range made it particularly suited for the long over-water flight required to attack the Japanese homeland from bases in China. During the last two months of 1944, B-29s began operating against Japan from the islands of Saipan, Guam and Tinian. With the advent of the conflict in Korea in June 1950, the B-29 was once again thrust into battle. For the next several years it was effectively used for attacking targets in North Korea. *((Information courtesy of the National Museum of the United States Air Force).*

Boeing KC-135R Stratotanker, New Hampshire Air National Guard
(Wikipedia photo)

Boeing KC-135R Stratotanker

The Stratotanker is a tanker/transport powered by four 18,000-lb thrust Pratt & Whitney TF33-P-5 turbofan engines. It has a maximum speed of 600 mph and a service ceiling of 35,000'. The KC-135 has evolved over 30 different variants. These roles vary greatly with KC-135s now performing as airborne command posts, weather aircraft, transports, and highly specialized electronic reconnaissance aircraft.

(The Complete Encyclopedia of World Aircraft)

The Stratotanker was developed from the prototype Boeing Model 707 commercial transport, although the military version has a smaller-diameter fuselage and the cabin windows have been deleted. All equipment for the tanker role is carried on the lower deck or normal cargo area, including pivoted Flying Boom refueling gear. This was modified in later variants to allow for a probe-and drogue refueling capability. More than 820 variants have been delivered. *((Information courtesy of the National Museum of the United States Air Force).*

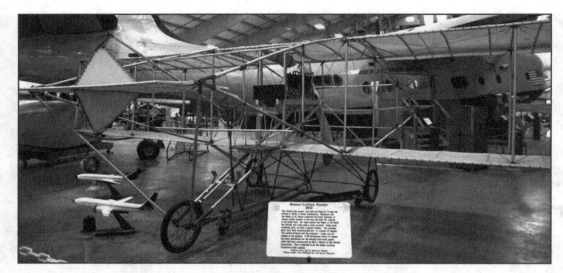

Bunce-Curtiss Pusher New England Air Museum
(Wikipedia photo)

Bunce-Curtiss Pusher

Young Howard Bunce would go wherever he could find a Curtiss pusher airplane, make sketches, then go home and make parts until he had assembled an airplane in 1912. He could not afford a Curtiss engine but used a 4-cylinder air-cooled Nelson built in New Britain, Connecticut. Wikipedia

Burnelli CBY-3 Loadmaster, New England Air Museum
(Author photo)

Burnelli CBY-3 Loadmaster

The Burnelli CBY-3 Loadmaster was an unconventional transport aircraft designed by United States engineer Vincent Burnelli and built in Canada in 1944 by Canadian Car and Foundry. The CBY-3 "lifting fuselage" was an evolution of the earlier Burnelli UB-14. Burnelli worked as a designer at Canadian Car and Foundry (CanCar) in Montreal, and the CBY-3 was intended for bush operations in northern Canada. The sole prototype was extensively tested but failed to gain a production contract.

Burnelli had a lifelong career devoted to exploiting the advantages of the lifting body airfoil concept that characterized many of his earlier aircraft designs. His last design, the CBY-3 was manufactured by CanCar in Montreal, but ownership reverted back to Burnelli, when the CBY-3 was unable to gain a production contract. The name of the aircraft, CBY-3, was derived from the name of the three partners involved in its creation: CanCar, Burnelli and Lowell Yerex and "3" from the number of partners involved. Lowell Yerex was a New Zealander who had formed TACA – *Transportes Aéreos Centroamericanos* (Central American Air Transport) in Honduras in 1931, and joined the project when Burnelli convinced him that the CBY-3 could be used as both a cargo and passenger aircraft.

A follow-up design in 1942 for the CC&F B-1000, a bomber using the same lifting body principles, remained a "paper project". Originally registered "CF-BEL-X" while still in the experimental stage, this one-off, twin-boom, aerofoil-section fuselage, high-lift airliner garnered significant interest from the industry. "CF-BEL-X" underwent rigorous testing and proving flights designed to show off its potential. Despite a trouble-free test program and glowing accolades from the press and industry observers, no production orders resulted and the prototype was later sold in the US as *N17N*.

Moving to Southampton, N.Y., Burnelli remained tireless in his determination to promote his airfoil-shaped fuselage transport planes. In 1955, he adapted the CBY-3 to carry an expedition of 20 passengers and 41 sled dogs, along with their equipment, to the North Pole, but the enterprise was canceled.

The Loadmaster continued to fly regularly as a commercial airliner both in northern Canada and South America; acquired with design rights by Airlifts Inc. in Miami, Florida, it went to Venezuela, and returned to Burnelli Avionics for refitting with Wright R-2600 engines, finally ended its flying days at Baltimore's airport in Maryland. In 1964 the CBY-3 air transport was retired to the New England Air Museum in Windsor Locks, Connecticut, where it is displayed outside. Wikipedia.

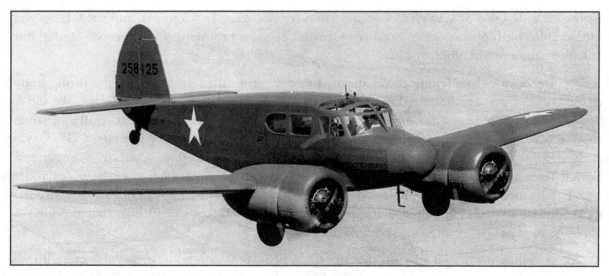

Cessna AT-17 Bobcat
(photo courtesy of the USAF)

Cessna AT-17/UH-78 Bobcat

The Bobcat is a five-seat light transport powered by two 245-hp Jacobs R-755-9 radial piston engines. The aircraft had a maximum speed of 195 mph, a service ceiling of 22,000', and a range of 750 miles. *The Complete Encyclopedia of World Aircraft.*

War-time expansion of Navy ferry squadrons and aircraft delivery units brought a need for small reliable transports to carry ferry pilots to and from their home bases at the end of delivery flights during World War II. Typical of the commercial types acquired by the Navy in 1942-43 to fill this need was the four/five seat Cessna T-50 bearing the Navy designation JRC-1 and affectionately called the Bamboo Bomber by those who flew it.

The aircraft was also acquired by the Army Air Forces under the designations of ATB and AT-17 and was used as a transition trainer for pilots who were going on to fly multi-engine type aircraft. *Information courtesy of the National Museum of Naval Aviation.*

The Collings Foundation's UC-78 was restored in the late 90's as a Navy JRC-1 by Bill Stookey. It won a 1998 Grand Champion Warbird award at Oshkosh for its fine restoration. It was brought to the Collings Foundation in October of 2001. *Information courtesy of the Collings Foundation).*

Cessna T-37B Tweet
(Wikipedia photo)

Cessna T-37B Tweet

The T-37 Tweet (designated Model 318 by Cessna) is a small, economical twin-engine jet trainer-attack type aircraft which flew for decades as a primary trainer for the United States Air Force (USAF) and in the air forces of several other nations. The A-37 Dragonfly variant served in the light attack role during the Vietnam War and continues to serve in the air forces of several South American nations.

The T-37 served as the US Air Force's primary pilot training vehicle for over 52 years after its first flight. After completing Primary in the Tweet, students moved on to other advanced Navy, Marine Corps or Allied trainers. 1,269 Cessna T-37s were built, with 419 still serving in the United States Air Force in 2006. Between 2001 and 31 July 2009 the USAF phased out the T-37 in favor of the T-6 Texan II. Wikipedia.

Chance Vought F4U Corsairs on deck
(Wikipedia photo)

Chance Vought XF4U-4 Corsair, New England Air Museum
(photo courtesy of Wikipedia)

Chance Vought F4U-4 Corsair

The Corsair is a single-seat carrier-based fighter powered by one 2,000-hp Pratt & Whitney R-2800-8 radial piston engine. It has a maximum speed of 417 mph, a service ceiling of 36,900', and a range of 1,015 miles. It is armed with six wing-mounted .50 cal machine-guns. *The Complete Encyclopedia of World Aircraft.*

The F4U Corsair saw service primarily in World War II and the Korean War. Brewster-built aircraft were designated F3A and Goodyear-built Corsairs FG. The Corsair served in smaller air forces until the 1960s, following the longest production run of any piston-engined fighter in US history (1942–1952). Some Japanese pilots regarded it as the most formidable American fighter of World War II. The US Navy counted an 11:1 kill ratio with the F4U Corsair.

Corsairs served with the US Navy, US Marines, Fleet Air Arm and the Royal New Zealand Air Force, as well the French Navy *Aéro-Navale* and other services postwar. It quickly became the most capable carrier-based fighter-bomber of World War II. Demand for the aircraft soon overwhelmed Vought's manufacturing capability, resulting in production by Goodyear (as the FG-1) and Brewster (as the F3A-1). From the first prototype delivery to the US Navy in 1940, to final delivery in 1953 to the French, 12,571 F4U Corsairs were manufactured by Vought, in 16 separate models. Wikipedia.

The F4U was equipped with a radial air-cooled engine mounted in the nose and fitted with a four-blade propeller. Its low-set wings were inversed-gullwing shaped. They were elliptical with rounded tips. An oval air intake was housed in the leading edge of either wing close to the fuselage. The tailplane was parabola-shaped and was set past the tail fin. The Corsair's landing gear with tail wheel and a hook was retractable.

The Corsair was conceived to use the most powerful engine and largest propeller a fighter plane ever had. Unfortunately, the long propeller blades caused ground clearance problems. The W or gull-shaped-wings helped to reduce the required length of the landing gear, and provided very good visibility to the sides. The long landing gear was fragile, and the first reports of carrier tests were unfavorable: *"This plane will never be a good carrier plane."* The Corsair was nicknamed the Ensign Eliminator. It would appear that the strong engine torque didn't make it an easy aircraft to land.

Developed in 1938 for the US Marine Corps, the first prototype XF4U-1 flew on 29 May 1940 and went into production in 1942. The main modifications included the F4U-1 which was the first production version; the F4U-1A which was an improved F4U-1; the F4U-1B, exported to the United Kingdom in 1943; the F4U-1C close air support version armed with guns rather than machine guns; the F4U-1D which was a fighter/bomber variant; the F4U-2 night fighter equipped with a radar which was housed in a fairing on the left wing; the XF4U-3 experimental high-altitude fighter with twin turbochargers; the F4U-4 fitted with a more powerful engine, and which could carry rockets; the XF4U-4 had a new engine and cowling; and the F4U-5 night fighter powered with a Pratt & Whitney R-2800 engine. By 1952, 12,681 Corsairs had been built. *Information courtesy of the National Museum of Naval Aviation;* Internet: http://www.sikorskyarchives.com/f4u.html).

Infantrymen nicknamed the Corsair "The Sweetheart of the Marianas" and "The Angel of Okinawa" for its roles in these campaigns. Among Navy and Marine aviators, however, the aircraft was nicknamed "Ensign Eliminator" and "Bent-Wing Eliminator" because it required many more hours of flight training to master than other Navy carrier-borne aircraft. It was also called simply "U-bird" or "Bent Wing Bird". The Japanese allegedly nicknamed it "Whistling Death", for the noise made by airflow through the wing root-mounted oil cooler air intakes. Wikipedia.

Classic Fighters Industries Inc Me 262 B-1c
(photo courtesy of the Collings Foundation)

Classic Fighters Industries Inc Messerschmitt Me 262 B-1c

The Me 262 B-1c reproduction (Serial No. 501241), Reg. No. N262AZ was a Me 262 Werk Number 501241 was a project that was started by Texas Aircraft Factory Inc. in conjunction with Classic Fighter Industries Inc and completed by the Me 262 Project in Everett, Washington. It first flew on 20 December 2002. The Me 262 B-1c is the 2-seat version of the Me 262. The Collings Foundation eventually plans to offer a flight training session on the Me 262 at over 100 locations nationwide each year.

The original Messerschmitt Me 262 Schwalbe ("Swallow") was the world's first operational jet-powered fighter aircraft. Design work started before World War II opened, but engine problems meant the aircraft did not reach operational status until mid-1944. Compared with Allied fighters of its day, including the jet-powered Gloster Meteor, it was much faster and better armed.

In combat, when properly flown, it proved difficult to counter due to its speed. Me 262 pilots claimed a total of 509 Allied kills (although higher claims are sometimes made) against the loss of about 100 Me 262s. The design was pressed into a variety of roles, including light bomber, reconnaissance and even experimental night fighter versions.

The Me 262 is considered to have been the most advanced German aviation design in operational use during World War II. The Allies countered its potential effectiveness in the air by relentlessly attacking the aircraft on the ground, or while they were taking off or landing. Maintenance during the deteriorating war situation and a lack of fuel also reduced the effectiveness of the aircraft as a fighting force. In the end, the Me 262 had a negligible impact on the course of the war due to its late introduction and the small numbers that were deployed in operational service. The Me 262 influenced the designs of post-war aircraft such as the North American F-86 and Boeing B-47.

After the end of the war, the Me 262 and other advanced German technologies were quickly swept up by the Americans (as part of the USAAF's Operation Lusty), British, and Soviets. Many Me 262s were found in readily-repairable condition and were confiscated. During testing, the Me 262 was found to have advantages over the early models of the Gloster Meteor. It was faster, had better cockpit visibility to the sides and rear (mostly due to the canopy frame and the discoloration caused by the plastics used in the Meteor's construction), and was a superior gun platform, as the early Meteors had a tendency to snake at high speed and exhibited "weak" aileron response. The Me 262 did have a shorter combat range than the Meteor.

The USAAF compared the P-80 Shooting Star and Me 262 concluding, "Despite a difference in gross weight of nearly 2,000 lb, the Me 262 was superior to the P-80 in acceleration, speed and approximately the same in climb performance. The Me 262 apparently has a higher critical Mach number, from a drag standpoint, than any current Army Air Force fighter." The Army Air Force also tested an example of the Me 262A-1a/U3 (US flight evaluation serial FE-4012), an unarmed photoreconnaissance version, which was fitted with a fighter nose and given an overall smooth finish. It was used for performance comparisons against the P-80. During testing between May and August 1946, the aircraft completed eight flights, lasting four hours and 40 minutes. Testing was discontinued after four engine changes were required during the course of the tests, culminating in two single-engine landings.

These aircraft were extensively studied, aiding development of early US and Soviet jet fighters. The F-86 Sabre, designed by the engineer Edgar Schmued, used the Me 262 airfoil (Messerschmitt Wing A) and a slat design similar to that of the Me 262.

In January 2003, the American Me 262 Project completed flight testing to allow for delivery of near-exact reproductions of several versions of the Me 262 including at least two B-1c two-seater variants, one A-1c single seater and two "convertibles" that could be switched between the A-1c and B-1c configurations. All are powered by General Electric J85 engines and feature additional safety features, such as upgraded brakes and strengthened landing gear. The "c" suffix refers to the new J-85 powerplant and has been informally assigned with the approval of the Messerschmitt Foundation in Germany (the Werk Number of the reproductions picked up where the last wartime produced Me-262 left off - a continuous airframe serial number run with a 50 year production break).

Flight testing of the first newly manufactured Me 262 A-1c (single-seat) variant was completed in August 2005. The first of these machines went to a private owner in the south-western United States, while the second was delivered to the Messerschmitt Foundation at Manching, Germany. This aircraft conducted a private test flight in late April 2006, and made its public debut in May at the ILA 2006. The new Me 262 flew during the public flight demonstrations. Me 262 Werk Number 501241 was delivered to the Collings Foundation as White 1 of JG 7. Wikipedia.

Consolidated B-24J Liberator, Collings Foundation
(photo courtesy of the Collings Foundation)

Consolidated B-24J Liberator

The Liberator is a long-range bomber and reconnaissance aircraft powered by four 1,200-hp Pratt & Whitney R-1830-65 Twin Wasp turbo-charged radial piston engines. It had a maximum speed of 290 mph, a service ceiling of 28,000', and a range of 2,100 miles. It was armed with ten .50 cal machine-guns (in nose, upper, ventral "ball" and tail turrets, and could carry a maximum bombload of 12,800 lbs, although its normal bombload was 5,000 lbs. *The Complete Encyclopedia of World Aircraft.*

The B-24 was employed in operations in every combat theater during World War II. Because of its great range, it was particularly suited for such missions as the famous raid from North Africa against the oil industry at Ploesti, Rumania on 1 August 1943. This feature also made the airplane suitable for long over-water missions in the Pacific Theater. More than 18,000 Liberators were produced, of which 6,678 were of the J model. *(Information courtesy of the National Museum of the United States Air Force).*

The Liberator was designed by Consolidated Aircraft Company of San Diego, California. Its mass production was brought into full force by 1943 with the aid of the Ford Motor Company through its newly constructed Willow Run facility, where peak production had reached one B-24 per hour and 650 per month in 1944. Other factories soon followed. The B-24 ended World War II as the most produced Allied heavy bomber in history, and the most produced American military aircraft at over 18,000 units, thanks in large measure to Henry Ford and the harnessing of American industry. It still holds the distinction as the most-produced American military aircraft. The B-24 was used by several Allied air forces and navies and by every branch of the American armed forces during the war, attaining a distinguished war record with its operations in the Western European, Pacific, Mediterranean, and China-Burma-India Theaters.

Often compared with the better-known B-17 Flying Fortress, the B-24 was a more modern design with a higher top speed, greater range, and a heavier bomb load; however, it was also more difficult to fly, with heavy control forces and poor formation-flying characteristics. Popular opinion among aircrews and general's staffs tended to favor the B-17's rugged qualities above all other considerations in the European Theater. The placement of the B-24's fuel tanks throughout the upper fuselage and its lightweight construction, designed to increase range and optimize assembly line production, made the aircraft vulnerable to battle damage.

The B-24 was notorious among American aircrews for its tendency to catch fire. Moreover, its high fuselage-mounted Davis wing also meant it was dangerous to ditch or belly land, since the fuselage tended to break apart. Nevertheless, the B-24 provided excellent service in a variety of roles thanks to its large payload and long range. The B-24's most famous mission was the low-level strike against the Ploesti oil fields, in Romania on 1 August 1943, which turned into a disaster due to attack waves getting out of sequence. Wikipedia.

The Collings Foundation B-24J was produced in August of 1944 by Consolidated Aircraft in Fort Worth, Texas, and was been delivered to the RAF two months later, in October. The RAF operated it in the Pacific in a multitude of roles, including bombing, anti-shipping, and resupplying resistance force operations, until the war had ended. Later acquired by India, it had served as a patrol bomber during the 20-year period from 1948 to 1968, after which it had remained abandoned until Doug Arnold, a British collector, had obtained it in 1981. Disassembled, it was returned to England in a Heavy Lift Cargo transport and advertised for sale in its "as is" condition, a purchase made by Dr. Robert F. Collings three years later, in 1984. Although only intended for static display after its three-week transatlantic crossing by sea, in sections, to Boston, it was decided it should be restored to flying condition because of the vastly increased exposure it would bring to the public.

Massachusetts volunteers began preliminary work on the restoration in 1985. This work entailed restoration to the armament, turrets, oxygen system, and radios, while Tom Reilly Vintage Aircraft of Kissimmee, Florida, carried out the major airframe and powerplant overhauls. Several companies donated equipment: Emerson Electric provided the nose turret, PPG Industries the turret glass, and United Technologies a Norden bombsight, while General Electric, Consolidated Aircraft's successor, had provided significant monetary support.

During the $1.3 million, 97,000 man-hour restoration, one-third of its outer skin had been replaced, 400,000 rivets had been reapplied, and 5,000 feet of hydraulic lines, control cables, and electrical wiring had been installed, along with the introduction of new, Kevlar fuel tanks to increase passenger safety. It resulted in the world's only airworthy Liberator.

First appearing in an "All American" livery in 1989 immediately after its restoration, it represented a B-24 of the 15th Air Force which had shot down 14 enemy fighters on a single mission and had been one of only two of 19 to have returned to base. It sported the "All American" paint scheme for more than nine years. It's second paint scheme, "Dragon and his tail," represented a B-24 which had been operated by the 43rd Bomb Group's 64th Bomb Squadron on 85 missions in its Pacific theater of operations.

The third and current color scheme, "Witchcraft," was been applied on 14 December 2004 and represented a Liberator which had been flown by the 8th Air Force in England and assigned to the 467BG, where it completed a record 130 combat missions. Robert G. Waldvogel, Internet: http://www.collingsfoundation.org/newsdb.

Convair F-102A Delta Dagger
(photo courtesy of Wikipedia)

Convair F-102A Delta Dagger

The Delta Dagger is a single-seat supersonic all-weather interceptor that is powered by one 17,200-lb after-burning thrust Pratt & Whitney J57-P-23 or –25 turbojet. It had a maximum speed of 825 mph, a service ceiling of 36,000', and a range of 1,350 miles. It was armed with two AIM-26 or 26A Falcon missiles, or one Falcon and two AIM-4C/D missiles in a weapons bay. *The Complete Encyclopedia of World Aircraft.*

The primary mission of the F-102 was to intercept and destroy enemy aircraft. It was the world's first supersonic all-weather jet interceptor and the USAF's first operational delta-wing aircraft. The F-102 made its initial flight on 24 October 1953 and became operational with the Air Defense Command in 1956. At the peak of deployment in the late 1950's, F-102s equipped more than 25 ADC squadrons.

Convair built 1,101 F-102s, 975 of which were F-102As. The USAF also bought 111 TF-102s as combat trainers with side-by-side seating. In a wartime situation, after electronic equipment on board the F-102 had located the enemy aircraft, the F-102's radar would guide it into position for attack. At the proper moment, the electronic fire control system would automatically fire the F-102's air-to-air rockets and missiles. *(Information courtesy of the National Museum of the United States Air Force).*

The F-102 was the first operational supersonic interceptor and delta-wing fighter of the USAF. It used an internal weapons bay to carry both guided missiles and rockets. As originally designed, it could not achieve Mach 1 supersonic flight until redesigned with area ruling. The F-102 replaced subsonic types such as the F-89 Scorpion, and by the 1960s, it saw limited service in Vietnam in bomber escort and ground attack roles. It was supplemented by F-101 Voodoos and, later, by F-4 Phantom IIs. Many of the F-102s were transferred to United States

Air National Guard duty by the mid-to-late 1960s, and the type was retired from operational service in 1976. The follow-on replacement was the Mach 2 class F-106 Delta Dart which was an extensive redesign of the F-102. Wikipedia.

Convair F-106A Delta Dart, Massachusetts ANG
(photo courtesy of Wikipedia)

Convair F-106A Delta Dart

The Delta Dart is a single-seat supersonic all-weather interceptor powered by one 24,500-lb afterburning thrust Pratt & Whitney J75-P-17 turbojet. It has a maximum speed of 1,525 mph, a service ceiling of 57,000', and a combat radius of 729 miles. *The Complete Encyclopedia of World Aircraft.*

The Dart was first introduced to the USAF in 1960 to counter the threat of a nuclear attack by supersonic Russian bombers. The Delta Dart cruised at a speed near Mach 2, and its fire-control system worked with a ground-based radar to guide the aircraft and its weapons towards its target.

The delta wing gave the F-106 both stability and low drag for Mach 2 flight. The F-106 all-weather interceptor was developed from the Convair F-102 Delta Dagger. Originally designated the F-102B, it was redesignated F-106 because it had extensive structural changes and a more powerful engine. The first F-106A flew on 26 December 1956, and deliveries to the Air Force began in July 1959. Production ended in late 1960 after 277 F-106As and 63 F-106Bs had been built. The F-106 uses a Hughes MA-1 electronic guidance and fire control system. After takeoff, the MA-1 can be given control of the aircraft to fly it to the proper altitude and attack position. Then it can fire the Genie and Falcon missiles, break off the attack run, and return the aircraft to the vicinity of its base. The pilot takes control again for the landing. *(Information courtesy of the National Museum of the United States Air Force).*

Convair C-131D Samaritan
(photo courtesy of Wikipedia)

Convair C-131D Samaritan

The Samaritan is a twin-engine transport aircraft powered by a pair of 2,500-hp Pratt & Whitney R-2800-CB16 or CB17 radial piston engines. It had a maximum speed of 300 mph, a service ceiling of 24,900', and a range of 470 miles. *The Complete Encyclopedia of World Aircraft.*

The Samaritan was first built March 1954. Its primary mission was air evacuation, and it has been used extensively by the Coast Guard. It was also used by military as a flying classroom. The Samaritan was a USAF transport version of the Convair 240/340/440 series commercial airliners. The first Samaritan, a C-131A derived from the Convair 240, was delivered to the Air Force in 1954. It was similar to the T-29 trainer (also based on the Convair 240) flown by the USAF since 1949 to instruct navigators, bombardiers and radio operators. The C-131 was acquired primarily for medical evacuation and personnel transportation. While some T-29s also saw duty as staff transports, a few C-131s likewise were used for training and testing. In fact, the first prototype of the Southeast Asia vintage side-firing Gunship program used the C-131 airframe. Nearly all of the USAF's C-131s left the active inventory in the late 1970s, but a few were still serving in Air National Guard units in the mid-1980s. *Information courtesy of the National Museum of the United States Air Force.*

The Navy's C-131 (R4Y) aircraft is the military version of Convair's 340 model commercial airliner which in turn is a newer design of the 240 model with a greater wing-span, wing area and weight; longer fuselage and a more powerful engine. First flown on 5 October 1951, the Convair 340 proved quite successful in the commercial field with sixteen American and foreign airlines placing orders for 160 production models in 1952 alone.

Delivery of 36 R4Y-1 aircraft (later redesignated C-131 in 1962) to the Navy began in 1952 and these were assigned to Navy and Marine Corps fleet support squadrons as logistic and administrative support aircraft. Capable of carrying up to 44 passengers and a freight payload of 12,000 lbs, the C-131 could also be employed as an aerial ambulance with a 27-bed capacity. A single R4Y-1Z had a VIP interior with 24 seats and became the VC-131F. Another was equipped with an extensive array of radar and electronic equipment (including radomes) for use as a countermeasures research and development aircraft. *Information courtesy of the National Museum of Naval Aviation.*

C-131D Samaritan (Serial No. 54-2810) is on display at the 158th FG, Vermont ANG, Burlington, Vermont.

Curtiss JN-4D Jenny,
(photo courtesy of the USN)

Curtiss JN-4D Jenny

The Jenny was the standard two-seat pilot trainer of WWI. It was powered by a liquid-cooled 90-hp V-8 90 HP OX-5 inline engine. It had a maximum speed of 75 mph and a service ceiling of 6,500'. *The Complete Encyclopedia of World Aircraft.*

The first air mail was flown in a Jenny between New York and Washington, D.C. on the 15th of May 1918. It was also the mainstay of the US Signal Corps and the barnstormers of the 1920's and early 1930's. One of American's most famous airplanes, the Jenny was developed by combining the best features of the Curtiss J and N models. A 1915 version, the JN-3, was used in 1916 during Pershing's Punitive Expedition into Mexico. Its poor performance, however, made it unsuited for field operations.

The JN-3 was modified in 1916 to improve its performance and redesignated the JN-4. With America's entry into World War I on April 6, 1917, the Signal Corps began ordering large quantities of JN-4s, and by the time production was terminated after the Armistice, more than 6,000 had been delivered, the majority of them JN-4D.

The Jenny was generally used for primary flight training, but some were equipped with machine guns and bomb racks for advanced training. After World War I, hundreds were sold on the civilian market. The airplane soon became the mainstay of the Barnstormer of the 1920s, and some Jennies were still being flown in the 1930s. *(Information courtesy of the National Museum of the United States Air Force).*

In the 1916 time-frame the Army and the Navy were becoming disturbed by the increasing accident rate in pusher-type aircraft. In the summer of 1916 in Pensacola, a series of fatal crashes resulted in the condemnation of many of the pushers on hand nearly bringing flying to a halt. Glenn Curtiss was in England to develop a tractor-type trainer to replace the Curtiss pushers then in service. In England and in Europe, tractor-type development was well ahead of that in the US. To gain time, Curtiss hired on a British engineer whose work resulted in the Model J which was produced in Hammondsport. This design was tried as both a landplane and a single-float seaplane. This was followed by the Model N differing primarily in the wing airfoil. Combining the best of both later resulted in the Model JN and the Model J was discontinued. But the Model N was continued and by World War I was further developed as the N-9.

The Navy's first Jennies were JN-1W single-float seaplanes. Even though they were modern in appearance, they still retained the old Curtiss shoulder-yoke aileron control. When the JN-4s were introduced, they were equipped with the stick-type controls. An advanced pilot training and gunnery trainer was developed with a 150 hp Wright-Hispano engine designated JN-4H and JN-4HG, respectively, and popularly referred to as the Hisso. The Jenny was also used in Canada to train US Naval Aviators.

Production of the Jenny' reportedly reached nearly 5000 in the US and Canada. After the war, large numbers of Jennies were declared surplus and purchased by pilots, most of whom had learned to fly during the war. Many then went out into the world to make a living flying in any way they could. This was the beginning of the barnstorming era. *Information courtesy of the National Museum of Naval Aviation.*

Curtiss XF15C-1, Quonset Air Museum
(USN photo)

Curtiss XF15C-1

The XF15C-1 was a mixed-propulsion fighter prototype of the 1940s. It is an all-metal aircraft with a cantilever low wing that folds for storage aboard an aircraft carrier. It is equipped with a tricycle undercarriage and the cockpit has a bubble canopy. The initial prototype had a conventional low-wing horizontal stabilizer but due to problems with this arrangement the model on display is equipped with a T-tail.

Powered by both a 2,100 hp (1,566 kW) Pratt & Whitney R-2800-34W 18-cylinder two-row radial, 2,100 hp (1,566 kW) propeller engine, and an Allis-Chalmers (licensed DeHavilland H-1B) J36 turbojet with 2,700 lbf (1,226 kN) thrust, the aircraft was in theory the fastest fighter in the US Navy at that time. The turbojet was intended for use only when climbing and in combat. It had a maximum speed of 469 mph (755 km/h), a range of 1,385 miles (2,228 km), a ceiling of 41,000' with the P&W engine only, and a rate of climb of 5,020 ft/min (25.5 m/s). It was armed with four wing-mounted 20 mm (.79 in) cannon.

By the late 1940s, the United States Navy was interested in the mixed-power concept for its shipborne fighters - i.e. aircraft with a mixture of propeller and turbojet engines, such as the FR Fireball. As such, an order was placed with Curtiss on 7 April 1944 for delivery of three mixed-power aircraft, designated the F15C.

The first flight of the first prototype was on 27 February 1945, without the turbojet installed. When this was completed in April of the same year, the aircraft flew several mixed-power trials, however on 8 May it crashed on a landing approach, killing test pilot Lloyd Child. The second prototype flew for the first time on 9 July, again in 1945, and was soon followed by a third prototype. Both aircraft showed promise, however by October 1946 the Navy had lost interest in the mixed-power concept and cancelled further development. Wikipedia.

The XF15C on display in the Quonset Air Museum was the third and final prototype (BuNo. 01215), and has the distinction of being the last Curtiss-Wright aircraft manufactured for the US Navy. (*Information courtesy of the Quonset Air Museum*).

Dassault HU-25A Guardian, USCG
(photo courtesy of Wikipedia)

Dassault HU-25A Guardian

The HU-25 Guardian is a USCG version of the Dassault Falcon 20, a French business jet which was the first of a family of business jets built by Dassault Aviation. Marcel Dassault gave the go-ahead for production of an eight or ten seat executive jet or military liaison aircraft the Dassault-Breguet Mystère 20 in December 1961.

The Mystère 20 was a low-wing monoplane with two rear-mounted Pratt & Whitney JT12A-8 engines. The prototype, registered F-WLKB, first flew on the 4 May 1963 at Bordeaux-Merignac. Under the influence of Pan American the aircraft was re-engined with two General Electric CF700 engines and some dimensions were increased. Pan American signed a contract to distribute the Mystère 20 in the western hemisphere and ordered 40 aircraft with options on 120. The re-engined aircraft first flew on 10 July 1964. The first production aircraft flew on 1 January 1965 and both French and American certification was awarded in June 1965. Deliveries began to the Pan American outfitting facility at Burbank Airport, California. In 1966 the company re-designated the American-delivered aircraft as the Fan Jet Falcon; this later became the Falcon 20. Military orders from Australia and Canada were received. All non-American aircraft were fitted out before delivery at Bordeaux-Merignac. In 1967 Pan American Business Jets Division increased their firm orders to 160 aircraft.

The improved Falcon 200 featured more advanced jet engines and other major improvements to increase range, capacity and comfort. The aircraft proved to be so popular that production did not end until 1988, being superseded by more advanced developments of the Falcon family. The United States Coast Guard operates a model called the HU-25 Guardian which is used as a high-speed spotter aircraft to locate shipwreck survivors and direct slower-moving aircraft and rescue vessels, and interdict aerial and shipborne drug trafficking.

Later developments of the Falcon 20 include the smaller Falcon 10, the larger 30-seat Falcon 30 (not developed) and Falcon 50, an improved three-engined development.

Three versions of the Guardian were built for the USCG: HU-25A Guardian, USCG version of the Falcon 20G; HU-25B Guardian, Pollution control version for the US Coast Guard equipped with side-looking airborne radar (SLAR); and HU-25C Guardian, Drug interdiction version for the US Coast Guard, equipped with a Westinghouse APG-66 search radar and WF-360 infrared turret. Wikipedia.

DeHavilland D.H.100 Vampire
(photo courtesy of Wikipedia)

DeHavilland D.H.100 Vampire

The D.H.100 Vampire was Britain's first single-seat jet fighter-bomber, entering RAF service in 1946. The DH.100 Vampire was commissioned by the Royal Air Force during the Second World War, and was the second jet fighter to enter service with the RAF, after the pioneering Gloster Meteor. Although the Vampire arrived too late to see combat during the war, it served with front line RAF squadrons until 1955, and continued in use as a trainer until 1966. The Vampire also served with many air forces worldwide, and set aviation firsts and records.

The Mk. 6 was powered by one 3350 lb D.H. Goblin 3 turbojet, and could reach a maximum speed of 548 mph. It had a service ceiling of 42,800', and a range of 1,220 miles. The Vampire is armed with four 20mm cannon mounted in the nose and has underwing pylons capable of carrying eight 60lb rockets or two 1,000lb bombs or drop tanks. *The Complete Encyclopedia of World Aircraft.*

Almost 3,300 Vampires were built, a quarter of them under license in other countries. The Vampire design was also developed into the DeHavilland Venom fighter-bomber as well as naval Sea Vampire variants. Wikipedia. The Quonset Air Museum has a former Swiss Air Force Vampire on display.

DeHavilland Canada U6A Beaver, New England Air Museum
(Author photo)

DeHavilland Canada DHC-2/U6A Beaver

The Beaver is a light utility transport powered by one 450-hp Pratt & Whitney R-985 Wasp Junior radial piston engine. It has a maximum speed of 163 mph, a service ceiling of 18,000', and a range of 733 miles.

The Beaver was developed as a short take-off and landing (STOL) transport in 1946 and made its first flight in 1947, and served primarily as a bushplane. The YS bought 980, which went into service as the U-6 in 1962. The British Army also purchased 46. The Beaver has been in use by at least 50 different countries. It has room for a pilot and in advanced versions, up to seven passengers. It is also operated on skis and floats. (*The Complete Encyclopedia of World Aircraft*)

DeHavilland Canada C7A Caribou, New England Air Museum
(Author photo)

DeHavilland C7A Caribou

The C-7A is a twin-engine, short takeoff and landing (STOL) utility transport built by DeHavilland Aircraft of Canada, Ltd. The C7 is powered by a pair of 1,450-hp Pratt & Whitney R-2000-7M2 Twin Wasp radial piston engines or a pair of General Electric GEYT-64 engines. It has a maximum speed of 216 mph, a service ceiling of 24,800', and a range with maximum payload and reserves of 242 miles. *The Complete Encyclopedia of World Aircraft.*

The Caribou is primarily used for tactical airlift missions in forward battle areas with short, unimproved airstrips. It can carry 26 fully equipped paratroops or up to 20 litter patients. As a cargo aircraft the Caribou can haul more than three tons of equipment. *Information courtesy of the Canadian Forces Archives.*

The Caribou made its first flight in 1958. In 1959, the US Army flew several prototypes for evaluation and, in 1961 the first 22 out of a total of 159 production versions were delivered to the Army. Originally designated AC-1, the aircraft was redesignated CV-2 in 1962 and retained that designation for the remainder of its US Army career. In January 1967, when responsibility for all fixed-wing tactical transports was transferred to the US Air Force, the Caribou received the designation C-7. During the Southeast Asian conflict, the Caribou's STOL capability made it particularly suitable for delivering troops, supplies, and equipment to isolated outposts. *(Information courtesy of the National Museum of the United States Air Force).*

Douglas C-47 Skytrain
(photo courtesy of the USN)

Douglas DC-3/C-47 Skytrain

The Skytrain is a short to medium range transport powered by a pair of 1,200-hp Pratt & Whitney R-1830-S1C3G Twin Wasp radial piston engines. It had a maximum speed of 230 mph, a service ceiling of 23,200', and a range of 2,125 miles. The Skytrain was also configured as a gunship, the AC-47D. The Spooky gunship variant was armed with three .3-in General Electric Miniguns firing through the fourth and fifth windows and from the open door on the port side of the fuselage. *The Complete Encyclopedia of World Aircraft.*

The Douglas C-47 cargo and passenger aircraft was the workhorse of the armed forces for many years. It carried heavy loads to high altitude and was used extensively in the China-Burma-India theater of WWII to fly supplies over the hump (The Himalayan Mountains). It was used by paratroopers and figured prominently in the European D-Day invasion.

Few aircraft are as well known or were so widely used for so long as the C-47 or Gooney Bird as it was affectionately nicknamed. The aircraft was adapted from the DC-3 commercial airliner which appeared in 1936. The first C-47s were ordered in 1940 and by the end of WW II, 9,348 had been procured for AAF use. They carried personnel and cargo, and in a combat role, towed troop-carrying gliders and dropped paratroops into enemy territory. After WW II, many C-47s remained in USAF service, participating in the Berlin Airlift and other peacetime activities. During the Korean War, C-47s hauled supplies, dropped paratroops, evacuated wounded and dropped flares for night bombing attacks. In Vietnam, the C-47 served again as a transport, but it was also used in a variety of other ways which included flying ground attack (gunship), reconnaissance, and psychological warfare missions. *(Information courtesy of the National Museum of the United States Air Force).*

Douglas C-54D Skymaster
(Wikipedia photo)

Douglas C-54D-1 Skymaster

The Skymaster is a long-range transport powered by four 1,350-hp R-2000-11 radial piston engines. It had a maximum speed of 280 mph, a service ceiling of 22,300', and a range of 2,500 miles carrying an 11,440-lb payload. 380 C-54Ds were built. *(The Complete Encyclopedia of World Aircraft)*

The USAAF accepted a grand total of 1,162 C-54's. Specifically, the C-54 program comprised 24 C-54s, 252 C-54As (56 to the Navy), 220 C-54Bs (30 to the Navy), 1 VC-54C specially modified to serve as Presidential transport for President Roosevelt (SACRED COW). 380 C-54Ds (86 to the Navy), 125 C-54Es (20 to the Navy) 162 C-54Gs (13 to the Navy) another 235 C-54Gs were cancelled after VJ-Day.

The C-54 and its sister, the DC-4, were designed in cooperation with five major United States airline companies. The Douglas design was bigger, longer ranged, and was powered by four engines. The prototype first flew in June 1938. The original design was considered too large for economical operations, resulting in a subsequent scaled down 42-passenger version.

When the United States entered World War II, the DC-4 was taken over by the Army Air Corps and redesignated the C-54. Maximum load was 28,000 pounds of cargo or 50 passengers. The first C-54 military transport flew in February 1942, and over 1,000 planes were produced. When the war ended, the growing airline industry demanded the C-54 as a suitable passenger plane. It was returned to the DC-4 configuration. During the Berlin Airlift in 1948, every C-54 the USAF had was pressed into service to supply the isolated city. Many C-54s were later converted into litter-carrying planes for use during the Korean War, returning 66,000 patients to the United States. *(Information courtesy of the Strategic Air and Space Museum)*

Douglas A-26C Invader
(photo courtesy of Wikipedia)

Douglas A-26C Invader

The Invader was the fastest three-seat USAAF light/medium bomber of WWII. It was powered by a pair of 2,000-hp Pratt & Whitney R-2800-27 or –79 Double Wasp radial piston engines. It had a maximum speed of 355 mph, a service ceiling of 22,100', and a range of 1,400 miles. It was armed with 10 .50 cal machine-guns and could carry up to 4,000-lbs of bombs. *The Complete Encyclopedia of World Aircraft.*

Some variants of the Invader such as the C model have a glazed nose for the bombardier, while other Attack variants were equipped with up to eight .50 caliber guns in the nose for the tactical role. The A-26, a follow-up airplane to the A-20 Havoc, made its first flight on July 10, 1942. Production delivery began in August 1943, and on November 19, 1944, it went into combat over Europe. It was used for level bombing, ground strafing and rocket attacks. By the time production halted after VJ-Day, 2,502 Invaders had been built.

The A-26 was redesignated the B-26 in 1948. During the Korean War, the airplane entered combat once again, this time as a night intruder to harass North Korean supply lines. Early in the Vietnam conflict, the Invader went into action for the third time. Also, the USAF ordered 40 modified B-26Bs having more powerful engines and increased structural strength. Designated the B-26K, the airplanes were designed for special air warfare missions. In 1966, the B-26K was redesignated the A-26A. *(Information courtesy of the National Museum of the United States Air Force).*

Douglas F4D-1 Skyray, New England Air Museum
(Author photo)

Douglas F4D-1 Skyray

The Skyray was the first short range, fast climbing, carrier-based interceptor. The Skyray is powered by one 14,500-lb thrust Pratt & Whitney J57-P-8B turbojet. It has a maximum speed of 7722 mph at sea level, a service ceiling of 55,000', and a range of 1,200 miles. It is armed with four fixed forward-firing 22mm cannon and can carry up to 4,000-lbs of stores, including auxiliary fuel, bombs, rockets or missiles on six underwing hardpoints. *The Complete Encyclopedia of World Aircraft.*

When the USAF accepted the Navy F4D into its domain its inventory it already had an F4 fighter so it designated the aircraft as a model F6A. Extensive wind tunnel tests led to the creation of the bat-like form with the horizontal flying controls attached to the wing trailing edge classifying it as tailless. It set a world speed record of 753.4 mph for a carrier plane.

The Skyray was one of the most effective interceptors of its era. In June 1947 Douglas Aircraft Corporation received a Navy contract for the study of a delta-wing fighter. Approval of preliminary designs and engineering concepts 18 months later led to a contract for two prototypes (XF4D-1s) that were delivered and first flown in January 1951. The XF4D-1 proved not to be a true delta-wing but rather a swept-wing with low aspect ratio. Testing trials followed by carrier suitability tests proved quite successful and full-scale production of 420 F4D Skyrays commenced thereafter. During test phases the XF4D-1 prototypes established speed records over the International 3-km course (755 mph) and the 100 km closed circuit course (728 mph).

Armed with 20 mm cannons and Sidewinder air-to-air missiles, the F4D was capable of carrying a weapons load compatible with its mission to intercept enemy aircraft before they reached their target. As an interceptor, the F4D established five world rate-of-climb records which, in turn, led to the assignment of a Navy all-weather F4D squadron at San Diego and one at Key West to the Air Force's North American Air Defense Command in an interceptor role. The San Diego unit earned honors as the best in NORAD for two years running.

The last of the short-ranged Skyrays served until 1964. The Museum's F4D-1 (BuNo. 134806) was received from NAS Patuxent River. *Information courtesy of the National Museum of Naval Aviation.*

Douglas A4D-1 Skyhawk, New England Air Museum
(Author photo)

Douglas A4D-1/A-4B/A-4F/A-4M/TA-4J Skyhawk

The Skyhawk is a single-seat carrier-based attack bomber, powered by one 11,200-lb thrust Pratt & Whitney J52-P-408A turbojet. It has a maximum speed of 670 mph, and a range with a 4,000-lb bomb-load of 340 miles. The aircraft was armed with two 20mm cannon and could carry up to 9,155 pounds of weapons on five external hard-points. *The Complete Encyclopedia of World Aircraft.*

The Skyhawk first flew on 22 June 1954. Its compact size allowed it to operate from a carrier without folding the wings. It added long range capability with bombs, atom bombs, missiles, rockets, guns and other weapons. It refueled by tanker aircraft and could itself be converted into a tanker by carrying external wing tanks. On the 15th of October 1955 it set a new F.A.I. world speed record for a 500 km closed course at an average speed of 695.163 mph. Later production models were equipped with electronic instrumentation for all weather navigation and weapon delivery. The Skyhawk replaced the Skyraider in USN and US Marine service and was widely employed as an attack aircraft over Vietnam. The Skyhawk was powered by Pratt & Whitney J52-P-408A turbojet. The aircraft was armed with two 20mm cannon and could carry up to 9,155 pounds of weapons on five external hard-points.

The Douglas A-4D Skyhawk was designed by the late Ed Heinemann in response to a Navy requirement for a fast (but compact) long-range, light-weight carrier jet aircraft capable of delivering a nuclear weapon. Prototype test results in 1954 confirmed that the Skyhawk exceeded all of the Navy's criteria. Because of its small size (wing span less than that of a Piper Cub) and ease with which flight deck personnel could handle it in comparison with other jet aircraft, A-4Ds became known variously as either Scooters, Tinker Toys or Heinemann's Hot Rod.

An A-4 set a world speed record of over 695-mph in 1959 for class C aircraft over a 500 km course. Fitted with two 150 gallon under wing drop tanks, two A-4Ds flew 2,082 miles non-stop without in-flight refueling in a demonstration of its long-range capability. While original specifications limited the aircraft to 30,000 lbs fully loaded, various weight-saving measures reduced that to 25,000 lbs. This was accomplished by elimination of a heavy duty battery in favor of a fuselage stored wind driven generator; back-up hydraulic system eliminated by gravity dropped gear; and installation of a simplified air conditioning system one third the weight of those then available.

The A-4 was stress limited to 24,500 lb total weight for catapult launches, and 5,000 lb ordnance loads on a center line and four wing racks ranging from conventional bombs, to sophisticated weapons such as the Gatling gun, Bullpup, Walleye, Shrike and, in one case, Sidewinder air-to-air missiles. Built into the aircraft were two 20mm cannons. The Skyhawk participated in the first raids of the Vietnam War and became one of the primary strike aircraft thereafter until replaced by the Ling-Tempco-Vought A-7 Corsair II in the 1969 timeframe. An A-4C is credited with shooting down a MiG -17 over Vietnam. The A4Ds endured the most losses of any carrier-based aircraft in Vietnam with the loss of 195 of them in combat including those piloted by Senator John McCain and Vice Admiral James Stockdale as well as the first two victims of surface-to-air guided missiles during that conflict. The A-4 also saw considerable combat action during the Arab/Israel and Falkland Island wars.

Nearly 3,000 A-4s were produced from 1956 to 1979 for use by the Navy and Marine Corps as well as Australia, Israel, Argentina and Kuwait. A two-seat trainer version was still used by the Navy until late 1999. *Information courtesy of the National Museum of Naval Aviation.*

The Collings Foundation TA-4J Skyhawk (C/N 13590) was delivered to the US Navy and accepted into the inventory on 24 July 1967 and assigned BuNo. 153524. It saw initial service with Marine Air Group 43 in 1968 before being transferred to Naval Test Pilot School at NAS Pax River where it saw extensive service. On 5 August 1994 it was flown to the Aircraft Maintenance and Regeneration Center (AMARC) at Tucson, Arizona where it was deemed to be in excess of US Navy requirements. Skyhawk "524" had completed her Naval service with a total of 6496.6 hours.

The Collings Foundation was allocated a Douglas TA-4 Skyhawk through Congressional action in October 2000. After looking at various aircraft that were held in storage at AMARC BuNo. 153524 was selected because the overall condition of the aircraft and its low airframe hours. The aircraft was removed from storage at AMARC, Tucson exactly one year after the legislation was signed into law. Negotiations with Navy attorneys were laborious as the Foundation struggled to complete the Deed of Gift and to transfer missing components. After four years of delays, the transfer of the needed components was finally completed in the spring and summer of 2004.

The Skyhawk was disassembled in Tucson and shipped by truck to the facilities of AvCraft in Myrtle Beach, SC, arriving on 3 October 2004. Reassembly and return to flight inspections along with needed repairs were begun immediately upon arrival. To expedite the process, it was decided to involve noted A-4 specialists from Safe Air Ltd. in New Zealand to add their expertise to the process of making it a restoration with the high quality the Collings Foundation expects of its flying collection. Specialists Ian Ginders, Norm Tse, and Dave Meikle reassembled the aircraft and completed both Phase A and B inspections. SafeAir is acknowledged as being the world's foremost Skyhawk experts and combined with help from AvCraft's specialty shops; the TA-4J project was on schedule for engine runs by December 2004. The Foundation is thankful to Ben Bartel, President of AvCraft for his generous underwriting of the project.

The first flight since "524"s initial retirement by the Navy was accomplished on 15 December 2004 at Myrtle Beach, South Carolina with Captain Bert Zeller (USNR) at the controls. The flight was made without incident and a few minor squawks were addressed upon landing. TA-4F Skyhawk BuNo 153524 then went to Av Source West, Midland, Texas, where it underwent repainting. Av Source West replicated the paint scheme carried by the aircraft of H&MS 11, "the Playboys", based at DaNang during the Viet Nam war. Hentzen Coatings of Milwaukee, Wisconsin, supplied the primer and paint to complete this project. The Collings Foundation is proud to honor the memory of all Vietnam Veterans by returning the Playboy colors to the sky. The Skyhawk is currently based in Houston, TX and it operates as part of the Collings Foundation Vietnam Memorial Flight. *Information courtesy of the Collings Foundation).*

Douglas F3D-2 Skyknight
(photo courtesy of Wikipedia)

Douglas F3D-2 Skyknight

The Skyknight is a carrier-based all-weather fighter powered by two 3,400-lb thrust Westinghouse J34-WE-36/36A turbojets. It had a maximum speed of 565 mph, a service ceiling of 38,200', and a range of 1,200 miles. It was armed with four fixed forward-firing 20mm cannon. *The Complete Encyclopedia of World Aircraft.*

In 1946, the Navy contracted with Douglas Aircraft Company for the development of a carrier based night-fighter. Specifications included twin-jet power, side-by-side seating for the pilot and radar operator, 500 mph top speed, 500 mile combat radius, an operating altitude of 40,000 ft, and an escape system that enabled the crew to depart downward through the bottom of the fuselage.

First flown in March 1948, the three prototype XF3D-1s confirmed the basic soundness of the design and led to the first production F3D-1s being delivered to the Navy in 1950. However, insufficient roll rate at high speed was a major deficiency of the F3D-1 and limited its production run to only 28 examples. These aircraft were delivered to the Navy's VC-3 and the Marine's VMF (N)-542 in late 1950 and were utilized primarily in a training role while awaiting delivery of the improved F3D-2 model. The -2 models incorporated new electronic and radar equipment, thicker bullet proof canopy, wing spoilers to improve rate-of-roll, an automatic pilot and provisions for air-to-air rocket weapons. Max speed and range were increased to 600 mph and 1200 miles respectively utilizing uprated versions of the basic model's J34 engines. First flown in February 1951, production of the F3D-2 totaled 237 examples including several conversions to special-duty variants.

Operational use of the F3D-2 was primarily by Marine squadrons. Deployed to Korea in August 1952, the Marine's VMF (N)-513 proved the effectiveness of the Skyknight by destroying both jet and prop aircraft in night engagements. Marine F3Ds were responsible for the destruction of more enemy aircraft than any other Navy/Marine Corps aircraft type. Scoring six and possibly seven kills, the Skyknight scored the first jet versus jet night kill in history and was later credited with the destruction of a MiG-15 jet fighter at night.

The Navy also deployed the Skyknight to the Korean theater, albeit in a more limited role. VC-4 Det 44N deployed four F3D-2 aircraft onboard USS Lake Champlain (CVA-39); the ship reaching Korean waters during the final months of the war. In the combat zone, the Detachment flew both carrier based and land based sorties (attached to VMF (N)-513) in support of the UN effort.

In the post-war years, missile and ECM versions were produced. In this capacity, the aircraft was utilized to train both all-weather pilots and Radar Intercept Officers, and as an electronic reconnaissance and countermeasure aircraft during the Cuban Missile Crisis and through much of the Vietnamese Conflict including combat missions in the latter. As a result, the Skyknight (redesignated the F-10 series in 1962) was the only tactical jet aircraft to see combat action in both the Korean and Vietnam War. The last of the Sky Knights were retired in 1970. *Information courtesy of the National Museum of Naval Aviation.*

The F3D-2 Skyknight (BuNo. 124620) on display in the Quonset Air Museum was assigned to VMF (N) – 513 in Korea during the Southeast Asian conflict. After the war it returned to the USA and was initially based in southern California, and then later at Cherry Point, North Carolina. This aircraft later served in Vietnam as an EF-10B counter-intelligence aircraft. *(Information courtesy of the Quonset Air Museum).*

Douglas A-3B Skywarrior, New England Air Museum
(Author photo)

Douglas A-3B Skywarrior

The Skywarrior is a carrier-based attack bomber powered by two 10,500-lb thrust Pratt & Whitney J57-P-10 turbojets. It had a maximum speed of 610 mph, a service ceiling of 41,000', and a range of 1,050 miles. It was armed with two 20mm cannon in a radar-controlled rear turret, and could carry up to 12,000 lbs of assorted weapons in an internal bomb bay. *The Complete Encyclopedia of World Aircraft.*

Designed in 1947 to fit the role of a heavy bomber capable of operating from carriers, the Skywarrior was intended to maximize the combination of jet-engine power and nuclear weapons delivery capability. The initial designed gross weight of 60,000 lbs (later increased to 82,000 lbs) made it the largest and heaviest plane ever projected for use from carriers then in service. The A-3 incorporated a 36-degree swept-wing design, podded engines, and an internal weapons storage bay capable of carrying 12,000 lbs of ordnance.

First flown on October 28, 1952, the first of fifty production models were delivered to the Navy on March 31, 1956. It was these aircraft (manned by three crewmen) that were instrumental in evaluating the total concept of carrier-based strategic bombers, and experimenting with their use aboard aircraft carriers. Because of its size, the A3D was known as the Whale. Unlike most jet aircraft, the A3D was not equipped with an ejection seat. Instead, the crew exited the A3D through a chute under the fuselage.

230 variants of this first version of the A3D would see service in a wide array of missions. The A3D-2 incorporated a change in the weapons bay in order to accommodate a wider range of weapons stores (including mines), as well as a 1,082-gallon in-flight refueling pack. The YA3D-1P photo-reconnaissance version and the A3D-2Q (EA-3B) radar countermeasures and electronic reconnaissance aircraft were also developed. The A3D-2T with a pressurized fuselage was employed as a trainer for radar/navigation crewmen and could accommodate six pupils plus an instructor and the pilot.

During the Vietnam War, the Skywarrior served in the tanker and countermeasures capacity. Navy squadrons operated the EA-3B as a radar countermeasures and electronic jamming aircraft while the KA-3B tanker was utilized to top up the fuel for carrier-based strike aircraft on their way to missions into Vietnam. About thirty aircraft became EKA-3Bs with the dual role of countermeasures as well as tanker aircraft. Significant records established by the A3D included:

Non-stop flight without refueling from Hawaii to Albuquerque, New Mexico.

Non-stop flight without refueling from a West coast carrier to Jacksonville, New England via Oklahoma City and winning the Douglas Trophy for the first leg of the flight at an average speed of 606 mph.

Two transcontinental speed records on a round trip flight from Los Angeles to New York and return and on a mainland to Hawaii flight.

Heaviest aircraft to launch from a carrier at 84,000 lbs.

Longest (6100 miles) nonstop flight by a carrier tactical aircraft from Naval Station Rota, Spain to NAS Alameda, CA.

The last of the A-3s was retired in 1993. The Museum's aircraft (BuNo. 135418) was received from the Naval Missile Center, NAS Patuxent River, MD. *Information courtesy of the National Museum of Naval Aviation.*

Etrich Taube
(Owls Head Transportation Museum photo)

Etrich Taube

The Etrich *Taube*, also known by the names of the various manufacturers who build versions of the type, for instance Rumpler *Taube*, was a pre-World War I monoplane aircraft, and the first mass-produced military plane in Germany. Being the Germans' first practical military plane, the *Taube* ("dove") was used for all common military aircraft applications, including as a fighter, bomber, surveillance plane and trainer from its first flight in 1910 until the beginning of World War I. The plane was very popular in the years immediately prior to the First World War, and was used by the air forces of Italy, Germany and Austria-Hungary. (Even the Royal Flying Corps operated at least one example in 1912.) By 1914, however, it quickly proved lacking as a serious warplane, and was soon superseded.

The Owls Head Transportation Museum is so far the only known museum to attempt the construction of a flyable reproduction of the Etrich Taube in North America. Their example first flew in 1990, and it still flies today with the power of a 200 hp Ranger L-440 inline-6 "uprighted" air-cooled engine. Wikipedia.

Fairchild A-10A Thunderbolt II, Massachusetts Air National Guard
(photo courtesy of Wikipedia)

Fairchild A-10A Thunderbolt II

The Thunderbolt is a single-seat close-support aircraft powered by a pair of 9,065-lb thrust General Electric TF34-GE-100 turbofans. It has a maximum speed of 439 mph, and an endurance rate of 1 hour and 40 minutes. The Thunderbolt II is armed with a General Electric GAU-8/A Avenger 30mm seven-barrel cannon. *The Complete Encyclopedia of World Aircraft.*

The A-10 is the first USAF aircraft designed specifically for close air support of ground forces. It is named for the famous P-47 Thunderbolt, a fighter often used in a close air support role during the latter part of WW II. The A-10 is designed for maneuverability at low speeds and low altitudes for accurate weapons delivery, and carries systems and armor to permit it to survive in this environment. It is intended for use against all ground targets, but specifically tanks and other armored vehicles.

The Thunderbolt II's great endurance gives it a large combat radius and/or long loiter time in a battle area. Its short takeoff and landing capability permits operation from airstrips close to the front lines. Service at forward area bases with limited facilities is possible because of the A-10's simplicity of design. The first prototype Thunderbolt II made its initial flight on May 10, 1972. A-10A production commenced in 1975. Delivery of aircraft to USAF units began in 1976 and ended in 1984. *(Information courtesy of the National Museum of the United States Air Force).*

In the photo illustration, an AGM-65 Maverick missile flies away from a USAF A-10 Thunderbolt attack aircraft from the 104th Fighter Wing, Barnes Air National Guard Base, Westfield, Massachusetts, over northwest Florida during a Combat Hammer Air-to-Ground Weapons System Evaluation Program (WSEP) mission. The missions are conducted by the 86th Fighter Weapons Squadron (FWS), from Eglin Air Force Base, Florida. Wikipedia.

Fieseler Fi-156 Storch, Collings Foundation
(photo courtesy of the Collings Foundation)

Fieseler Fi-156 Storch

The Storch is a two-seat army co-operation/reconnaissance aircraft powered by one 240-hp Argus As 10C-3 8-cylinder inverted Vee piston engine. It had a maximum speed of 109 mph, a service ceiling of 15,090', and a range of 239 miles. It was armed with one rear-firing 7.92mm machine-gun on a pivoted mount. *The Complete Encyclopedia of World Aircraft.*

The Storch (Stork) was designed in 1935 and was widely used during WW II by German military forces for reconnaissance, liaison, ambulance, and other duties and by high ranking officers as personal transports. Among its features was its maneuverability, extremely low stalling speed of 32 mph, and its short field takeoff and landing characteristics. Between 1937 and 1945, the German Air Force accepted almost 2,900 Starches. Other countries using the Fi 156 included Sweden, Finland, Switzerland, and Italy. The most famous Storch mission was the hazardous rescue of deposed Italian dictator Benito Mussolini in 1943 from a tiny rock-strewn plateau at a remote lodge high in the Apennine Mountains. *(Information courtesy of the National Museum of the United States Air Force).*

One of the most unique aircraft ever produced, the Fieseler Fi-156 Storch was an aircraft built for a specific task. Able to take off and land in literally twice its own length, it was perfect for forward air observation on battlefields and air ambulance work. Flying for the German Luftwaffe in WWII, it saw service on all fronts. The Fi-156 Storch flown by the Collings Foundation is based in Stow, MA and flies regularly. It can be seen at regional events and always attracts attention when it flies. *Information courtesy of the Collings Foundation).*

Fokker Dr.I replica, New England Air Museum
(Author photo)

Fokker Dr.I

The Fokker Dr.I Dreidecker (Triplane) was a World War I fighter aircraft built by Fokker-Flugzeugwerke. The Dr.I saw widespread service in the spring of 1918. It became renowned as the aircraft in which Manfred von Richthofen gained his last 20 victories, and in which he was killed on 21 April 1918. While no Dr.I airframes survive, large numbers of flying and static replicas have been built. Wikipedia.

Fokker C.IVA, Owls Head Transportation Museum
(photo courtesy of Wikipedia)

Fokker C.IVA

The C.IV was a 1920s Dutch two-seat reconnaissance aircraft designed and built by Fokker. The C.IV was developed from the earlier C.I but it was a larger and more robust aircraft. The C.IV was designed as a reconnaissance biplane with a fixed tailwheel landing gear and was originally powered by the Napier Lion piston engine. It had a wider fuselage and wider track of the cross-axle landing gear than the C.I.

Examples of the C.IV were delivered to both the Dutch Army Air Corps (30 aircraft) and the Dutch East Indies Army (10 aircraft). It was also exported; the USSR bought 55 aircraft and the United States Army Air Service acquired eight. Twenty aircraft were licensed built in Spain by the Jorge Loring Company for the Spanish Army. After service as reconnaissance machines the aircraft were then operated as trainers into the 1930s.

The last flying example of a C.IV is a C.IVA preserved at the Owls Head Transportation Museum in Owls Head, Maine. It was used in a trans-Pacific attempt in the late 1920s or early 1930s. They took out the seats in the passenger compartment and installed a large fuel tank. They also put a small cockpit just in front of the vertical stabilizer with a hand-powered fuel pump inside. In flight, the crew member sitting there would transfer fuel to the main tank in the wing, where it would be fed by gravity into the engine. In this trans-Pacific attempt they planned not to go straight across the Pacific but up the West Coast of North America to Alaska and down the chain of Aleutian Islands, proceeding down the Chinese coast to Tokyo. They took off from Tacoma, Washington and started to head north, but made it about 100 miles of the way to Vancouver, British Columbia when the engine vapor locked and forced a landing in a field. They had to dump most of their fuel to bring down the weight in order to take off from the field. Then they got back in the air, they started heading for the national airport to top off the tanks, but they crashed upon landing and decided to give up. They loaded the C.IV onto a Ford flatbed truck and brought it back to Tacoma. It sat until 1970, when one of the museum's trustees found it and restored it and donated it to the museum. It flies to this very day. Wikipedia.

Fouga CM 170R Magister
(Wikipedia photo)

Fouga CM 170R Magister

The Fouga Magister (company designation CM.170) is a 1950s French two-seat jet trainer. The related CM.175 Zéphyr was a carrier-capable version for the French Navy.

Although it is often lauded as the first purpose built two-seat turbojet-powered trainer aircraft, similar claims are made for the Fokker S.14 Mach trainer whose first flight, production, and service entry were all about year earlier. However, the Magister was much more successful than the Mach trainer, being produced in far greater numbers and being exported to many nations.

In 1948, Fouga designed a jet-powered primary trainer called CM.130 for the French Air Force (Armée de l'Air, AdA) to replace piston-engined Morane-Saulnier MS.475 aircraft. When AdA found the aircraft lacking in power from the two Turbomeca Palas turbojets, Fouga enlarged the basic design and used the more powerful Turbomeca Marboré engine. The distinctive V-tail of the new CM.170 Magister originated on the CM.8 glider Fouga was using to experiment with jet engines. In December 1950, AdA ordered three prototypes, with the first aircraft flying on 23 July 1952. A pre-production batch of 10 was ordered in June 1953 followed by the first production order for 95 aircraft on 13 January 1954. Fouga built a new assembly plant at Toulouse-Blagnac to produce the aircraft. The aircraft entered service with AdA in 1956. Due to different industrial mergers, the aircraft has been known as the "Fouga CM.170 Magister", "Potez (Fouga) CM.170 Magister", Sud Aviation(Fouga) CM.170 Magister" and "Aérospatiale (Fouga) CM.170 Magister" depending on where and when they were built.

The French Navy's Aeronavale adopted a derivative of the Magister, the CM.175 Zéphyr, as a basic trainer for deck landing training and carrier operations. These were preceded by two "proof of concept" prototypes designated the CM.170M Magister, which made their first flights in 1956/57.

An improved version of the Magister designated the CM.173 Super Magister was produced from 1960. It used a more powerful Turbomeca Marboré IV engine. Introduction of the Magister stopped in France in 1962 but continued to be built in Finland up to 1967. The development of the aircraft came to an end when the French Air Force selected the Alpha Jet as their new jet trainer.

The first export customer was Germany who ordered 62 aircraft from Fouga and Flugzeug Union Süd license built a further 188 aircraft. In addition the CM.170 was built under license by Valmet in Finland, and Israel Aircraft Industries in Israel, with a total of 929 built. Of these 286 were completed under license. Wikipedia.

Gee Bee Model A, New England Air Museum
(Author photo)

Gee Bee Model A

The Granville Gee Bee Model A is a two-place single engine biplane racing aircraft of the 1930s. Only nine were built. One survivor is on display in the New England Air Museum, Reg. No. N901K.

Gee Bee R1 Supersportster Racer, New England Air Museum
(Author photo)

Gee Bee R1 Supersportster Racer

The Granville Gee Bee Model Z was an American single engine monoplane racing aircraft of the 1930s, the first of the Super Sportster aircraft built by Granville Brothers Aircraft of Springfield, Massachusetts (*Gee Bee* stands for Granville Brothers), with the sole intent of winning the Thompson Trophy. In this it was successful, setting a speed record for land-based aircraft. However, it soon suffered a fatal crash during a world speed record attempt, starting the reputation of the Gee Bee aircraft as killers.

The Gee Bee Model R Super Sportster (also known as the GB Sportster), sometimes nicknamed *The Flying Silo* due to the short, fat fuselage resembling that type of farm storage building, was a special purpose racing aircraft.

The 1932 R-1 and its sister ship, the R-2, were the successors of the previous year's Thompson Trophy-winning Model Z. It was suspected by a few that the Model Z's crash during a speed run in December 1931 was due to an unexpected failure of the gasoline tank cap, which may have been ripped off of the fuel tank filler tube by the aerodynamic boundary layer of air immediately over the surface of the airplane's fuselage, resulting in the now-airborne gas cap smashing into the pilot's face. A bullet-proof windscreen and internal fuel caps were part of the new design.

Chief engineer Howell 'Pete' Miller and Zantford 'Granny' Granville spent three days of wind tunnel testing at NYU with aeronautical engineering professor Alexander Klemin. The aircraft had a very peculiar design. Granny reasoned that a teardrop-shaped fuselage would have lower drag than a straight-tapered one, so the fuselage was wider than the engine at its widest point (at the wing attachment point). The cockpit was located very far aft, just in front of the vertical stabilizer, in order to give the racing pilot better vision while making crowded pylon turns. In addition, it turned out that the fuselage acted as an airfoil, just like the 'lifting-body' designs of the 1960s. This allowed the plane to make tight 'knife-edge' turns without losing altitude. It was, in effect, a Pratt & Whitney R-1340 engine with wings and a tail on it. Wikipedia.

Goodyear ZNP-K Airship car
(Author photo)

Goodyear ZNP-K Airship

The ZNP-K Airship is one of the K-class non-rigid airships, a class of blimps built by the Goodyear Aircraft Company of Akron, Ohio for the US Navy. These blimps were powered by two radial air-cooled engines mounted on outriggers on the side of the control car that hung under the envelope. Before and during World War II 135 K-Class blimps were built, configured for patrol and anti-submarine warfare operations and were extensively used in the Navy's anti-submarine efforts in the Atlantic and Pacific Ocean areas.

The K-Class blimp was a product of the austere times of the American depression. In 1937, the K-2 was ordered from Goodyear as part of a contract that also bought the L-1. The L-Class was Goodyear's standard advertising and passenger blimp. The K-2 was the production prototype for future K-class airship purchases. K-2 flew for the first time at Akron, Ohio on 6 December 1938 and was delivered to the Navy at NAS Lakehurst, New Jersey on 16 December. The envelope capacity of the K-2 404,000 cubic feet (11,440 m³) was the largest for any USN blimp up to that time. K-2 was flown extensively as a prototype, and continued to operate testing new equipment, techniques, and performing whatever tasks were needed, including combat patrols in World War II.

On 24 October 1940, the Navy awarded a contract to Goodyear for six airships (K-3 through K-8) that were assigned the designation Goodyear ZNP-K. These blimps were designed for patrol and escort duties and were delivered to the Navy in late 1941 and early 1942. The K-3 through 8 had only minor modifications to the K-2 design; the only major change was in engines from Pratt & Whitney R-1340-16s to Wright R-975-28s. The Wright engine/propeller combination proved excessively noisy and was replaced in later K-ships with the Pratt & Whitney engines.

During the life of the K-Class airship the US Navy used three different designation systems. From 1922 through World War II the Navy used a four character designator. The K-Class blimps were designated ZNP-K where the "Z" signified lighter-than-air; "N" denoted non-rigid; "P" denoted a patrol mission; and "K" denoted the type or class of airship.

In April 1947, the General Board of the US Navy modified the designation system for airships. The second character of the designator was dropped as the Board dropped the code for rigid airships so that the "N" for non-rigid was no longer needed. The designation for the K-Class blimps then became ZPK. Wikipedia.

General Dynamics F-16A Fighting Falcon, Vermont ANG
(photo courtesy of the USAF)

General Dynamics F-16A Fighting Falcon

The Fighting Falcon is a single-seat front-line air-superiority and air-to-ground attack fighter, powered by a Pratt & Whitney F100-PW-220 engine, or by a General Electric F110-GE-100 after-burning turbofan. It has a maximum speed of more than 1,320 mph, a service ceiling above 50,000', and a range of 575 miles. *The Complete Encyclopedia of World Aircraft.*

The Falcon has been nicknamed the "Electric Jet", and it is highly maneuverable. Its strong, light, carbon-epoxy frame can with —stand 9 G's of pressure (about the maximum a pilot can take), and computerized "fly-by-wire" controls maximize the F-16's flight characteristics. A side-arm control mounted on an arm-rest helps the pilot keep hold of the stick under high Gs, and head-up instrumentation enables him to keep his eyes on the target. The USAF Thunderbird Air Demonstration Team has been flying the F-16 since 1983.

The F-16 evolved from a 1972 USAF Lightweight Fighter (LWF) prototype program which sought a small, lightweight, low cost, air-superiority day fighter designed for high performance and ease of maintenance. It achieved combat-ready status in October 1980. Many foreign nations, including Belgium, Denmark, Turkey, Egypt and Israel, have purchased the F-16. *(Information courtesy of the National Museum of the United States Air Force).*

The photo shows a pair of General Dynamics F-16 Fighting Falcons flown by the Vermont Air National Guard "The Green Mountain Boys" 158th Fighter Wing.

Grumman TBF-1 Avenger
(photo courtesy of the USN)

Grumman TBF-1/General Motors TBM-3E Avenger

The Avenger is a three-seat carrier-based torpedo-bomber. The TBM-3 variant is powered by one 1,750-hp Wright R-2600-20 Cyclone 14-cylinder radial engine. It had a maximum speed of 267 mph, a service ceiling of 23,400', and a range of 1,130 miles. It was armed with two forward-firing .50 cal machine-guns, one .50 cal machine-gun in a dorsal turret and on .3-in machine-gun in a ventral position. It could carry 2,000 lbs of weapons in the bomb bay, and later variants could be armed with rocket projectiles, drop-tanks or equipped with a radar pod mounted under the wing. *The Complete Encyclopedia of World Aircraft.*

The Avenger was the workhorse of the USN during WWII. Avengers remained in service until the mid-1950s. It served in virtually every carrier and was employed for torpedo attack, level bombing and spotting/reconnaissance. Many are used in the water-bomber role today.

In response to a 1939 requirement for a carrier-based torpedo-bomber to replace the TBD Devastator, Grumman Aircraft Engineering Corporation produced the TBF Avenger equipped with an electrically powered gun turret and an internal bomb-bay for four 500 lb bombs or an aerial torpedo. Crewed by a pilot, radioman and gunner, the TBF could cruise at 145 mph. In 1942 General Motors also built the TBF known as the TBM. A total of 9,842 TBF/TBM Avengers were produced, the last of which were retired in 1954.

The combat debut of the TBF occurred during the Battle of Midway when six of them were launched from Midway without fighter escort to attack the approaching Japanese fleet. Jumped by Zeros during their torpedo runs, five were shot down while the sixth was so badly shot-up (pilot/radioman wounded, gunner killed) that it was scrapped after landing at Midway with bomb-bay doors open and only one wheel extended.

In 1944 while flying from an aircraft carrier on a bombing mission against a Japanese radio station on Chichi Jima, the TBM of LTJG George Bush was severely damaged by anti-aircraft fire. Despite a flaming engine, he continued his dive to score a direct hit before being forced to bail-out over water where he was picked up by a submarine and subsequently returned to his squadron to fly additional combat missions. Both of his crewmen failed to survive.

Other combat highlights involving the Avenger included the sinking of six Japanese transports in one day by aircraft from a single squadron; the sinking of the world's largest battleships, the Musashi and Yamato; shooting down ninety-eight planes in aerial combat; and sinking thirty-one German submarines in the Atlantic.

In 1945, five TBMs from NAS Fort Lauderdale on a routine training flight disappeared in an area known as the Bermuda Triangle. Their location remains a mystery to this day. *Information courtesy of the National Museum of Naval Aviation.*

The TBM-3 Avenger on display in the Quonset Air Museum (QAM) was acquired from Hick and Lawrence Aerial Applicators, Ontario, Canada, where it had been used as a spruce budworm sprayer. The aircraft made a forced landing in the northwest Maine wilderness due to engine problems in 1972, where is remained until the QAM learned of its existence in 1989. The QAM's Historic Aircraft Recovery Team made four expeditions to the crash site to prepare the aircraft for recovery. On 18 September 1991, the Connecticut Army National Guard airlifted the Avenger out of the Maine wilderness with a Sikorsky CH-54B Tarhe (Skycrane) and it was then flown to the Presque Isle, Maine, airport for transportation to the Quonset Air Museum. *(Information courtesy of the Quonset Air Museum).*

The TBM Avenger owned by the Collings Foundation is a TBM-3E built by Eastern in 1944. It was thoroughly restored to wartime condition after serving as a fire-bomber in the early 80's. It is based at Stow, MA and can be seen at airshows on the East Coast. This Avenger has been noted as being the most accurately restored example of the TBM available on the airshow circuit. *Information courtesy of the Collings Foundation).*

Used in Korea as a carrier-based fighter and night fighter, the Corsair's technologically advanced features enabled it to survive in an era where propeller-driven fighters were being replaced by jets. The F4U-5NL-5NL Corsair owned by the Collings Foundation is one of these Korean warriors. It was restored by American Aero Services in New Smyrna Beach, FL, and was completed in the fall of 2003. *Information courtesy of the Collings Foundation).*

Grumman F6F-3 Hellcats
(photo courtesy of the USN)

Grumman F6F-3 Hellcat

The Hellcat was a single-seat carrier-borne day or night-fighter that replaced the Wildcat in 1943. This aircraft operated primarily from carriers in the Pacific against the Japanese during WWII. The Hellcat was powered by one 2,000-hp Pratt & Whitney R-2800-10W Double Wasp 18-cylinder radial piston engine. It had a maximum speed of 380 mph, a service ceiling of 37,300', and a range of 1,530 miles. It was armed with six .50 cal machine-guns, although later models were equipped with two 20mm cannon in place of two of the machine-guns. The Hellcat could also be armed with two 1,000-lb bombs or six 5-in rockets. *The Complete Encyclopedia of World Aircraft.*

In 1942, Grumman Aircraft Engineering Corporation began mass production of the F6F Hellcat fighter as replacement for the F4F/FM-2 Wildcat which had been carrying the burden of fighter operations in the Pacific. The results obtained from testing a captured Japanese Zero restored to flyable condition were utilized in refining design features of the production F6F to enable it to engage the Zero on equal terms and thus dictate the rules of combat. At one time during the war, Grumman was delivering a Hellcat at the rate of one per hour around the clock for a grand total of 12,275 deliveries from 1942 to 1945.

While the F6Fs capability for carrying bombs and rockets was widely utilized in air support of friendly ground forces as well as the destruction of enemy airfield installations and shipping, it is best known for its role as a fighter. All in all, the Hellcat was credited with destroying 5,156 enemy aircraft in air-to-air combat (75% of all Navy aerial kills) with a kill ratio of 19:1. Notable combat stories of F6F encounters with enemy aircraft during World War II are legendary and include:

A division of four pilots from the first squadron to receive the F6Fs accumulated 50 kills without the loss of a single aircraft. A Marine night fighter squadron shot down twenty-two aircraft over a two month period.

David McCampbell (Navy's leading ace with 34 aerial kills and 20 on the ground) accounts for seven aircraft from a flight of 80 in a single encounter; and, later attacked a flight of 60 aircraft with a single wingman, shooting down nine while his wingman accounted for 7 others. McCampbell received the Medal of Honor.

A flight of F6Fs fed into the landing pattern of 49 Japanese aircraft on Guam and shot down 30 while the balance crashed on landing. Following the war, F6Fs were used as advanced flight trainers and radio controlled drones as targets and explosive laden aircraft flown against installations in North Korea. *Information courtesy of the National Museum of Naval Aviation.*

Grumman F6F-5 Hellcat (Serial No. 79192) is on display in the New England Air Museum. Grumman F6F-5 Hellcat (Serial No. 70185) is being restored at the Quonset Air Museum, and a ¾-scale Hellcat (Serial No. 1), Reg. No. N6FN, built by Al Sparling is also on display.

Hellcat (BuNo. 70185) in the Quonset Air Museum was recovered by QAM in December, 1993 off the coast of Martha's Vineyard, Massachusetts. This Hellcat had been assigned to NACTULANT (Night Air Combat Training Unit Atlantic) which was headquartered at NAAF Charlestown, Rhode Island.

According to Navy Crash records, this F6F was on a familiarization flight out of NAAF Westerly, Rhode Island on 3 April 1945. The aircraft was one of seven aircraft on a ground control intercept flight. The aircraft were in the vicinity of Nantucket Sound when the Pilot, Ensign Vincent A. Frankwitz, USNR, radioed a loss of oil pressure. He was ordered to turn towards Martha's Vineyard where there was a small Navy Auxiliary landing field. He descended rapidly to below the 600 foot overcast and at this point his wingman noted that Frankwitz's engine seized.

The aircraft appeared to make a successful ditching and Ensign Frankwitz was seen to exit the aircraft. The aircraft sank in approximately one minute. Ensign Frankwitz was sighted several times in the water in the midst of the oil slick before his wingman was ordered back to base. Ensign Frankwitz was never rescued. The water temperature was 42 degrees. This Grumman F6F-5 Hellcat is to be dedicated and restored in his memory. 70185 is an early production F6F-5 that retains the small windows behind the cockpit. Of the 7,869 F6F-5 Hellcats produced, only 1,404 were built before the rear windows were deleted. *(Information courtesy of the Quonset Air Museum).*

Grumman HU-16E Albatross
(Author photo)

Grumman HU-16E Albatross

The Albatross is a twin-engine general purpose amphibian aircraft with good short take-off and landing characteristics and a range of 4600 km. It could also carry 10 passengers or 12 stretcher patients. The Albatross was powered by a pair of 1,425-hp Wright R-1820-76A or 76B Cyclone 9-cylinder radial piston engines. It has a maximum speed of 236 mph, a service ceiling of 21,500', and a range of 2,850 miles. *The Complete Encyclopedia of World Aircraft.*

The versatile Albatross amphibian was designed to meet a Navy requirement for a utility aircraft which could operate from land or water and, with skis, from snow and ice. The prototype first flew on October 24, 1947 and soon after the USAF ordered a quantity for air-sea rescue duties as SA-16As. (In 1962 the USAF designation was changed to HU-16.) Grumman delivered 297 -As to the Air Force; most were assigned to the Air Rescue Service.

In 1955, Grumman developed an improved version with a 16 ½ foot increase in wing span and larger aileron and tail surfaces. Beginning in 1957, many -As were converted to the -B configuration with these improvements.

The Albatross is best known as a rescue aircraft. During the Korean War, Albatrosses rescued almost 1,000 United Nations personnel from coastal waters and rivers, often behind enemy lines. They also made numerous dramatic and hazardous rescues in Southeast Asia, on occasion taxiing many miles over rough, open water when unable to take-off. *(Information courtesy of the National Museum of the United States Air Force).*

Begun in 1944 as a general purpose amphibian to replace the Grumman JRF Goose which served throughout WW II, the HU-16 (UF) Albatross was another example of Grumman's ten year experience in building amphibians. Flown in 1947, it featured a conventional two-step hull, full amphibian capability, a high wing with fixed stabilizing floats, and a single tail unit. Three variations of the aircraft were produced, including the winterized UF-1L for Antarctic operations, the dual-control UF-1T for use as a trainer, and the general purpose UF-1. The

US Air Force also procured the Albatross as the SA-16 for air-sea rescue duties, and signed an agreement in which the Air Force and Coast Guard would train Navy pilots in the techniques of operating the HU-16 in Search and Rescue.

The Albatross established three record flights for amphibians in September 1962 that included two separate altitude flights carrying 1,000 and 2,000 kg loads to 29,460' and 27,380' respectively, and a new world 5,000 km. speed record carrying a 1,000 kg load with a speed of 151.4 mph in a UF-2G. The last operational HU-16 Albatross made a final water landing on Pensacola Bay on 8 August 1976 and was then turned over to the NMNA. *Information courtesy of the National Museum of Naval Aviation.*

The USCG Air Station, Race Point Beach, Cape Cod, Massachusetts has a Grumman HU-16E Albatross on display. The New England Air Museum has Grumman HU-16E Albatross (Serial No. 51-7228), marked USCG 7228, on display.

Grumman S2F-3 Tracker
(photo courtesy of the USN)

Grumman S2F-3 Tracker

The Tracker is a twin engine aircraft powered by a pair of 1,525-hp Wright R-1820-82WA Cyclone 9-cylinder radial piston engines. It had a maximum speed of 265 mph, and a range of 1,300 miles. The Tracker combined the roles of anti-submarine warfare (ASW) and search and strike in one patrol aircraft. The aircraft could be equipped with 32 sonobuoys in engine nacelles, an APS-38 search radar in a retractable radome, and magnetic anomaly detection (MAD) gear in a boom which extended behind the tail. Armament included a fuselage weapons-bay for one Mk. 57 or Mk. 101 nuclear depth bomb or 60 echo-sounding depth charges carried in the fuselage, and six underwing pylons capable of handling depth-bombs, torpedoes or rockets. *The Complete Encyclopedia of World Aircraft.*

The Grumman S2F/S-2A Tracker was developed and first flown in 1952 to replace hunter/killer aircraft for anti-submarine warfare operations. Design criteria required that the aircraft accommodate air-to-underwater guided missile torpedoes and associated electronic equipment, and be capable of long-range search missions at low altitudes while flying in all-weather conditions from an aircraft carrier.

The first of 755 production model S-2s entered service in 1954 and soon established themselves as the Navy's front line carrier based ASW air-craft. Later versions carried Jezebel passive long-range acoustic search equipment and Julie explosive echo-sounding equipment.

The Tracker was manned by a crew of four (two pilots, two radar operators). The last front-line Trackers were retired from active duty in 1976. A training version, the TS-2A, remained in service until 1979. *Information courtesy of the National Museum of Naval Aviation.*

Grumman C-1A Trader (modified), Quonset Air Museum
(Author photo)

Grumman C-1A Trader

The Trader is a derivative of the S-2 Tracker which first appeared in 1955 as the Grumman C-1, powered by two 1,525-hp Wright R-1820-82WA Cyclone 9-cylinder radial piston engines. The C-1A grossed out at 27,900 lbs, had a top speed of 253 mph and a maximum range of 1150 miles. The Trader was designed as a Carrier Onboard Delivery (COD) aircraft to provide passenger, mail and cargo services to deployed carriers. The C-1A could be configured to carry up to nine passengers or up to 4,800 lbs of high priority cargo whose dimensions were compatible with those of the cargo area and/or the fuselage access doors (this included small jet engines). *The Complete Encyclopedia of World Aircraft.*

The Traders normally operated from overseas shore-based VR (transport) squadrons and, in many situations, as detachments from other foreign military fields, e.g., Philippines, Turkey, Greece, Norway, etc., to support naval requirements. Some aircraft carriers had a C-1A permanently assigned to provide proficiency time for eligible ship's pilots.

The C-1A was the last piston driven carrier aircraft in the Navy and served until 30 September 1988. When operating as a COD, the crew consisted of two pilots and an aircrewman who performed in the capacity of a plane captain, mechanic and loadmaster. *Information courtesy of the National Museum of Naval Aviation.*

The US Navy needed an advanced carrier-based aircraft suitable for flying with a large radar assembly, the Hazeltine AS/APS-82 and Grumman chose to redesign the C-1 to carry it. In 1956 Grumman modified the C-1 tail assembly, replacing the single vertical fin and rudder with new twin fins and rudders attached to a modified horizontal stabilizer. The bobbed centre tail provided support for the rear fairing of the large 20' by 30' radome. TF-1 (BuNo. 136792) was used to test the flight characteristics of the design, proving that large over the fuselage radomes could be practically flown and operationally deployed. This knowledge led directly to the design, production and operational deployment of the Grumman E-2 Hawkeye and the Boeing E-3 Sentry AWACs aircraft.

When "792" test flying duties came to an end, the aluminum "dummy" radome it carried was removed and the aircraft was transferred to the Overhaul and Repair Department (O & R) of the Quonset Point Naval Air Station on 11 September 1969. On 3 April 1974, "792" made the last official Navy flight from Quonset NAS. The aircraft was retired from NAES Lakehurst, New Jersey on 3 February 1983. *(Information courtesy of the Quonset Air Museum).*

Grumman E-1B Tracer, New England Air Museum
(Author photo)

Grumman E-1B Tracer

To provide the Navy with an airborne early-warning aircraft capable of operating from aircraft carriers, Grumman began development of a variant of the S-2A Tracker in 1954. This was designated as the WF-2, based on the C-1A and subsequently redesignated E-1B Tracer, more often being known as Willy Fudd to its pilots and crewmen. Powered by two 1,525-hp

Wright R-1820-82WA Cyclone 9-cylinder radial piston engines, the Tracer had a maximum speed of 265 mph, and an endurance with maximum fuel of 9 hours. Its ferry range was 1,300 miles. The E-1B has a crew of four, and grosses out at 26,200 lbs. *The Complete Encyclopedia of World Aircraft.*

The first flight, in March 1957, was by a C-1A modified as an aerodynamic prototype to be the first major type of naval aircraft to carry a massive dish-type radome above the fuselage. The other major external change consisted of a new tail unit with twin fins and rudders and a central fin. Delivery of 88 production models began in February 1958 and operated until replaced by the Grumman E-2 Hawkeye.

Detachments of two aircraft along with crews and other supporting personnel from a parent squadron were deployed on aircraft carriers operating overseas. The New England Air Museum has E-1B Tracer (Serial No. 147217) on display. *Information courtesy of the National Museum of Naval Aviation.*

Grumman OV-1A Mohawk
(photo courtesy of Wikipedia)

Grumman OV-1A Mohawk

Grumman OV-1 Mohawk is a two-seat multi-sensor observation aircraft powered by a pair of 1,400-lb Avco Lycoming T53-L-701 turboprops. It has a maximum speed of 289 mph, and a maximum range of 1.011 miles. The Mohawk was used as a combat team in concert with the AC-119K gunship. It improved the lethality of the gunship by acting as a target seeker. Once a target was identified, the gunship would be called in for the attack. Two versions of the OV-1 were used, the OV-1B carrying a Side Looking Airborne Radar (SLAR) and the OV-1C with an infra-red (IR) detector. *The Complete Encyclopedia of World Aircraft.*

The Army OV-1's flew out of Udorn Royal Thai Air Base and conducted nightly reconnaissance patrols of the Plain of Jars (or Barrel Roll) area of Laos. The IR equipped OV-1C's could detect heat from the engines of trucks and even camp fires. The SLAR equipped OV-

1B's were used to detect moving objects. In many cases, the targets identified by the OV-1's were gone by the time the recorded reconnaissance data was gathered, interpreted and analyzed. The idea was to relay the near real-time target data appearing on the OV-1 monitors to AC-119K gunships operating in the area. The Mohawk was also called the Spud.

The first test period of the OV-1 Seeker and AC-119K Destroyer (or Hunter Killer) teams was done between 27 April and 23 May 1970. Intelligence data indicated most enemy troop movements were conducted in the late evening so the evaluation missions were flown between 8 and 11 PM. When the OV-1 detected a target, the information was passed the Airborne Battlefield Command and Control Center (ABCCC). The ABCCC or Alleycat was a Lockheed HC-130 flying over Laos used to coordinate aircraft flying within its zone. If a gunship was available (support of troops in contact (TIC) took precedence over all other missions), and target validation could be obtained, the ABCCC relayed the information to the gunship. The AC-119K then flew to the target area and attempted to identify the target using its Forward Looking Infrared (FLIR) or Night Observation Device (NOD). The test was relatively successful when all the equipment worked properly; however, this was rare. The SLAR system on the OV-1B was prone to failure and there was only one aircraft assigned to the Army detachment at Udorn. The AC-119K systems were also prone to failure. There were only three Stinger assigned at Udorn and each was scheduled (fragged) for a mission every night. The season was changing from dry season to wet season and some missions were canceled due to bad weather. Furthermore, the IR detection capability of the OV-1C was reduced with increased moisture. Wet weather virtually eliminated the IR detection capability of the AC-119K.

The most serious problem was the OV-1 / AC-119K seek and destroy team was the rules of engagement. Because of several friendly fire incidents, nearly all targets identified by the OV-1 were reported to the ABCCC which in turn relayed the information to the US embassy in Laos for validation. Once validated, the target information was relayed back to the ABCCC which would then call for the gunship. The gunship would then be cleared to attack to coordinates of the original sighting, but if the target had moved, the entire validation process had to begin again.

The second test period for the OV-1/AC-119K teams was between 19 September and 19 November 1971, 16 months after the initial test. The second test was formed in an ad hoc manner at the start of the fall dry season. A large column of enemy trucks was detected on the morning of September 19th and the Army urgently requested gunship support. The OV-1's were still based at Udorn, but the AC-119 had moved to Nakhon Phanom (NKP) Air Base in Thailand. Although the tactics were essentially the same during the second test period, the results were not. The OV-1 advisories amounted to a very small number of successful attacks. The AC-130 Spectre gunships were in use by this time and were very effective at finding their own targets and destroying them without the cumbersome relay and validation scheme used for OV-1 identified contacts. With the failure of the second Hunter Killer test, the concept was dropped. *(Information courtesy of the National Museum of the United States Air Force).*

Grumman A-6B Intruder
(Author photo)

Grumman A-6B Intruder

The Intruder is a two-seat (side-by-side) sub-sonic carrier or shore-based all-weather attack bomber, capable of day and night operations using an internal, fully integrated attack/navigation system. It is powered by a pair of 9,300-lb thrust Pratt & Whitney J52-P-8B turbojets. It has a maximum speed of 644 mph, a service ceiling of 42,400', and a range with maximum payload of 1,011 miles. It is equipped with one under-the-fuselage and four underwing attachment points for weapons and stores and is capable of carrying an external load of 18,000 pounds. *The Complete Encyclopedia of World Aircraft.*

The Intruder had an excellent slow-flying capability and a combat radius of 1,100 miles. Grumman Aerospace Corporation produced 693 Intruders, which flew for the Navy and the Marines between 1963 and 1967. The Navy's experience in the Korean War showed the need for a new long-range strike aircraft with a high subsonic performance at tree-top height to permit under-the-radar penetration of enemy defenses and capable of finding and hitting small targets in any weather. The result was the Grumman A-6 Intruder.

Manned by a pilot and bombardier/navigator seated side-by-side, the A-6 was designed to be powered by two engines which gave the Intruder far better reliability and performance than a single engine design and was heartily endorsed by flight crews because of the added margin of safety. The concept of incorporating tilting tailpipes to provide for a STOL (Short Takeoff and Landing) was abandoned when it was determined that tilting tailpipes only reduced landing speeds by 7 mph at normal approach weights which the Navy considered acceptable.

The first of the A-6 series (A-6A) were delivered to the Navy in 1963 and to the Marines in 1964. The first operational squadron to receive the A-6As was VA-75 that began its support of US forces in Vietnam flying initially from USS Independence. The Digital Integrated Attack and Navigation Equipment (DIANE) and its subsystems incorporated into the aircraft enabled the crew to attack preselected targets or targets of opportunity at night or under adverse weather conditions without the crew having to look out of the cockpit from launch to recovery.

As the A-6 aircraft were produced from the -6A through the -6E, developments in sophisticated electronics and delivery hardware were incorporated. These developments included Low Light Level TV (LLLTV), Forward Looking Infrared (FLIR), targeting with laser beam, and Moving Target Identification (MTI) which enabled the crew to detect and destroy land or sea targets moving at a speed greater than 10 mph. Properly used, the Intruders produced disproportionate results as illustrated when two A-6s made a night strike with 26-500 lb bombs against a North Vietnam power plant. The damage was such that the Vietnamese were convinced that B-52s had been at work. A Navy Cross was awarded for this mission as was done for a number of other similar ones.

Subsequent to Vietnam, equally effective all-weather strikes were made by A-6s against targets in Libya during the Gulf of Sidra crisis, Iranian gun boats in the Persian Gulf, and Iraqi installations during Desert Storm operations. The last of the A-6E Intruders were retired in 1997 although the EA-6B Prowler variants are still in service. *Information courtesy of the National Museum of Naval Aviation.*

The A-6B Intruder (BuNo. 155629) on display in the Quonset Air Museum is one of only 19 Intruders of the 700 built to be modified to the A-6B Wild Weasel configuration. This aircraft saw combat in Vietnam with Attack Squadron VA-165 "Boomers" aboard the USS America (CVA-66) during their 1969-1970 combat deployment. This Intruder was flown to the Quonset Air Museum on 7 December 1994 from US Navy Attack Squadron VA-34 "Blue Blasters" based at Naval Air Station Oceana, Virginia Beach, Virginia. *(Information courtesy of the Quonset Air Museum).*

Grumman F-14A Tomcat, New England Air Museum
(Author photo)

Grumman F-14A Tomcat

The Tomcat is a two-seat carrier-based multi-role fighter powered by two 20,900-lb thrust Pratt & Whitney TF30-P-412A afterburning turbofans. It has a maximum speed of 1,564 mph, a service ceiling of over 50,000' and a range of 2,000 miles. It is armed with one General Electric M61A-1 20mm cannon in the forward fuselage and can carry various combinations of bombs or missiles, including the Phoenix, Sidewinder and Sparrow. It can also carry a tactical reconnaissance pod or ECM equipment. *The Complete Encyclopedia of World Aircraft.*

Failure of the General Dynamics F-111B to meet US Navy requirements for an advanced carrier-based air superiority fighter left a significant gap in the Navy's inventory. Following its cancellation in April 1968, the Navy launched a new design contest in which the finalists were Grumman and McDonnell with the former declared the winner with its proposed variable geometry, two-seat twin-engined aircraft. Designated the F-14 and eventually named Tomcat, procurement began in 1969 for 700 aircraft for completion in the early nineties. Deliveries to the Navy began in June 1972 with deployment of operational carrier squadrons in 1974.

The ability to sweep its wings aft 43 degrees from the horizontal, coupled with twin 21,000 lb thrust engines enables the F-14 to achieve speeds in excess of twice the speed of sound. The degree of variable sweep is a function of aircraft speed and is computer controlled. As aircraft speed bleeds off for whatever reason (high-g's, landing, etc.), the computer automatically compensates by extending the wing for more lift to prevent a stall from occurring.

The F-14As made a brief appearance over Vietnam, flying protective patrols for helicopters effecting the final evacuation of US forces from Saigon with no opposition from enemy fighters. The Middle East was to become the scene of the Tomcat's combat initiation during encounters with Libyan fighters over the Gulf of Sidra in 1981 when several Sukhoi SU-22 "Fitter" fighters were shot down. In its interceptor roll, the F-14 proved invaluable during the gulf war providing cover for airborne Navy and USAF support aircraft as well as blocking Iraqi aircraft from flying to safe-havens in Iran.

The F-14 with its Phoenix air-to-air missile coupled with airborne early warning aircraft is able to simultaneously intercept, engage and destroy up to five incoming enemy aircraft out to distances in excess of five hundred miles from a carrier task force. The F-14 is now used in the attack role, as well.

Reduction of force requirements and concurrent cuts in defense spending has necessitated gradual replacement by the year 2008 of the F-14s by F/A-18 Hornets. While the latter aircraft lacks the long-range air defense capability of the F-14, it is cheaper to produce and costs less to operate per flight hour. *Information courtesy of the National Museum of Naval Aviation.*

Grumman F-14B Tomcat (BuNo. 162591) was flown to the Quonset Air Museum on 25 January 2002, where it is currently on display. It is a former "Top Gun" aircraft from the US Navy's training facility in Nevada. Grumman F-14B Tomcat (BuNo. 162926) is on display in the New England Air Museum.

Gyrodyne QH-50 DASH
(Wikipedia photo)

Gyrodyne QH-50 DASH

The Gyrodyne QH-50 DASH (Drone Anti-Submarine Helicopter) is a small, drone helicopter built by Gyrodyne Company of America for use as a long-range anti-submarine weapon on ships that would otherwise be too small to operate a full-sized helicopter. It remained in production until 1969. Several are still used today for various land-based roles.

DASH was a major part of the United States Navy's Fleet Rehabilitation and Modernization (FRAM) program of the late 1950s. FRAM was started because the Soviet Union was building submarines faster than the US could build anti-submarine frigates. Instead of building frigates, the FRAM upgrade series allowed the US to rapidly catch up by converting older ships that were otherwise less useful in modern naval combat. The Navy was able to inexpensively upgrade the sonar on World War II-era destroyers, but needed a stand-off weapon to attack out to the edge of the sonar's range. The old destroyers had little room for add-ons like a full flight deck. The original DASH concept was a light drone helicopter that could release a nuclear depth charge or torpedoes. The aircraft was considered expendable.

The manned Gyrodyne XRON Rotorcycle program of the mid-1950s provided prototype work for the DASH, and ultimately the Rotorcycle was modified to produce the initial drone version, the DSN-1/QH-50A. The DSN-1 was powered by a Porsche YO-95-6 72 hp piston engine and carried one Mark 43 homing torpedo. The next developmental version was the DSN-2/QH-50B that was powered by two Porsche YO-95-6 engines and also carried one Mk 43 homing torpedo. Serial production of the DASH began with the third version, the DSN-3/QH-50C, in which a 255 hp (190 kW) Boeing T50-4 turboshaft engine replaced the piston engine and the payload was increased to two Mk 44 torpedoes. Three hundred and seventy eight QH-50C were produced before production ended in January 1966. Wikipedia.

Hiller OH-23G Raven Helicopter, New England Air Museum
(Author photo)

Hiller OH-23G Raven Helicopter

The OH-23G Raven was a three-seat light reconnaissance helicopter powered by one 323-hp Avco Lycoming VO-540-A1B flat-six piston engine. It had a maximum speed of 95 mph, a service ceiling of 13,200', and a range of 205 miles. Ravens replaced the Bell-47 Sioux. *The Complete Encyclopedia of World Aircraft.*

In 1949 the Hiller Aircraft Corporation produced a two-seat, two-bladed helicopter that employed a new control system design called Rotor-Matic Control which made it easy to handle as well as providing a high degree of stability. Designated as the Model 360 (and later by the Navy as the HTE-1 and the UH-12), success came instantly and by 1950 it had become the largest selling helicopter in the world. A model of it became the first helicopter to make a transcontinental commercial flight.

With the beginning of the Korean War, production shifted to the military with the Navy ordering a limited number in comparison to the hundreds purchased by the Army. Equipped with a 200 hp power-plant, it became the most powerful light utility helicopter in the world at that time and was employed by both the Army and Navy as medical evacuation, observation, and utility aircraft in Korea.

About 2,200 production versions of this Hiller helicopter were built in the first production run. In the 1970s it appeared in four versions, two of which employed turbine engines. *Information courtesy of the National Museum of Naval Aviation.*

The H-23 Raven was the Army version and performed as a utility, observation, and Medevac helicopter during the Korean War. Model numbers ranged A through D, F and G. The H-23A had a sloping front windshield. The H-23B was used as a primary helicopter trainer. Beginning with the UH-23C, all later models featured the "Goldfish bowl" canopy similar to the Bell 47; it also featured a unique cyclic control system, through two paddles offset 90 degrees to the main rotor blades. The OH-23 had a speed of 97 mph (84 knots). The Raven had a two-bladed main rotor, a metal two-bladed tail rotor. Both the OH-23B and the OH-23C were powered by one Franklin O-335-5D engine.

The OH-23D was a purely military version with a 0-435-23C engine and a more reliable transmission. Most OH-23Ds were replaced by the OH-23G, the most common version of the Raven, with a more powerful Lycoming O-540-9A six-cylinder, horizontally opposed, air cooled 305 hp engine. The OH-23G could seat three. The MEDEVAC version carried two external skid-mounted litters or pods. The Raven saw service as a scout during the early part of the Vietnam War before being replaced by the OH-6A Cayuse in early 1968. The Raven could be armed with twin M37C .30 Cal. machine guns on the XM1 armament subsystem or twin M60C 7.62 mm machine guns on the M2 armament subsystem. The XM76 sighting system was used for sighting the guns. Wikipedia.

Hiller OH-23G Raven (Serial No. 62-23812) is on display in the New England Air Museum.

Hughes OH-6A Cayuse
(photo courtesy of Wikipedia)

Hughes OH-6A Cayuse

The Hughes Helicopters OH-6 Cayuse (nicknamed "Loach", after the requirement acronym LOH - light Observation Helicopter) is a single-engine light helicopter with a four-bladed main rotor used for personnel transport, escort and attack missions, and observation. Hughes also developed the Model 369 as a civilian helicopter, the Hughes Model 500, currently produced by MD Helicopters.

First flown in 1963, the Cayuse has a top speed of 175 mph, a range of 267 miles and a service ceiling of 15,995'. It can be armed with two M60 or M134 Minigun 7.62 mm machine guns; two .50 cal (12.7 mm) MG pods; fourteen 2.75 in (70 mm) Hydra 70 rockets in two pods; or four TOW missiles in two pods; or four Hellfire missiles in two pods. 1,420 OH-6As were built. Internet: Wikipedia.

The Quonset Air Museum's OH-6A served in Vietnam with the 17th Cavalry, Troop C, from February 1969 to February 1970, and with the 5th AVN Det., AVN TNG Team, 8th Cavalry, F Troop, 17th Cavalry, H Troop, May 1971 to January 1973. It then served with NASA from January to May 1973, and with the Connecticut Air National Guard from November 1975 to October 1976. *(Information courtesy of the Quonset Air Museum).*

Hughes OH-6A Cayuse (Serial No. 67-16127) is on display in the New England Air Museum.

Kaman HH-43A Huskie Helicopter
(Author photo)

Kaman HH-43A Huskie Helicopter

The HH-43 Huskie is a twin-engine inter-meshing rotor helicopter initially used as a trainer. The HH-43 had a cabin seating up to 8 passengers and was powered by an 815-hp Avco Lycoming T53-L-1B turboshaft engine. *The Complete Encyclopedia of World Aircraft.*

The Huskie was used primarily for crash rescue and aircraft fire-fighting. It was in use with the US Navy when delivery of the H-43As to the USAF Tactical Air Command began in November 1958. Delivery of the -B series began in June 1959. In mid-1962, the USAF changed the H-43 designation to HH-43 to reflect the aircraft's rescue role. The final USAF version was the HH-43F with engine modifications for improved performance. Some -Fs were used in Southeast Asia as aerial fire trucks and for rescuing downed airmen in North and South Vietnam. Huskies were also flown by other nations including Iran, Colombia, and Morocco.

A Huskie on rescue alert could be airborne in approximately one minute. It carried two rescuemen/fire-fighters and a fire suppression kit hanging beneath it. It often reached crashed airplanes before ground vehicles arrived. Foam from the kit plus the powerful downwash air from the rotors were used to open a path to trapped crash victims to permit their rescue. *(Information courtesy of the National Museum of the United States Air Force).*

Kaman K-16B V-STOL
(Author photo)

Kaman K-16B V-STOL

The Kaman K-16B was one of the first "tilt wing" VTOL experiments. Each propeller blade has provisions for variable camber to allow it to function like a helicopter rotor when the wing is in the vertical position. This approach was one of many to address the VTOL/STOL requirements, but was not altogether successful.

The project was initiated by the US Navy which contracted the Kaman Aviation Corporation to design and build a tilt-wing VTOL vehicle, the program being given the company designation of K-16B. To put the project together in a minimal amount of time, Kaman turned to existing parts and pieces for the construction of the prototype. It was decided that the fuselage of the Grumman JRF Goose, a flying boat configuration, would exactly serve the purpose for this application, along with the fact that it was already available and wouldn't have to be fabricated from scratch.

The tilting wing was fabricated in-house. The wing carried a 34-foot span, but unlike other such tilt-wing designs which rotated to the full 90 degrees, the Kaman design would only move to a maximum 50-degree position. The lifting effect was enhanced because the wing contained large trailing edge flaps that enhanced the downward force effect of the wing when it was in the partially tilted attitude. Small controllable flaps on the propeller/rotors gave the pilot control of the aircraft at speeds up to 50mph when the conventional control surfaces were not yet effective. Above 50mph the flap control phased out automatically and the conventional controls took over. The flaps were operated by a cyclic control system so that the propellers could effectively be operated as rotors. The longitudinal cyclic pitch was used to control yaw, while roll was controlled by changes in propeller pitch.

The K-16B was powered by a pair of General Electric T58-GE-2A turboprops, each driving giant 15-foot diameter propellers, with a projected horizontal speed of up to 300mph. There was also some contribution from the Deflected Slipstream technique as there was a lift enhancement from the large flaps. As promising as this aircraft appeared, it would never take to the air. It was, however, tested In the NASA Ames wind tunnel during 1962. The reason it didn't move into a powered flight test stage is not known. Undoubtedly, the number of promising VTOL programs of the time has to play heavily in the decision. Wikipedia and S. Markman & B. Holder, "Straight Up: A History of Vertical Flight", 2000.

Kaman K-225 Helicopter, New England Air Museum
(photo courtesy of Wikipedia)

Kaman K-225 Helicopter

Kaman K-225 was an experimental helicopter developed by Kaman Aircraft. One was modified to become the world's first gas turbine powered helicopter. The K-125 was Charles Kaman's first helicopter, which utilized intermeshing rotors and Kaman's patented servo-flap stability control. The K-125 first flew on 15 January 1947.

The K-225 was an improved version of the K-125, which first flew in July 1949. The US Navy bought two and the Coast Guard one for $25,000 each. Later, they received the H-22 designation.

A modified K-225 equipped with a Boeing 502 (YT50) engine became the world's first gas turbine powered helicopter in December 1951. This aircraft is now at the Smithsonian. Wikipedia.

Learjet C-21A
(photo courtesy of Wikipedia)

Learjet C-21A

The Learjet Model 35 and Model 36 are a series of American multi-role business jets and military transport aircraft. When used by the United States Air Force they carry the designation C-21A. The C-21A is an "off the shelf" military variant of the Learjet 35A, with room for eight passengers and 42 ft³ (1.26 m³) of cargo. In addition to its normal role, the aircraft is capable of transporting litters during medical evacuations.

The aircraft are powered by two Garrett TFE731-2 turbofan engines. Its cabin can be arranged for 6-8 passengers. The Model 36 has a shortened passenger area in the fuselage, in order to provide more space in the aft fuselage for fuel tanks. It is designed for longer-range mission capability. The engines are mounted in nacelles on the sides of the aft fuselage. The wings are equipped with single-slotted flaps. The wingtip fuel tanks distinguish the design from other aircraft having similar functions.

Delivery of the C-21A fleet began in April 1984 and was completed in October 1985. Dyncorp International provides full contractor logistics support at seven worldwide locations. There are 38 Air Force active duty aircraft, and 18 Air National Guard aircraft in the C-21A fleet. On 1 April 1997, all continental U.S.-based C-21As were realigned under Air Mobility Command, with the 375th Airlift Wing at Scott Air Force Base, Illinois, as the lead command. C-21As stationed outside the continental United States are assigned to the theater commanders. Wikipedia.

On 24 December 1996, a Learjet 35A crashed in New Hampshire, leading to the longest missing aircraft search in that state's history, lasting almost three years, and eventually resulting in Congressional legislation mandating improved emergency locator transmitters (ELTs) be installed in U.S.-registered business jets. Wikipedia.

Ling-Tempco-Vought A-7D Corsair II, Quonset Air Museum
(Author photo)

Ling-Tempco-Vought A-7D Corsair II

The Corsair II is a carrier-based attack bomber powered by a 14,500-lb thrust Allison TF41-A-2 turbofan, or by a Pratt & Whitney J57-P-20A turbojet. It has a maximum speed of 698 mph, and a tactical radius with typical weapon load of 700 miles. It is armed with one 20mm M61A1 multi-barreled cannon, two Sidewinder missiles and an under-fuselage rocket pack. It can also carry 15,000-lbs of mixed stores externally. *The Complete Encyclopedia of World Aircraft.*

The Ling-Temco-Vought design consortium developed the Corsair II based on the F-8 Crusader. The Corsair II first entered service with training squadrons in 1966. The aircraft is a sub-sonic machine, which can carry up to 20,000 pounds of offensive weapons. The A-7D is a single-seat, tactical close air support aircraft. Although designed primarily as a ground attack aircraft, it also has limited air-to-air combat capability. It was derived from the A-7 originally developed by LTV for the US Navy.

The first A-7D made its initial flight on 5 April 1968 and deliveries of production models began on 23 December 1968. When A-7D production ended in 1976, 459 had been delivered to the USAF. In 1973, the USAF began assigning A-7Ds to the Air National Guard (ANG), and by 1987 they were being flown by ANG units in ten states and Puerto Rico. The A-7D demonstrated its outstanding capability to attack ground targets while flown by the 354th Tactical Fighter Wing at Korat RTAFB, Thailand, during the closing months of the war in Southeast Asia. The Corsair II achieved its excellent accuracy with the aid of an automatic electronic navigation and weapon delivery system. *(Information courtesy of the National Museum of the United States Air Force).*

The A-7D Corsair II on display in the Quonset Air Museum was the next to last A-7D built. It had been assigned to the 162nd Tactical Fighter Group, Arizona Air National Guard in 1977, where it was flown until assigned to the 104th TFG, Massachusetts Air National Guard at the Barnes Municipal Airport, Westfield, Massachusetts. This unit used the Corsair II for training at Instructional Airframes for Battle Damage Repair. The A-7D (Serial No. 75-0408) was acquired through the GSA-DRMO system in January 1995. The aircraft was towed 115 miles from Westford, Massachusetts to the Quonset Air Museum on 24 January 1995. *(Information courtesy of the Quonset Air Museum).*

Lockheed L-10A Electra, New England Air Museum
(photo courtesy of Wikipedia)

Lockheed L-10A Electra

The Electra was a twin-engine short-range light transport fitted with a pair of 450-hp Pratt & Whitney Wasp Junior SB radial piston engines. A few were temporarily fitted with Wright R-975-E3 engines as the Model 10-B. They had a maximum speed of 202 mph, a service ceiling of 19,400', and a range of 810 miles.

The Model L-10 is a cantilever low-wing monoplane of all-metal construction, retractable landing gear and a tail unit incorporating twin fins and rudders. It provided accommodation for 10 passengers. The first prototype was flown on 23 February 1934, and 148 production aircraft followed. A number were also pressed into service with the USAAF. *(The Complete Encyclopedia of World Aircraft)*

The Lockheed Electra is perhaps most notable for being the aircraft type in which Amelia Earhart made her ill-fated attempt to fly around the world in 1937. It represented Lockheed's entry into the era of streamlined all-metal planes and as such very ably filled the growing demand for fast, safe, and reliable twin-engined passenger planes. It was used by various airlines in Europe and in North and South America. *(Information courtesy of the Pima Air & Space Museum)*

Lockheed L-1649A-98 Starliner
(photo courtesy of Wikipedia)

Lockheed L-1649A Starliner

The L-1649A Starliner was an improved variant of the Lockheed Constellation ("Connie") propeller-driven airliner powered by four 18-cylinder radial Wright R-3350 engines. It was built by Lockheed between 1943 and 1958 at its Burbank, California, USA, facility. A total of 856 aircraft were produced in four models, all distinguished by a triple-tail design and dolphin-shaped fuselage. The Constellation was used as a civilian airliner and as a US military air transport plane, seeing service in the Berlin Airlift. It was the presidential aircraft for US President Dwight D. Eisenhower.

The initial military versions carried the Lockheed designation of L-049; as World War II came to a close, some were completed as civil L-049 Constellations. The L-1649 Starliner had an all new wing and L1049G fuselage. Military versions included the C-69 and C-121 for the Army Air Forces/Air Force and the R7O R7V-1 (L-1049G) WV-1 (L-749A) WV-2 (L-1049H) (widely known as the Willie Victor) and many variant EC-121 designations for the Navy. **Wikipedia.**

Lockheed T-33A Shooting Star, New England Air Museum
(Author photo)

Lockheed T-33A/TV-2 Shooting Star

The two-place T-33 jet was designed for training pilots already qualified to fly propeller-driven aircraft. It was developed from the single-seat F-80 fighter by lengthening the fuselage slightly more than three feet to accommodate a second cockpit. Originally designed the TF-80C, the T-33 made its first flight in March 1948. Production continued until August 1959 with 5,691 T-33s built. In addition to its use as a trainer, the T-33 has been used for such tasks as drone director and target towing, and in some countries even as a combat aircraft. The RT-33A version, reconnaissance aircraft produced primarily for use by foreign countries, had a camera installed in the nose and additional equipment in the rear cockpit. The Lockheed TV-2 Shooting Star is the USN version of the T-33A.

The T-33 is one of the world's best known aircraft, having served with the air forces of more than 20 different countries for almost 40 years. Many were supplied to foreign nations under the Military Aid Program, and are still in use throughout the world. A total of nearly 6,000 were built. The Canadian Forces (CF) used a license-built version with a Rolls-Royce Nene engine. *(Information courtesy of the National Museum of the United States Air Force)*.

Lockheed F-94C Starfire, New England Air Museum
(Author photo)

Lockheed F-94C Starfire

The Starfire is a two-seat all weather jet fighter powered by one 6,350-lb thrust Pratt & Whitney J48-P-5 turbojet and 8,750-lb thrust with afterburning. It has a maximum speed of 640 mph, a service ceiling of 51,400', and a range of 805 miles. Its armament consisted of 24 folding-fin rockets in the nose, plus 24 similar rockets in two wing pods. *(The Complete Encyclopedia of World Aircraft)*

The F-94 series all-weather interceptors were developed from the Lockheed F-80 Shooting Star. The prototype F-94 first flew on July 1, 1949. The Starfire was subsequently produced in the -A, -B, and -C series. The F-94C (originally designated the F-97A) was a fundamental redesign of the F-94B and made its first flight on the 18th of January 1950. Improvements in the F-94C included a higher thrust engine, single point refueling, a redesigned wing, a swept-back horizontal stabilizer, upgraded fire-control and navigation systems and, later, mid-wing rocket pods. Twenty-four rockets were carried in the nose in a ring around the radome, shielded by retractable doors, with an additional 24 in the wing pods, if installed. The F-94C carried no guns.

Starfires were employed in the air defense of the Continental US in the 1950s. In the F-94A form, they served as the first all-jet all-weather interceptor for the Air Defense Command. The last F-94Cs were withdrawn from USAF service in 1959. *((Information courtesy of the National Museum of the United States Air Force).*

Lockheed F-104A Starfighter
(Wikipedia photo)

Lockheed F-104A Starfighter

The F-104 Starfighter was a tactical strike fighter built for the USAF Tactical Air Command. It was powered by one 15,800-lb afterburning thrust J79-GE-7 engine and was armed with Sidewinder missiles or with bombs or rocket pods for conventional or nuclear strike missions. It was fitted with an in-flight-refueling probe. 77 were built.

On 14 December 1959, an F-104C set a world altitude record of 103,395 feet. The Starfighter was the first aircraft to hold simultaneous official world records for speed, altitude and time-to-climb. *(The Complete Encyclopedia of World Aircraft)*.

The F-104D was a combat training version of the F-104C. 21 were built for the USAF and 20 for the Japanese Self Defense Force under the F-104DJ. The Lockheed F-104B and D models were combat-capable two-place trainer versions used by the USAF. The 20mm cannon was removed from the aircraft to make room for the second cockpit. The two-seat versions also had a much wider vertical stabilizer. Finally, the nose landing gear was relocated to the front of the wheel well and retracted aft instead of forward as on the -A model.

26 F-104Bs were built. The USAF bought 21 improved versions as F-104Ds (Serial Nos. 57-1314 to 57-1334) in 3 production blocks. The -D model is easily distinguished from the -B model by the spacer present between the canopies on the -D model. In addition, -D models starting with Serial No. 57-1320 were fitted with a refueling probe. *((Information courtesy of the National Museum of the United States Air Force)*.

Lockheed P2V-7 Neptune
(Wikipedia photo)

Lockheed SP-2H/P2V-7 Neptune

The Neptune is a long-range maritime patrol aircraft powered by a pair of Wright R-3350-32W Turbo Compound radial piston engines, plus two Westinghouse J34-WE-36auxiliary turbojets. The P2V-7 Neptune had a maximum speed of 403 mph, a service ceiling of 22,000', and a range of 3,685 miles. *The Complete Encyclopedia of World Aircraft.*

The Neptune was designed in 1942 by Vega Aircraft Corp., a subsidiary of Lockheed, as a land based photo-reconnaissance and anti-submarine duty aircraft. Lockheed dissolved Vega in 1943 and an XP2-1 made its first flight in May 1945. A P2V named the Truculent Turtle flew from Perth Australia Sept. 29, 1946 to Columbus Ohio, 11255.6 miles, in 55 hours and 17 minutes breaking the world distance record without refueling. Although designed for land operation this aircraft was flown from carriers. Successive models progressed from the P2V-1 to the P2V-7. In 1962 the P2-Vs were re-designated as P-2s.

The P2V-s became the P-2 E and the P2V-7 became the P-2H. More than 1,000 Neptunes were built for the USN and other services for maritime patrol duties. The land-based Neptune led to the development of the current US P-3 Orion. Improved versions of the Neptune were equipped with jet engines attached outboard of the regular engines. *Information courtesy of the National Museum of Naval Aviation.*

The Lockheed SP-2H (P2V-7) was the last and most sophisticated derivative of the P-2 models built for the Navy for the primary mission of anti-submarine warfare (ASW) and a secondary mission of aerial mining. First flown in early 1954, the SP-2H was the only production model of the Neptune to be equipped with underwing jet pods and to introduce the Jezebel and Julie submarine detection gear. Two hundred and sixteen SP-2H aircraft were produced for the Navy.

The SP-2H saw considerable Vietnam War service in Market Time surveillance missions off the coast of Vietnam. Inland, the Neptunes were deployed experimentally by the Air Force as night attack aircraft, and some versions dropped electronic sensors on truck routes in Laos in hopes of detecting enemy convoys.

The Neptunes were fitted with skis for use in Antarctic and Arctic operations. In their arctic role as cargo transports, they incorporated a unique system in which the cargo was carried in a specially designed module that was fitted into the bomb bay of the aircraft. When inserted, the module became the bottom of the aircraft's fuselage.

The last ASW P2V in the Navy made its final flight on 20 February 1970. Co-pilot for the flight was Rear Admiral Tom Davies, who twenty-four years earlier, had been the pilot of the Truculent Turtle, the Neptune that set a long distance record. Following the flight it joined others in service as utility aircraft in Naval Reserve Squadrons. *Information courtesy of the National Museum of Naval Aviation.*

Lockheed P2V-7 Neptune (BuNo. 131427), VP-21, is on display at Naval Air Station Brunswick, Main, located near the Main Gate.

Lockheed P-3C Orion
(Wikipedia photo)

Lockheed P-3C Orion

The P-3C is a four-engine turboprop land-based, long-range, anti-submarine warfare (ASW) patrol aircraft. Powered by four 4,910-hp Allison T56-A-14turboprops, the Orion has a maximum speed of 473 mph, and a range of 2,738 miles. It can remain on station for three hours at 1,500 feet. The P-3 has a crew of 11, and is armed with 20,000-lbs of ordnance which can include *Harpoon* (AGM-84D) cruise missile, SLAM (AGM-84E) missiles, *Maverick* (AGM 65) air-to-ground missiles, MK-46/50 torpedoes, rockets, mines, depth bombs, and special weapons. It has advanced submarine detection sensors such as directional frequency and ranging (DIFAR) sonobuoys and magnetic anomaly detection (MAD) equipment. The P-3's avionics system is integrated by a general purpose digital computer that supports all of the tactical displays, monitors and automatically launches ordnance and provides flight information to the pilots. In addition, the system coordinates navigation information and accepts sensor data inputs for tactical display and storage. The P-3C can carry a mixed payload of weapons internally and on wing pylons.

To provide a replacement for the P-2 Neptune, the Navy called for design proposals in 1957 for a new high-performance anti-submarine patrol aircraft and suggested that manufacturers seek to meet the requirement with a variant of an aircraft already in production. Lockheed won the design contest by adapting its commercial Electra turboprop, retaining the wings, tail unit, power plant as well as much of the fuselage structure which was shortened by about seven feet and incorporated a weapons-bay together with extensive new electronics and other systems. A prototype of the ASW aircraft (designated YP3V-1 and later changed to P-3) was first flown in late 1959. The name Orion was adopted in late 1960. Delivery of P-3A production models to fleet units began in August 1962.

The Orion was fully equipped for its ASW role, with extensive electronics in the fuselage plus stowage for search stores, and a 13 ft-long unpressurized bomb-bay equipped to carry torpedoes, depth-bombs, mines or nuclear weapons. Ten external pylons under the wings could carry mines or rockets. A searchlight was located under the starboard wing.

Variants of the P-3 included weather reconnaissance aircraft and electronic reconnaissance aircraft that carried special radar, with radomes in long fairings above and below the fuselage and an additional ventral radome forward of the wing. P-3A models were followed and replaced in quick succession by the P-3B and P-3C models each of which incorporated improved electronics. A limited number of P-3s were produced for export under the Military Assistance Program. *Information courtesy of the National Museum of Naval Aviation.*

Lockheed P-3A Orion (BuNo. 152156) is on display at Naval Air Station Brunswick, Main, located near the Main Gate.

Lockheed Martin C-130J Super Hercules,
Rhode Island Air National Guard
(photo courtesy of Wikipedia)

Lockheed Martin C-130J Super Hercules

The C-130J "Super" Hercules is a four-engine turboprop military transport aircraft. The C-130J is a comprehensive update of the venerable Lockheed C-130 Hercules, with new engines, flight deck, and other systems. The Hercules family has the longest continuous production run of any military aircraft in history. During more than 50 years of service, the family has participated in military, civilian and humanitarian aid operations. The Hercules has outlived several planned successor designs, most notably the Advanced Medium STOL Transport contestants. Wikipedia.

The original C-130 Hercules was a medium to long-range combat transport. The C-130A is powered by four 3,750-hp Allison T56-A-1A turboprop engines and was first flown on 7 April 1955. The Hercules has a maximum cruising speed of 374 mph, a service ceiling of 33,000', and a range with maximum payload of 2,487 miles. The Hercules is in service with many nations in many variations, and continues to be upgraded and developed. *(The Complete Encyclopedia of World Aircraft)*

The C-130J is the newest version of the Hercules and the only model still in production. Externally similar to the classic Hercules in general appearance, the J model sports considerably updated technology. These differences include new Rolls-Royce AE 2100 D3 turboprops with Dowty R391 composite scimitar propellers, digital avionics (including Head-Up Displays (HUDs) for each pilot) and reduced crew requirements (two pilots and one loadmaster - no navigator or flight engineer).

The aircraft can also be configured with the "enhanced cargo handling system". The system consists of a computerized load masters station from where the user can remotely control the under floor winch and also configure the flip floor system to palletized roller or flat floor cargo handling. The cargo compartment is approximately 41 feet (12.5 m) long, 9 feet (2.7 m) high, and 10 feet (3.0 m) wide, and loading is from the rear of the fuselage. Initially developed for the USAF, this system enables rapid role changes to be carried out and so extends the C-130J's time available to complete taskings. These combined changes have improved performance over its C-130E/H siblings, such as 40% greater range, 21% higher maximum speed, and 41% shorter take-off distance. Wikipedia.

Lockheed Martin F-35 Lightning II
(photo courtesy of Wikipedia)

Lockheed Martin F-35 Lightning II

The F-35 Lightning II is a family of fifth-generation, single-seat, single-engine stealth multirole fighters. When it enters service it will be the most advanced fighter aircraft in the world and will perform ground attack, reconnaissance, and air defense missions. The F-35 has three main models; one is a conventional takeoff and landing variant, the second is a short take off and vertical-landing variant, and the third is a carrier-based variant. It has a speed of Mach 1.67 (1,283 mph, 2,065 km/h), a range of 1,200 nmi (2,220 km) on internal fuel, a combat radius over 590 nmi (1,090 km) on internal fuel, and a service ceiling of 60,000 ft (18,288 m).

The F-35 is descended from the X-35, the product of the Joint Strike Fighter (JSF) program. JSF development is being principally funded by the United States, with the United Kingdom and other partner governments providing additional funding. It is being designed and built by an aerospace industry team led by Lockheed Martin. The F-35's first flight took place on 15 December 2006.

The United States intends to buy a total of 2,443 aircraft for an estimated US$323 billion, making it the most expensive defense program ever. The USAF's budget data in 2010, along with other sources, projects the F-35 to have a flyaway cost that ranges between US$89 million and US$200 million over the planned production of F-35's, depending on the variant.

In July 2010, the Secretary of the Air Force announced he has selected the Vermont National Guard to be the first Air Guard unit to base the F-35 Joint Strike Fighter. Burlington is one of two preferred choices for F-35 operations, along with Hill Air Force Base in northern Utah, and Luke Air Force Base in Arizona is the top pick for training. Final basing decisions will be made later in the ongoing selection process. Under the current production schedule, the planes could begin arriving in Vermont in the 2018 federal fiscal year.

The F-35 appears to be a smaller, slightly more conventional, single-engine sibling of the sleeker, twin-engine F-22 Raptor, and indeed drew elements from it. The exhaust duct design was inspired by the General Dynamics Model 200 design, which was proposed for a 1972 supersonic VTOL fighter requirement for the Sea Control Ship. For specialized development of the F-35B STOVL variant, Lockheed consulted with the Yakovlev Design Bureau, purchasing design data from their development of the Yakovlev Yak-141 "Freestyle". Although several experimental designs have been built and tested since the 1960s including the Navy's unsuccessful Rockwell XFV-12, the F-35B is to be the first operational supersonic STOVL fighter. With takeoff weights up to 60,000 lb (27,000 kg), the F-35 is considerably heavier than the lightweight fighters it replaces. In empty and maximum gross weights, it more closely resembles the single-seat, single-engine Republic F-105 Thunderchief, which was the largest single-engine fighter of the Vietnam era. However the F-35's modern engine delivers over 60% more thrust in an aircraft of the same weight.

The F-35 is designed to be America's "premier surface-to-air missile killer and is uniquely equipped for this mission with cutting edge processing power, synthetic aperture radar integration techniques, and advanced target recognition." Lockheed Martin has suggested that the F-35 could also replace the USAF's F-15C/D fighters in the air superiority role and the F-15E Strike Eagle in the ground attack role. Wikipedia.

The F-35's main engine is the Pratt & Whitney F135. STOVL versions of both power plants use the Rolls-Royce LiftSystem, patented by Lockheed Martin and built by Rolls-Royce. The F-35's armament includes a GAU-22/A four-barrel 25mm cannon. The cannon will be mounted internally with 180 rounds in the F-35A and fitted as an external pod with 220 rounds in the F-35B and F-35C. The gun pod for the B and C variants will have stealth features. This pod could be used for different equipment in the future, such as EW, reconnaissance equipment, or possibly a rearward facing radar.

Internally (current planned weapons for integration), up to two air-to-air missiles and two air-to-air or air-to-ground weapons (up to two 2,000 lb bombs in A and C models (BRU-68); two 1,000 lb bombs in the B model (BRU-67)) can be carried in the bomb bays. At the expense of being more detectable by radar, many more missiles, bombs and fuel tanks can be attached on four wing pylons and two near wingtip positions.

The F-35 has a low radar cross section primarily due to the materials used in construction, including fibre-mat. The F-35 also has a more stealthy shape than past fighters, including a zigzag-shape weapons bay and landing gear door. In spite of being smaller than the F-22, the F-35 has a larger radar cross section. It is said to be roughly equal to a metal golf ball rather than the F-22's metal marble.

While the United States is the primary customer and financial backer, the United Kingdom, Italy, the Netherlands, Canada, Turkey, Australia, Norway and Denmark have agreed to contribute US$4.375 billion toward the development costs of the program. The nine major partner nations plan to acquire over 3,100 F-35s through 2035, making the F-35 one of the most numerous jet fighters.

The F-35 was originally planned to be built in three different versions to suit various combat missions. A fourth variant, the F-35I export version for Israel has since been added.

The F-35A is the conventional takeoff and landing (CTOL) variant intended for the US Air Force and other air forces. It is the smallest, lightest F-35 version and is the only variant equipped with an internal cannon, the GAU-22/A. This 25 mm cannon is a development of the GAU-12 carried by the USMC's AV-8B Harrier II. It is designed for increased effectiveness against ground targets compared to the 20 mm M61 Vulcan cannon carried by other USAF fighters. The A variant is primarily intended to replace the USAF's F-16 Fighting Falcon, beginning in 2013, and replace the A-10 Thunderbolt II starting in 2028.

The F-35B is the short takeoff and vertical landing (STOVL) variant of the aircraft. Similar in size to the A variant, the B sacrifices some fuel volume to make room for the vertical flight system. Takeoffs and landing with vertical flight systems are by far the riskiest, and in the end, a decisive factor in design. Like the AV-8B Harrier II, the B's guns will be carried in a ventral pod. Whereas F-35A is stressed to 9 g, the F-35B is stressed to 7 g. Unlike the other variants, the F-35B has no landing hook; the "STOVL/HOOK" button in the cockpit initiates conversion instead of dropping the hook. The United Kingdom's Royal Air Force and Royal Navy plan to use this variant to replace their Harrier GR7/GR9s. The United States Marine Corps intends to purchase 340 F-35Bs to replace all current inventories of the F/A-18 Hornet (A, B, C and D-models), and AV-8B Harrier II in the fighter, and attack roles. The USMC is investigating an electronic warfare role for the F-35B to replace the service's EA-6B Prowlers.

The F-35C carrier variant has a larger, folding wing and larger control surfaces for improved low-speed control, and stronger landing gear and hook for the stresses of carrier landings. The larger wing area allows for decreased landing speed, increased range and payload, with twice the range on internal fuel compared with the F/A-18C Hornet, achieving much the same goal as the heavier F/A-18E/F Super Hornet. The United States Navy will be the sole user for the carrier variant. It intends to buy 480 F-35Cs to replace the F/A-18A, B, C, and D Hornets. The F-35C will also serve as a stealthier complement to the Super Hornet. Wikipedia.

Martin RB-57A Canberra, New England Air Museum
(photo courtesy of Wikipedia)

Martin RB-57A Canberra/Night Intruder

The Canberra is a twin engine night intruder powered by a pair of 7,200-lb thrust Wright J65-W5 turbojets. It has a maximum speed of 582 mph, a service ceiling of 48,000', and a range of 2,300 miles. The Canberra is armed with eight .50 cal machine-guns or four 20mm cannon, 16 underwing rockets and up to 6,000 lbs of bombs carried in an internal bomb-bay. *The Complete Encyclopedia of World Aircraft.*

The English Electric Canberra was the first jet bomber to be built in Britain and the first to serve with the RAF. The USAF made use of the Canberras as bomber and reconnaissance aircraft over Southeast Asia. First flown on 23 April 1950, the Canberra held the World Height Record of 65,889 feet in August 1955. The B-57 is a modified version of the English Electric Canberra, which was first flown in Britain on 13 May 1949, and later produced for the Royal Air Force (RAF). After the Korean Conflict began in 1950, the USAF looked for a jet medium bomber to replace the aging Douglas A-26 Invader. In March 1951, the USAF contracted with the Glenn L. Martin Co. to build the Canberra in the US under a licensing agreement with English Electric. The Martin-built B-57 made its first flight on the 20th of July 1953, and when production ended in 1959, a total of 403 Canberras had been produced for the USAF. *(Information courtesy of the National Museum of the United States Air Force).*

McDonnell F-101B Voodoo
(photo courtesy of Wikipedia)

McDonnell F-101B Voodoo

The F-101 Voodoo was a two-seat all-weather long-range interceptor flown by the USAF and the RCAF. The Voodoo was powered by two 14,880-lb thrust afterburning Pratt & Whitney J57-P-55 turbojets. It had a maximum speed of 1,221 mph, a service ceiling of 40,000' and a range of 1,550 miles. It was armed with two MB-1 Genie missiles with nuclear warhead and four AIM-4C, -4D or 04G Falcon missiles or six Falcon missiles. *The Complete Encyclopedia of World Aircraft.*

Initially designed by McDonnell Aircraft as a long-range bomber escort (known as a *penetration fighter*) for the Strategic Air Command (SAC), the Voodoo was instead developed as a nuclear armed fighter bomber for the Tactical Air Command (TAC), and as a photo reconnaissance aircraft based on the same airframe. Extensively modified versions were produced as an all-weather interceptor aircraft, serving with the Air Defense Command, later renamed the Aerospace Defense Command (ADC), the Air National Guard, the Royal Canadian Air Force and the unified Canadian Forces after 1968.

The Voodoo's career as a strike fighter was relatively brief, but the reconnaissance versions served for some time. Along with the US Air Force's U-2 and US Navy's RF-8 Crusaders, the RF-101 reconnaissance variant of the Voodoo was instrumental during the Cuban Missile Crisis and saw extensive service during the Vietnam War. Interceptor versions served with the Air National Guard until 1982, and in Canadian service they were a front line part of NORAD until their replacement with the CF-18 Hornet in the 1980s.

While the Voodoo was a moderate success, it may have been more important as an evolutionary step towards its replacement in most roles, the F-4 Phantom II, one of the most successful Western fighter designs of the 1960s. The Phantom would retain the twin engines, twin crew for interception duties, and a tail mounted well above and behind the jet exhaust. Both aircraft were influenced by the same company's F-3 Demon, a carrier-based naval fighter-interceptor that served during the 1950s and early 1960s.

All models of the aircraft were known by the nickname "One-oh-Wonder" and this was reflected on the aircraft type patches worn by crews. Wikipedia.

Developed from the XF-88 penetration fighter, the F-101 originally was designed as a long-range bomber escort for the Strategic Air Command (SAC) (now known as Strategic Command). However, when high-speed, high-altitude jet bombers such as the B-52 entered active service, escort fighters were not needed. Therefore, before production began, the F-101's design was changed to fill both tactical and air defense roles. The F-101 made its first flight on Sep. 29, 1954. The first production F-101A became operational in May 1957, followed by the F-101C in September 1957 and the F-101B in January 1959. By the time F-101 production ended in March 1961, McDonnell had built 785 Voodoos including 480 F-101Bs, the two-seat, all-weather interceptor used by the Air Defense Command. In the reconnaissance versions, the Voodoo was the world's first supersonic photo-recon aircraft. These RF-101s were used widely for low-altitude photo coverage of missile sites during the 1962 Cuban Missile Crisis and during the late 1960s in Southeast Asia.

The F-101 lineage included several versions: low-altitude fighter-bomber, photo-reconnaissance, two-seat interceptor and transition trainer. To accelerate production, no prototypes were built, the first Voodoo, an F-101A, made its initial flight on September 29, 1954. When production ended in March 1961, nearly 800 Voodoos had been built. Development of the unarmed RF-101, the world's first supersonic photo-recon aircraft, began in 1956 while 35 RF-101As and 166 RF-101Cs were produced, many earlier single-seat Voodoos were converted to the reconnaissance configuration. *(Information courtesy of the National Museum of the United States Air Force).*

McDonnell F-4D Phantom II, Collings Foundation
(photo courtesy of Wikipedia)

McDonnell Douglas F-4D Phantom II

The two-place Phantom II a tandem two-seat, twin-engined, all-weather, long-range supersonic jet interceptor fighter/fighter-bomber with advanced armament originally developed for the United States Navy by McDonnell Aircraft. It is powered by a pair of 17,900-lb afterburning thrust General Electric J79-GE-17 turbojets, with a maximum speed of 1,485 mph, a service ceiling of 62,250', and a combat radius of 595 miles. *The Complete Encyclopedia of World Aircraft.*

The Phantom II first entered service in 1960 with the US Navy. Proving highly adaptable, it was adopted by the US Marine Corps and US Air Force by the mid-1960s and became a major part of their air wings.

The Phantom is a large fighter with a top speed of over Mach 2. It can carry over 18,000 pounds (8,400 kg) of weapons on nine external hardpoints, including air-to-air and air-to-ground missiles, and various bombs. The F-4, like other interceptors of its time, was designed without an internal cannon, but later models incorporated a cannon. Beginning in 1959, it set 15 world records, including an absolute speed record, and an absolute altitude record.

The F-4 was used extensively by these three US services during the Vietnam War, serving as the principal air superiority fighter for both the Navy and Air Force, as well as being important in the ground-attack and reconnaissance roles by the close of US involvement in the war. The Phantom has the distinction of being the last US fighter flown to attain ace status in the 20th century. During the Vietnam War, the USAF had one pilot and two WSOs, and the US Navy one pilot and one RIO, become aces in air-to-air combat. It continued to form a major part of US military air power throughout the 1970s and 1980s, being gradually replaced by more modern aircraft such as the F-15 Eagle and F-16 Fighting Falcon in the US Air Force; the F-14 Tomcat and F/A-18 Hornet in the US Navy; and the F/A-18 in the US Marine Corps.

The F-4 Phantom II remained in use by the US in the reconnaissance and Wild Weasel (suppression of enemy air defenses) roles in the 1991 Gulf War, finally leaving service in 1996. It was also the only aircraft used by both US flight demonstration teams: the USAF Thunderbirds (F-4E) and the US Navy Blue Angels (F-4J). The F-4 was also operated by the armed forces of 11 other nations. Israeli Phantoms saw extensive combat in several Arab–Israeli conflicts, while Iran used its large fleet of Phantoms in the Iran–Iraq War. Phantoms remain in front line service with seven countries, and in use as an unmanned target in the US Air Force. Phantom production ran from 1958 to 1981, with a total of 5,195 built, making it the most numerous American supersonic military aircraft. Wikipedia.

The armament loaded on a typical F-4C consists of four AIM-7E and four AIM-9B air-to-air missiles, and eight 750 lb. Mk. 117 bombs. The aircraft is also carrying two external 370-gallon fuel tanks on the outboard pylons and one ALQ-87 electronic countermeasures (ECM) pod on the right inboard pylon. This was one of the typical armament configurations for the F-4C during the Vietnam War in the summer of 1967.

The Phantom is one of the most versatile aircraft in USAF and USN history, serving in fighter-attack, reconnaissance and interceptor roles. Based on its combat record the Phantom may be considered to be the most significant American fighter to take to the skies in combat since WWII. The USAF and the USN Phantoms scored 72% of all victories over North Vietnam between 1965 and 1973.

The Phantom is the only aircraft credited with six MiG kills since the Korean War. Captain Steve Ritchie made his first and fifth kills a Phantom which is currently on display at the USAF Academy in Colorado Springs. The Collings Foundation F-4D carries the same colors shown in the photo above,

First flown in May 1958, the Phantom II originally was developed for US Navy fleet defense and entered service in 1961. The USAF evaluated it for close air support, interdiction, and counter-air operations and, in 1962, approved a USAF version. The USAF's Phantom II, was designated the F-4C and made its first flight on 27 May 1963. Production deliveries began in November 1963. In its air-to-ground role the F-4 can carry twice the normal bomb load of a WW II B-17. USAF F-4s also fly reconnaissance and Wild Weasel anti-aircraft missile suppression missions. Phantom II production ended in 1979 after over 5,000 had been built--more than 2,600 for the USAF, about 1,200 for the Navy and Marine Corps, and the rest for friendly foreign nations. In 1965 the first USAF Phantom II's were sent to Southeast Asia (SEA). The first USAF pilot to score four combat victories with F-4s in South East Asia was then Col. Robin Olds, a WW II ace. Col. Olds, the aircraft commander, and Lt. Stephan B. Croker, the backseat pilot, scored two of those victories in a single day, on 20 May 1967. *(Information courtesy of the National Museum of the United States Air Force).*

After losing out to the F8U Crusader in a competitive bid for a Navy Supersonic air-superiority fighter, McDonnell began a company funded project in 1952 to produce a carrier-borne fighter-bomber as a replacement for its F3H Demon. The outcome was the single-seat, multi-role (i.e., fighter, attack, photo-reconnaissance, ECM) AH-1 aircraft with a top-speed of Mach 1.5. After the purchase of two AH-1 prototypes in 1954, Navy specifications were revised to provide for two-crew manning (pilot and Radar Intercept Officer), the Sparrow III (and eventually the Sidewinder) guided missile weapons system, and two GE J-79 engines with 17,000 lbs thrust each for Mach 2+ speed. The combined thrust of the two engines in after-burner gave it a thrust-to-weight ratio greater than one, which meant that the F-4 could climb straight up after take-off. The aircraft designation was then changed from AH-l to F4H-l and named the Phantom II, one of the most famous aircraft in the history of military aviation. Its maiden flight occurred in 1958 with deliveries to Navy and Marine squadrons beginning in 1960.

In the space of about twenty-eight months since its introduction, the F-4 had established 15 world aviation records including altitude (98,500 ft), time-to-climb and speed (Mach 2.59). These factors coupled with a demonstrated capability to lift a load of up to 22,000 lbs convinced the Air Force to procure the aircraft whose performance qualities were as good as or better than their best fighters.

Navy, Marine Corps and Air Force F-4s were used extensively during the Vietnam conflict as high and low altitude bombers delivering a wide array of ordnance, and as fighters downing 107 enemy aircraft in aerial combat. Three MiG-17s, including one flown by the leading ace of North Vietnam, were downed on a single mission by a Navy pilot and his RIO - the Navy's only MiG ace of the war. The F-4s also saw significant combat with the Israel air force in the same roles during the Israel/Arab wars.

Over 5,000 F-4s were produced of which 1500 were still in use by 1992 and second only to the MiG-21 in numbers produced. It has served the Air Forces of twelve foreign countries and is the only aircraft to be flown concurrently by the Navy and Air Force flight demonstration teams. While Navy and Marine Corps F-4's were replaced by the Grumman F-14 Tomcat, the Air Force still retains some for special mission roles. All-in-all, the F-4 has quite a record for an aircraft variously referred to as the Big Ugly, Flying Anvil, and Big Iron Sled. *Information courtesy of the National Museum of Naval Aviation.*

After Vietnam, the F-4's continued to serve with the US military forces around the world. The next major conflict involving the F-4 was Operation Desert Storm, where Air Force "Wild Weasel" Phantoms participated in carrying out strategic strikes against Iraqi military installations. Finally, in 1996 (nearly forty years after its inception), the F-4 was retired from the Air Force, the last branch to use the aircraft. This retirement threatened to end the chance for people to see an aircraft in flight that contributed so much to the history of America. However, the Collings Foundation of Stow, and the Vietnam Memorial Flight have preserved one in flying condition to prevent that tragedy from occurring.

A few years ago, foreign warbird jets were starting to emerge as the powerful force in the future of vintage aviation. However, major legal obstacles were encountered when individuals made efforts to acquire non-demiled (demiled combat jets are not flight-worthy) US-built combat jets in America or from abroad. Despite these obstacles, the Collings Foundation decided to try acquiring and restoring a Phantom for flight exhibition. Accordingly, it took an act of Congress by means of an amendment to the Defense Authorization Bill of 1999 to allow the Collings Foundation to acquire its F-4 Phantom.

Available Phantoms that were stored at Davis Monthan AFB had baked in the hot Arizona sun for over nine years. To make the situation worse, the F-4's had been operated under highly demanding and stressful conditions for decades, such use had taken its toll. In order to rectify problems encountered from two conditions, a lot of work was undertaken to make the old warrior airworthy. A major 600 hour inspection was conducted, engines were replaced with zero-time units, avionics upgraded, hydraulic systems and components were overhauled, structural items tested and repaired, ejection seats located, and much more. After thousands of hours of labor, the Collings F-4 took to the sky in August of 1999.

Considering that hundreds of thousands of servicemen flew, maintained, and supported the Phantom and that countless others benefited from its close support in its forty-year life-service span, interest in the aircraft is. Currently, the fighter jet soars across America for displays around the country, helping to educate a nation about its past history. *Information courtesy of the Collings Foundation.*

McDonnell Douglas F-15A Eagle
(photo courtesy of Wikipedia)

McDonnell Douglas F-15A/C Eagle

The Eagle is a single-seat all-weather air-superiority fighter powered by two Pratt and Whitney F-100 turbofan engines which produce high performance, high maneuverability, and enable it to quickly achieve Mach 2.5. Each engine has 23,000 pounds of thrust. The Eagle can climb to 50,000 feet in one minute. It is armed with one M61A1 20mm six-barreled cannon and four AIM-9 Sidewinder, four AIM-7 Sparrow or eight AMRAAM air-to air missiles. The Eagle can also carry 6,000 lb of weapons externally. It is an extremely maneuverable aircraft which entered UASF service on 14 November 1974. *The Complete Encyclopedia of World Aircraft.*

The McDonnell Douglas (now Boeing) F-15 Eagle was designed to gain and maintain air superiority in aerial combat. It is considered among the most successful modern fighters with over 100 aerial combat victories with no losses in dogfights. Following reviews of proposals, the United States Air Force selected McDonnell Douglas' design in 1967 to meet the service's need for a dedicated air superiority fighter. The Eagle first flew in July 1972, and entered service in 1976. The F-15 is expected to be in service with the US Air Force until 2025.

Since the 1970s, the Eagle has also been exported to Israel, Japan, and Saudi Arabia. Despite originally being envisaged as a pure air superiority aircraft, the design proved flexible enough that an all-weather strike derivative, the F-15E Strike Eagle, was later developed, and entered service in 1989. Wikipedia.

First flown on 27 July 1972, the Eagle began entering the USAF inventory on 14 November 1974. It was the first US fighter to have engine thrust greater than the normal weight of the aircraft, allowing it to accelerate while in a vertical climb. This, combined with low aircraft weight compared to wing area, made the Eagle highly maneuverable. The Eagle has been produced in single-seat and two-seat versions. During Operation Desert Storm F-15Cs conducted counter-air operations over Iraq. They escorted strike aircraft over long distances and scored 36 of the 39 USAF aerial victories during the conflict. The F-15C was also used to search out and attack Scud ballistic missile launchers. *(Information courtesy of the National Museum of the United States Air Force).*

McDonnell Douglas AV-8B Harriers, USMC
(photo courtesy of Wikipedia)

McDonnell Douglas AV-8B Harrier

The Harrier was the first jet aircraft capable of vertical take-off and landing in the RAF. The Harrier is powered by one 21,500-lb thrust Rolls-Royce Pegasus Mk. 103 vectored-thrust turbofan engine. It has a maximum speed of 737 mph, a service ceiling of 50,000', and a range with one in-flight refueling of 3,455 miles. Broadly equivalent to the RAF's Harrier GR 3, the AV-8C entered US Marine Corps service in 1973. *The Complete Encyclopedia of World Aircraft.*

The Harrier is a second-generation vertical/short takeoff and landing or *V/STOL* ground-attack aircraft of the late 20th century. It is an Anglo-American development of the Hawker Siddeley Harrier and Sea Harrier. I t is primarily used for light attack or multi-role tasks, typically operated from small aircraft carriers, large amphibious assault ships and during combat, forward operating bases.

Although the AV-8B Harrier II shares the designation with the earlier AV-8A/C Harrier, the AV-8B was extensively redesigned from the previous-generation Harrier GR.1A/AV-8A/C by McDonnell Douglas. British Aerospace joined the improved Harrier project in the early 1980s, and it has been managed by Boeing/BAE Systems since the 1990s.

The AV-8B is used by the United States Marine Corps. The British Harrier GR7/GR9 versions are used by the Royal Air Force and Royal Navy. Versions are also used by NATO countries: Spain and Italy. The Harrier family models are referred to commonly as the "Harrier Jump Jet'. Wikipedia.

The dream for a military aircraft able to take-off and land vertically like a helicopter and then transition to conventional flight was realized in the British made AV-8A Harrier. First flown and deployed by the RAF in 1969, it utilizes the concept of Vectored Thrust in which turbine by-pass air is routed to one of two pairs of nozzles at the wing roots, while jet exhaust is directed through the second pair.

The combined thrusts enable the Harrier to either hover or fly normally depending on the position of the nozzles which can be rotated in unison along the longitudinal axis anywhere from straight aft for forward flight to a little forward of straight down for hover. A single lever near the throttle controls nozzle positions. To control the aircraft in the hover mode and thus going too slowly for normal flap, elevator and rudder surfaces to be operable, a reaction control system cuts in which enables high pressure bleed air to be routed to exhaust ducts at the wing tips, nose and tail called puffers or puff pipes. When the pilot moves the stick forward, the puffer under the tail emits air causing the nose to go down; and when he pulls it back, the puffer under the nose emits air causing the nose to go up. Similarly, side-to-side movement of the stick operates the puffers at the wing tips (inversely of course) causing the plane to roll; and puffers at the tail operated by the rudder pedals, blow air sideways to control yaw. As far as the pilot is concerned, the controls continue to operate normally.

As developed, the Harrier became the first successful V/STOL (Vertical/Short Take Off and Landing) aircraft with the ability not only to make vertical take-offs and landings but also to hover, rotate around its vertical axis, and even to fly sideways and backwards.

Designed primarily for ground attack and support carrying all armament under the wings, it is also capable of near supersonic speeds (approximately 600 knots). Harriers were tested in combat during the Falkland Islands War during which 42 were deployed for ground support, air defense, ship strikes, and reconnaissance. They shot down at least 20 enemy planes (Mirages, A-4 Skyhawks, and a Canberra bomber), most with Sidewinders and some with 30 mm, without a single air-to-air loss. Five were lost to ground fire and four to adverse weather. It is said that the British victory probably would not have happened without the Harriers.

The US Marine Corps saw the Harrier as the perfect aircraft for the support of its ground forces and ordered 102 AV-8A Harriers and two 2-seat trainers (TAV-8A) in 1970, forming the first squadron in April, 1971. These aircraft were basically the same as the RAF Harriers but with American avionics, flight control systems and weapons systems. The last of this batch was delivered in 1976, and the last AV-8A was retired in 1986.

The US government was reluctant to have American military aircraft manufactured outside of the U.S, therefore a licensing agreement was made between Hawker-Siddeley (later British Aerospace) and McDonnell-Douglas for the manufacture of the follow-on AV-8B (Harrier II) designed to give the Harrier the payload, range, and accuracy of the most modern conventional aircraft. Testing was so successful that the initial production order of 12 AV-8Bs was placed before the program was completed, and delivered to the Marines in January 1984. While outwardly resembling the earlier Harriers, the AV-8B was a new and totally different aircraft that incorporated a higher thrust engine (21,500 lbs vs. 20,000 lbs) giving about the same speed, but a much greater payload. It had a new supercritical wing holding more fuel and with six payload wing pylons instead of four, plus a fuselage station. The cockpit was entirely different, being similar to the F/A-18 Hornet with state of the-art electronics and a bubble canopy for better visibility.

With wing tanks half full, the AV-8B can lift about 7,000 lbs nearly vertically, or carry an external load of 9,200 lbs with a take-off run of about 850 ft (it is customary to operate with a short take-off for more payload and land vertically when fuel and weapons have been expended). Payloads would include various bombs and other weapons, plus additional fuel, or a 25mm cannon with 300 rounds in two pods under the fuselage. It also has radar, a warning system, flare and chaff dispensers, night vision capability, Angle Rate Bombing Set (ARBS) for laser or TV guided weapons delivery, Heads Up Display (HUD), and with an electronic countermeasures pod available. For battle conditions, it has its own ground starting and oxygen generating equipment. Being without afterburner and with deflected jet blast, the AV-8B has a low infra red signature, making it a more difficult target for heat seeking missiles.

From an air-to-air standpoint, its vectored thrust and puffers enable the AV-8B to perform maneuvers impossible with a conventional fighter such as VIFFing (Vectoring In Forward Flight), whereby the pilot deflects the nozzles downward, causing the plane to decelerate suddenly.

During Desert Storm operations, four USMC Harrier squadrons (86 aircraft), operating from land and shipboard bases, flew 3,380 sorties for 4,038 hours, and delivered over 5.95 million lbs of ordnance (mainly Rockeye cluster bombs, 500 lb iron bombs and napalm). The Marine Corps is pleased with its Harriers, with seven Attack Squadrons and one Training Squadron flying them, and it is expected that they will be operational well into the next century. Harriers are also used by the British, Spanish, and Italian Navies. *Information courtesy of the National Museum of Naval Aviation.*

McDonnell Douglas AV-8C Harrier (BuNo. 158710) is on display at the Quonset Air Museum.

MiG-15 Fagot, New England Air Museum
(Author photo)

Mikoyan-Gurevich MiG-15 Fagot

The MiG-15 was a single-seat high altitude fighter/bomber/interceptor with a swept-wing. Nicknamed the Fagot, the MiG-15 was powered by one 5,952-lb thrust Klimov VK-1 turbojet (a Soviet version of the Rolls-Royce Nene jet engine). It had a maximum speed of 668 mph, a service ceiling of 50,855', and a range of 1,156 miles. *The Complete Encyclopedia of World Aircraft.*

Designed by the Mikoyan/Gurevich team, it made its first flight on 30 December 1947. Designed as a bomber interceptor, it suffered from a slow cyclic rate of fire in the air-to-air fighting in Korea. It was armed with one 37mm cannon mounted on the right and two 23mm cannon mounted on the left. The MiG-15 had an excellent rate of climb of 10,000' per minute, much better that the best Sabre, the F-86F at 9.300' per minute. The MiG-15 also had a service ceiling advantage of some 7,000'.

Americans flying Sabres fought MiG pilots in Korea who came from many different countries, including the former Warsaw Pact, China and Russia. Sometimes they brought their own aircraft, as US pilots reported seeing almost every type of Iron Curtain national insignia on the MiGs. The better Red units had, as with US units, a variety of colorful markings, including lightning bolts, command stripes, entire tails of red, as well as wing stripes. One of the best units to fly in Korea was believed to be a Russian unit that camouflaged their aircraft in an overall coppery-tan color. Taking to the air in early 1953, they did shoot down some Sabres, but were eventually decimated and withdrawn by April 1953. The great Russian ace Kozhedub led the Red units for a year in the 1951-52 period.

Lt. Kum Suk No, who defected with his MiG to Kimpo in 1953, reported that Red air strength was slightly over 900 MiGs (400 Russian, 400 Chinese, and two North Korean units of about 125 MiGs). This enemy complement of fighters was faced by the American Sabre contingent which consisted of seven aircraft in December 1950 but which grew to six squadrons in 1952 to 12 squadrons with about 300 F-86s at the war's end. Lt. No reported that the North

Koreans had lost over 800 aircraft by the end of the war. Larry Davis, MiG Alley, Squadron/ Signal Publications, Warren, Michigan, 1978, p. 71. The Quonset Air Museum has a MiG-15 on display.

MiG-17 Fresco
(Author photo)

Mikoyan-Gurevich MiG-17F Fresco C

The MiG-17 is a single-seat day fighter powered by one Klimov VK-1F turbojet with afterburning thrust of 7,452 lb. It had a maximum speed of 711 mph, a service ceiling of 54,460', and a range of 1,230 miles. It is armed with one N-37 37mm and two or three 23mm NR-23 cannon and can carry up to 1,102 lbs of weapons on underwing hardpoints. *The Complete Encyclopedia of World Aircraft.*

The MiG-17 is a refined version of the famous MiG 15 of the Korean War. Although similar in appearance to the MiG-15, the MiG-17 has more sharply swept wings, an afterburner, better speed and handling characteristics and is about three feet longer. The first flight of a MiG-17 prototype took place in January 1950 and production began in late 1951. The first operational MiG-17s appeared in 1952 but were not available in sufficient quantities to take part in the Korean War. Five versions of the aircraft eventually were produced. The MiG-17 has served in the air arms of at least 20 nations throughout the world--including nations friendly to the US--and was flown against US aircraft during the Vietnam War. Between July 10, 1965, and February 14, 1968, USAF F-105s and F-4s downed 61 MiG-17s. *(Information courtesy of the National Museum of the United States Air Force).*

The Quonset Air Museum has a MiG-17 on display.

Nieuport 28
(Wikipedia photo)

Nieuport 28

The Nieuport 28 was a single-seat biplane fighter powered by one 160-hp Gnome 9N rotary piston engine. It had a maximum speed of 121 mph, a service ceiling of 16,405', and a range of 248 miles. It was armed with two fixed forward-firing .303in Vickers machine-guns. *The Complete Encyclopedia of World Aircraft.*

The Nieuport 28 (N.28C-1) was the first fighter airplane flown in combat by pilots of the American Expeditionary Forces (AEF) in WWI. Its second armed patrol with an AEF unit on 14 April 1918 resulted in two victories when Lieutenants Alan Winslow and Douglas Campbell (the first American-trained ace) of the 94th Aero Squadron each downed an enemy aircraft. Although the Nieuport 28 was considered obsolete at the time, American pilots maintained a favorable ratio of victories to losses with it. The Nieuport was more maneuverable than the sturdier SPAD XIII that replaced it, but it had a reputation for fragility and a tendency to shed its upper wing fabric in a dive. Even so, many American aces of WW I - including 26-victory ace Capt. Eddie Rickenbacker - flew the French-built Nieuport at one time or another in their careers. *(Information courtesy of the National Museum of the United States Air Force).*

Making its debut in June 1917, the French built Nieuport 28 fighter was an upgraded version of the Nieuport 17 designed to compete with the recently arrived S.P.A.D. series of French fighters. Despite its increased maneuverability, the Nieuport 28 retained the same problems as its predecessor in that the fighter's wing surfaces tended to shed in prolonged power dives and was very unforgiving of pilot error.

While only a limited number were produced for the French Flying Service, it found a customer in the Allied Expeditionary Force (AEF) and became the aerial tool of some of

America's greatest aces in World War I including Eddie Rickenbacker who scored many of his 26 kills in this aircraft. Despite these early successes, the wing fabric problems remained and the Americans eventually followed their French counterparts in obtaining the sturdier S.P.A.D. fighters.

In 1919 the US Navy acquired twelve Nieuport 28s for service with the fleet as part of the shipboard fighter concept in which the fighters were considered expendable and war surplus aircraft were favored in lieu of newer American built models. Thus, the Nieuports entered service flying from platforms built on the forward turrets of battleships and were equipped with flotation gear for recovery should they be forced to ditch at sea. They were also used extensively in formation flying and combat tactics training. *Information courtesy of the National Museum of Naval Aviation.*

The Owls Head Transportation Museum has a Nieuport 28 replica in flying condition on display.

North American AT-6 Texan
(photo courtesy of Wikipedia)

North American AT-6D/AT-6F/SNJ-5 Texan

The T-6 Texan was a single-engine two-seat advanced trainer aircraft used to train pilots of the United States Army Air Forces, United States Navy, Royal Air Force and other air forces of the British Commonwealth during World War II and into the 1950s. Designed by North American Aviation, the T-6 is known by a variety of designations depending on the model and operating air force. The USAAC designated it as the "AT-6", the US Navy the "SNJ", and British Commonwealth air forces, the Harvard, the name it is best known by outside of the United States. It remains a popular warbird aircraft. Wikipedia.

The Texan is powered by a 550-hp Pratt & Whitney R-1340-AN-1 radial piston engine. It had a maximum speed of 205 mph, a service ceiling of 21,500', and a range of 750 miles. The Complete Encyclopedia of World Aircraft.

The AT-6 advanced trainer was one of the most widely used aircraft in history. Evolving from the BC-1 basic combat trainer ordered in 1937, 15,495 Texans were built between 1938 and 1945. The USAAF procured 10,057 AT-6s; others went to the Navy as SNJs and to more than 30 allied nations. Most AAF fighter pilots trained in AT-6s prior to graduation from flying school. Many of the Spitfire and Hurricane pilots in the Battle of Britain trained in Canada in Harvards, the British version of the AT-6. To comply with neutrality laws, US built Harvards were flown north to the border and were pushed across. In 1948, Texans still in USAF service were re-designated as T-6s when the AT, BT, and PT aircraft designations were abandoned. To meet an urgent need for close air support of ground forces in the Korean Conflict, T-6s flew mosquito missions spotting enemy troops and guns and marking them with smoke rockets for attack by fighter-bombers. *(Information courtesy of the National Museum of the United States Air Force).*

Built as a private venture by North American Aircraft in 1935, the SNJ became the Navy's advanced trainer from 1936 through the forties and its primary trainer during much of the fifties. Of the approximately 16,000 models produced, the majority saw service with the Army Air Forces and numerous foreign countries while the Navy accounted for 4,800 of them. The SNJ is considered to be the most successful training aircraft ever produced.

Ordered by the Navy in 1936, the NJ represented a transition from the slower, less complex trainers to a high performance type that would prepare student aviators for the more advance fleet aircraft. The Texan's speed and performance figures were much greater than that of the N2S Kaydet, the N3N Yellow Peril, and the SNV Valiant. It was not only heavier and larger than these predecessors, but also incorporated retractable landing gear. Later versions were also fitted with arresting hooks as well as more powerful electrical systems to accommodate instrument-training requirements.

In addition to its training role, the SNJs were used as command and staff transports. An SNJ played an important role in the development of the modern aircraft carrier when it was utilized in 1953 to test day/night touch-and-go and arrested landings and takeoffs in winds of varying force and direction on the Navy's first angled deck aircraft carrier, the USS Antietam. Army versions were used in Korea as armed spotters for UN ground troops, and many a Hollywood war movie used SNJs to portray the Japanese Zero, which had a similar silhouette. *Information courtesy of the National Museum of Naval Aviation.*

North American A-36A Apache
(photo courtesy of Wikipedia)

North American A-36A Apache

The A-36A dive-bomber was the first AAF version of the "Mustang" developed for Britain in 1940. The Apache is powered by one 1,325-hp Allison V-1710 piston engine. It had a maximum speed of 365 mph, a cruising speed of 250 mph, a service ceiling of 25,100', and a range of 550 miles. It is armed with six .50-cal. machine-guns and can carry 1,000 lbs of bombs externally.

The A-36 first flew in October 1942; production of 500 A-36As was completed by March 1943. Unofficially named "Invaders," A-36As were assigned to the 27th and 86th Bombardment Groups (Dive), later re-designated as Fighter-Bomber Groups. In June 1943, the plane went into action from North Africa. During the Italian campaign, A-36A pilots flew bomber escort and strafing missions as well as ground support bombing attacks. A-36As also served with the 311th Fighter Bomber Group in India. Dive brakes in the wings gave greater stability in a dive, but they were sometimes wired closed due to malfunctions. In 1944, AAF A-36As were replaced by P-51s and P-47s when experience showed that these high-altitude fighters, equipped with bomb racks, were more suitable for low-level missions than the A-36As. *(Information courtesy of the National Museum of the USAF).*

The Collings Foundation is restoring North American A-36A Apache (Serial No. 15956), Reg. No. N4607V, at New Smyrna Beach, Florida.

North American P-51C Mustang "Betty Jane"
(photo courtesy of the Collings Foundation)

North American P-51C Mustang

The P-51 Mustang was an American long-range single-seat World War II interceptor and long-range day-fighter powered by one 1,695-hp Packard Merlin V-1650-7 V-12 piston engine. It has a maximum speed of 437 mph, a service ceiling of 41,900', and a range of 2,080 miles. It is armed with six .50 cal machine-guns mounted in the wings, and can carry two 1,000-lb bombs or six .5in rocket projectiles. *The Complete Encyclopedia of World Aircraft.*

The P-51 was designed as the NA-73 in 1940 at Britain's request. The design showed promise and AAF purchases of Allison-powered Mustangs began in 1941 primarily for photo recon and ground support use due to its limited high-altitude performance. But in 1942, tests of P-51s using the British Rolls-Royce Merlin engine revealed much improved speed and service ceiling, and in December 1943, Merlin-powered P-51Bs first entered combat over Europe. Providing high-altitude escort to B-17s and B-24s, they scored heavily over German interceptors and by war's end, P-51s had destroyed 4,950 enemy aircraft in the air, more than any other fighter in Europe, while losing 2,500 of their own. Mustangs served in nearly every combat zone, including the Pacific where they escorted B-29s to Japan from Iwo Jima. *(Information courtesy of the National Museum of the United States Air Force).*

During the war several of the razorback Mustangs were modified in the field to carry a passenger in a second cockpit just behind the pilot. These former fighter aircraft were used as a high speed transport and gave the Mustang pilot the ability to share the joy of flying the world's greatest fighter with their trusted ground crews. One of the most famous of these modified two seat fighters was used by Dwight Eisenhower and was named "The Stars Look Down". Ike rode in the back seat of that Mustang over the beaches of Normandy to direct the invasion during D-Day.

The Collings Foundation will be offering flight training in the world's only fully dual control TP-51C Mustang (Serial No. 42-103293), Reg. No. N251MX, "Betty Jane", New Smyrna Beach, Florida. Participants can actually fly the Mustang on half hour or hour long introductory flights. Special training flights allow a true once in a lifetime opportunity to fly the most recognizable fighters from WWII. Information courtesy of the Collings Foundation). P-51C Mustang (Serial No. 42-103740), Reg. No. N309PV is currently registered to Clarke L. Hill, in Wentworth, New Hampshire.

North American P-51D Mustang
(photo courtesy of Wikipedia)

North American P-51D Mustang

The P-51D Mustang was powered by the Packard V-1650, a two-stage two-speed supercharged version of the legendary Rolls-Royce Merlin engine, and was armed with six .50 caliber (12.7 mm) M2 Browning machine guns.

Between 1941 and 1945, the AAF ordered 14,855 Mustangs (including A-36A dive bomber and F-6 photo recon versions), of which 7,956 were P-51Ds. During the Korean War, P-51Ds were used primarily for close support of ground forces until withdrawn from combat in 1953.

The Mustang began the Korean War as the United Nations main fighter, but was relegated to a ground attack role when superseded by jet fighters early in the conflict. Nevertheless, it remained in service with some air forces until the early 1980s. As well as being economical to produce, the Mustang was a fast, well-made, and highly durable aircraft. The definitive version was the P-51D. (Information courtesy of the National Museum of the United States Air Force).

While the government originally paid almost $40,000 for a P-51, they could be bought for less than $5,000 when they were sold surplus after the war. After World War II and the Korean War, many Mustangs were converted for civilian use, especially air racing. The Mustang's reputation was such that, in the mid-1960s, Ford Motor Company's Designer John Najjar proposed a new youth-oriented coupe automobile be named after the fighter. Wikipedia.

P-51D Mustang (Serial No. 44-84753), Reg. No. N251BP is registered to Cielos LLC, Holderness, New Hampshire and P-51D Mustang (Serial No. 44-84745), Reg. No. N851D is registered to Stallion 51 Corp, Nashua, New Hampshire.

North American B-25H Mitchell
(Collings Foundation photo)

North American B-25J Mitchell, New England Air Museum
(Wikipedia photo)

North American B-25H/J Mitchell

The B-25 Mitchell was an American twin-engined medium bomber manufactured by North American Aviation. It was used by many Allied air forces, in every theater of World War II, as well as many other air forces after the war ended, and saw service across four decades.

The B-25J variant was powered by two 1,700-hp Wright R-2600-95 Cyclone 14-cylinder air-cooled radial engines and was equipped with Holley 1685HA carburetors or Bendix Stromberg carburetors. The Mitchell had a maximum speed of 272 mph, a service ceiling of 24,200', and a range of 1,350miles. The Complete Encyclopedia of World Aircraft.

The B-25J was armed with two 0.50-inch machine guns in individual blisters on the left and right-hand side of the fuselage with 400 rpg. Another two 0.50-inch machine guns were mounted in a top turret, with 400 rpg, and two more 0.50-inch machine guns were mounted in the waist position with 200 rpg. Two 0.50-inch machine guns were mounted in the tail gunner's position with 600 rpg. The Mitchell's normal bomb load was 3000 pounds, but a maximum bombload of 4000 pounds could be carried on short-range missions. Some aircraft were fitted with underwing racks for eight 5-inch high velocity aircraft rockets (HVARs).

The B-25 was named in honor of General Billy Mitchell, a pioneer of US military aviation. The B-25 is the only American military aircraft named after a specific person. By the end of its production, nearly 10,000 B-25s in numerous models had been built. These included a few limited variations, such as the United States Navy's and Marine Corps' PBJ-1 patrol bomber and the United States Army Air Forces' F-10 photo reconnaissance aircraft. Wikipedia.

The twin-engine B-25 gained great fame when 16 of the B models took off from the aircraft carrier Hornet in March 1942 to successfully bomb the Japanese homeland for the first time after the attack on Pearl Harbor.

Some of the B-25Js were assigned to training units, but most were issued to units in action in the Southwest Pacific. The first B-25Js arrived at Townsville, Australia and Nadzab, New Guinea depots in the summer of 1944. They were issued to the 38th Bombardment Group. The 345th BG received its B-25Js in September 1944. Despite volume production, it was hard to meet the demand, and the 42nd Bombardment Group did not get its B-25Js to replace its aging C and D models until late 1944. In the Mediterranean theater, the B-25J was issued to operational bomb groups on an as-required basis.

In April 1944, the 310th Bombardment Group based on Corsica received its first B-25Js. The remaining groups in the 57th Bombardment Wing of the 12th Air Force transitioned to the B-25J throughout the remainder of 1944. The US Marine Corps ordered 255 B-25Js under the designation PBJ-1J. The transparent nose for the bombardier could be replaced by a factory built solid gun nose that was equipped with eight 0.50-inch machine guns.

With its maximum armament of eighteen guns, the solid-nosed B-25J was one of the most heavily-armed attack aircraft in the Allied arsenal. Sometimes, however, the package guns on the sides of the fuselage were deleted, the remaining fourteen guns being more than enough. The last B-25J was delivered to the USAAF in August of 1945. The day after the war in the Pacific ended, the Kansas City plant was closed. By late 1945, the B-25 Mitchell outnumbered all other medium bombers in service with the USAAF. Most examples of its Martin B-26 Marauder stablemate had been scrapped immediately after the war was over. During the immediate post-war years, substantial numbers of B-25s were stripped of their combat equipment and used as advanced pilot trainers. They remained in service with the Air Force for many years thereafter, the last example not being struck off the USAF rolls until January of 1959. Internet: http://www.b25.net.

North American B-25H Mitchell (Serial No. 43-04999) is on display in the New England Air Museum. This B-25 is the only surviving example of the aircraft having the distinction of being the most heavily armed aircraft used by the allies in World War II. It had a 75 mm cannon in the nose, 8 forward firing .50 caliber machine guns, and 6 other .50 caliber machine guns in the dorsal, waist ant tail turrets. *(Information courtesy of the New England Air Museum)*.

The Collings Foundation's B-25J (Serial No. 44-28932), was produced in August of 1944 by North American Aviation in Kansas City, Kansas. Accepted by the United States Army Air Corps on 3 August of that year, it served in the US in the AAF Flying Training Command Program, serving 12 different air bases until January of 1959, at which time it had been declared surplus and had been deleted from the US Air Force inventory. Converted into a fire bomber, it fought forest fires for another 25 years.

Acquired by the Collings Foundation in 1984, and restored by Tom Reilly Vintage Aircraft over a two-year period, the B-25J, the first World War II bomber in the collection, has been flown in air shows in the Boston area for a decade, after which it was ferried to Chino, California, in late 2001, for a secondary restoration by Carl Scholl of Aero Trader, Inc. Subsequently repositioned to Midland, Texas, it was painted by AVSource West in its current

"Tondelayo" livery after a B-25 which had been operated by the Air Apache 345th BG of the 5th Air Force in the Pacific Theater against targets in New Guinea, the 500th BS of the 5th Air Force itself having been the fourth squadron of the 345th BG to have attacked shipping in Vunapope near Rabaul on 18 October 1943.

The Tondelayo name had been inspired by Hedy Lamarr's character in the 1943 movie *White Cargo* and chosen by the crew of Lieutenant Ralph Wallace. The three-aircraft formation, comprised of the B-25 "Snafu" and flown by Captain Lyle Anacker, the "Tondelayo" flown by Lieutenant Wallace himself, and the "Sorry Satchul" flown by Lieutenant Paterson, claimed the sinking of three Japanese ships, but avenging fighters attacked "Sorry Satchul," hitting its port engine and forcing it to ditch, and "Tondelayo," damaging its right engine. Shut down and feathered, the engine almost wrenched itself free from its mountings because of severe vibration.

Flying over Cape Gazelle toward home base, the B-25 duo, maintaining a tight formation, was targeted again, this time by some 50 Japanese fighters. "Sorry Satchul" was so badly damaged that it was forced to head for shore and ditch and "Tondelayo," despite its own critical wounds and hovering only 30 feet above the water, managed to shoot down five additional enemy aircraft. Limping into base at Kiriwina, the aircraft was subsequently repaired and patched, receiving a new right wing, engine, propeller blades, and radio equipment, and its crew was awarded the Silver Star. Robert G. Waldvogel, Internet: http://www.collingsfoundation.org/newsdb.

North American F-86H Sabre, Hanscom AFB
(photo courtesy of Jonathan Mooney, Wikipedia photo)

North American F-86H Sabre, New England Air Museum
(Author photo)

North American F-86H Sabre

The F-86 Sabre is a single-seat transonic all-weather/night jet fighter-bomber/interceptor powered by one 7,500-lb thrust afterburning GE J-47-13 turbojet engine. It had a maximum speed of 707 mph, a service ceiling of 54,600', and a range of 835 miles. It was armed with six .50 cal nose-mounted machine-guns. *The Complete Encyclopedia of World Aircraft.*

The Sabre is best known for its Korean War role where it was pitted against the Soviet MiG-15. Although developed in the late 1940s and outdated by the end of the 1950s, the Sabre proved adaptable and continued as a front line fighter in air forces until the last active front line examples were retired by the Bolivian Air Force in 1994.

Its success led to an extended production run of more than 7,800 aircraft between 1949 and 1956, in the United States, Japan and Italy. It was by far the most-produced Western jet fighter, with total production of all variants at 9,860 units. Variants were built in Canada and Australia. The Canadair Sabre added another 1,815 airframes, and the significantly redesigned CAC Sabre (sometimes known as the Avon Sabre or CAC CA-27), had a production run of 112. Wikipedia.

The Sabre was the first US fighter to be developed using captured German swept-wing technology. It had been discovered that the build-up of shock waves on the leading-edge of the wing could be postponed by sweeping it aftwards, so that the angle formed by the wing's leading edge and fuselage was less than 90 degrees.

The F-86F version of the Sabre had a much improved high speed agility, coupled with a higher landing speed of over 145 mph (233 km/h). The F-35 block had provisions for a new task: the nuclear tactical attack with one of the new small "nukes" ("second generation" nuclear ordnance). The F-40 had a new slatted wing, with a slight decrease of speed, but also a much better agility at high and low speed with a landing speed reduced to 124 mph (200 km/h). The USAF upgraded many of previous F versions to the F-40 standard.

The F-86F-2 was the designation for ten aircraft modified to carry the M39 cannon in place of the M3 .50 caliber machine gun "six-pack". Four F-86E and six F-86F were production-line aircraft modified in October 1952 with enlarged and strengthened gun bays, then flight tested at Edwards Air Force Base and the Air Proving Ground at Eglin Air Force Base in November. Eight were shipped to Japan in December, and seven forward-deployed to Kimpo Airfield as "Project Gun Val" for a 16-week combat field trial in early 1953. Two were lost to engine compressor stalls after ingesting excessive propellant gases from the cannons. Wikipedia.

The F-86H was the last fighter, as opposed to interceptor, variant of the Sabre. It had the classic lines of the Sabre fighter, but with a muscular appearance due to the fit of a General Electric J73-GE-3 turbojet engine with 41.2 kN (4,195 kgp /9,250 lbf) dry thrust. The bigger engine required expansion of the intake and fuselage, with a 15 centimeter (6 inch) splice end to end to increase depth. The exhaust was extended 60 centimeters (two feet), and the tailfin was raised by 7.6 centimeters (3 inches). Other changes included the fit of the "clamshell" canopy designed for the F-86D, making the F-86H the only Sabre fighter variant not to have a sliding canopy; the new ejection seat designed for the F-86D; and a unitary flat "slab" tailplane.

475 F-86Hs were manufactured in all, including the two prototypes. However, the advance of aircraft design at the time was so rapid that even though the F-86H was superior in almost all respects to its F-86A ancestor, it was still obsolescent, and the "Hawg Sabre" or "Sabre Hog" was fazed out of first-line service to the Air National Guard by mid-1958. The F-86H would linger in ANG service until the early 1970s. After they had been retired, the US Navy purchased some for "aggressor training" to simulate MiG-17s, though they did not operate for long in this role. Internet: Greg Goebel, http://www.vectorsite.net/avf86_2.html#m5.

North American F-100D Super Sabre, Connecticut ANG
(Wikipedia photo)

North American F-100D Super Sabre, New England Air Museum
(Author photo)

North American F-100D Super Sabre

The Super Sabre is a single-seat fighter bomber was a supersonic jet fighter aircraft that served with the United States Air Force (USAF) from 1954 to 1971 and with the Air National Guard (ANG) until 1979. The first of the Century Series collection of USAF jet fighters, it was the first USAF fighter capable of supersonic speed in level flight. The F-100 was originally designed as a higher performance follow-on to the F-86 Sabre air superiority fighter.

Adapted as a fighter bomber, the F-100 would be supplanted by the Mach 2 class F-105 Thunderchief for strike missions over North Vietnam. The F-100 flew extensively over South Vietnam as the Air Force's primary close air support jet until replaced by the more efficient subsonic LTV A-7 Corsair II . The F-100 also served in several NATO air forces and with other US allies. In its later life, it was often referred to as "the Hun," a shortened version of "one hundred." Wikipedia.

F-100D was powered by one 17,000-lb afterburning thrust Pratt & Whitney J57-P-21A turbojet. It has a maximum speed of 864 mph, a service ceiling of 46,000', and a range of 600 miles. It is armed with four 20mm cannon and can carry a weapon-load of 7,500 lbs on underwing pylons including bombs, missiles and rockets. *The Complete Encyclopedia of World Aircraft.*

The Super Sabre was the USAF's first operational aircraft capable of flying faster than the speed of sound (760 mph) in level flight. It made its initial flight on the 25th of May 1953 and the first production aircraft was completed in October 1953. North American built 2,294 F-100s before production ended in 1959. Designed originally to destroy enemy aircraft in aerial combat, the F-100 later became a fighter-bomber. It made its combat debut during the Vietnam conflict where it was assigned the task of attacking such targets as bridges, river barges, road junctions, and areas being used by infiltrating enemy soldiers. The F-100C, which made its first flight in 1955, featured such advances as an in-flight refueling system, provisions for extra fuel drop tanks and bombs under the wings and an improved electronic bombing system. *(Information courtesy of the National Museum of the United States Air Force).*

North American T-28B Trojan
(photo courtesy of Wikipedia)

North American T-28A/T-28B/T-28D Trojan

The Trojan is a two-seat basic trainer powered by one 1,425-hp Wright Cyclone R-1820-86 radial piston engine. It has a maximum speed of 343 mph, a service ceiling of 35,500', and a range of 1,060 miles. *The Complete Encyclopedia of World Aircraft.*

The T-28C was built by North American Aviation Inc. This type of aircraft made its first flight on the 15ᵗʰ of September 1956. It was designed to be used for training of pilots in transition to high-speed aircraft.

Originally produced by North American for the Air Force, the all metal, tricycle landing gear T-28A Trojan made its maiden flight on September 26, 1949. With a top speed of 292 mph, 800 nm range and service ceiling of 31,650 ft, the Navy began evaluating it as a replacement for the SNJ Texan trainer. The results showed that the Navy version required a more powerful engine and North American responded with the T-28B that was fitted with a 1,425 hp Wright R-1820 engine which upped the speed to 343 mph. First flown on 6 April 1953, the delivery of 489 of this model began in 1954 to ultimately equip eleven training squadrons in both the primary and basic training roles.

The success of the T-28Bs resulted in the placement of an order for the tailhook equipped T-28C with a strengthened rear fuselage to absorb the tremendous stress of carrier landings. Making its first flight on 19 September 1955, the T-28C became the center-piece for all Navy flight training, including basic, primary, instrument, and carrier qualifications.

The T-28 was actively utilized in the Viet Nam war as the T-28D Nomad equipped to carry a variety of weapons ranging from bombs and rockets to napalm and used for counterinsurgency missions throughout Southeast Asia. It was especially effective in night operations against targets not protected by radar controlled anti-aircraft batteries and as armed escorts of A-26 attack aircraft and helicopters. They also operated in hunter/killer teams with O-1 aircraft that used starlight scopes to locate enemy convoys and then call in the T-28s to attack.

On 23 June 1976, the first of the Navy T-28s began to be replaced by the T-34 Mentor. The last was retired from active duty in the spring of 1984, ending twenty-nine years of active service. *Information courtesy of the National Museum of Naval Aviation.*

North American AGM-28 Hound Dog Missile
(photo courtesy of Wikipedia)

North American AGM-28 Hound Dog Missile

The North American Aviation Corporation AGM-28 Hound Dog was a supersonic, jet powered, air-launched cruise missile. The Hound Dog was initially given the designation B-77, later re-designated GAM-77, and finally being designated AGM-28. Hound Dog was originally envisioned as a temporary stand-off weapon for the B-52, to be used until the AGM-48 Skybolt air launched ballistic missile could be deployed. Instead, the Skybolt was canceled and the Hound Dog was deployed for 15 years until the missile was replaced by newer weapons, including the AGM-69 SRAM and the AGM-86 ALCM. Wikipedia.

The Hound Dog is an air-launched supersonic missile designed to destroy heavily-defended ground targets. Two AGM-28s were carried on specially modified B-52s, one beneath each wing. No AGM-28s were ever used in combat, but on a typical mission an AGM-28 would be launched at an altitude of 45,000 feet, climb to over 56,000 feet, cruise to the target area, and then dive to the target. The missile has a range of more than 600 miles, allowing stand-off launch hundreds of miles from the target, thus reducing the risk to the launch aircraft.

The first AGM-28 was launched on 23 April 1959 and production missiles entered service with the Strategic Air Command (SAC) in December of that year. In 1960 SAC developed a method for using the missiles' jet engines to provide extra power for the B-52 carrier in flight or on takeoff. The missiles could then be refueled in flight from the bomber's fuel tanks.

The AGM-28B, an advanced version of the -A, first flew in May 1961. It incorporates an improved guidance system and has greater range. Almost 700 AGM-28s were built before production ended in 1963; 428 of them were -Bs. Several hundred Hound Dog missiles were still in operational use in 1977. *(Information courtesy of the National Museum of the United States Air Force).*

Northrop F-89J Scorpion
(photo courtesy of Wikipedia)

Northrop F-89J Scorpion

The Scorpion was a two-seat, twin-engine, all-weather fighter-interceptor designed to locate, intercept, and destroy enemy aircraft by day or night under all types of weather conditions. It carried a pilot in the forward cockpit and a radar operator in the rear who guided the pilot into the proper attack position. The Scorpion was powered by a pair of after-burning thrust Allison J35-A-35, -33A, -41, or –47 turbojets, which gave it a maximum speed of 636 mph, a service ceiling of 49,200', and a range of 2,600 miles. The Scorpion was armed with 104 70mm rockets in wingtip pods or 27 rockets plus 3 Falcon missiles. *The Complete Encyclopedia of World Aircraft.*

The first F-89 made its initial flight in August 1948 and deliveries to the Air Force began in July 1950. Northrop produced 1,050 F-89s. On 19 July 1957, a Genie test rocket was fired from an F-89J, the first time in history that an air-to-air rocket with a nuclear warhead was launched and detonated. Three hundred and fifty F-89Ds were converted to J models, which became the Air Defense Command's first fighter-interceptor to carry nuclear armament. *(Information courtesy of the National Museum of the United States Air Force).*

Northrop T-38A Talon,
(photo courtesy of NASA)

Northrop T-38A Talon

The Talon is a two-seat supersonic jet trainer powered by a pair of 5,000-lb after-burning thrust General Electric J-38-GE-5A turbojets. It has a maximum speed of 1,083 mph, a service ceiling of 51,880', and a range of 1,543 miles. *(The Complete Encyclopedia of World Aircraft)*

In the mid-1950s, the USAF required a trainer with higher performance than the T-33 to better prepare student pilots for the latest tactical aircraft that were then coming into service. The aircraft chosen was the T-38A, because it offered high performance with low maintenance and operating costs. The T-38A became the USAF's first supersonic trainer. The T-38A prototype first flew on 10 April 1959, and production continued until 1972. A total of 1,189 T-38As were built. Some were later modified into AT-38Bs with external armament for weapons training purposes.

Jacqueline Cochran set eight performance records in the fall of 1961 flying a production T-38A and in February 1962 a T-38A set four international time-to-climb records. The USAF Thunderbirds used T-38As from 1974 to 1982 because of their economic operation and high performance. Other users of the T-38A include the US Navy in their Top Gun combat simulation program and the National Aeronautics and Space Administration (NASA). *((Information courtesy of the National Museum of the United States Air Force).*

The Talon was the world's first supersonic trainer and to date, is also the most produced. It remains in service as of 2010 in air forces throughout the world, although the USAF is the largest user. In addition to USAF pilots, the T-38 is used in the United States by NASA astronauts, with the aircraft loaned to NASA from the USAF. The US Naval Test Pilot School is the principal US Navy operator (other T-38s were previously used as USN aggressor aircraft until replaced by the similar F-5 Tiger II), as well as some NATO pilots participating in joint training programs, also fly the T-38. A few are also under civilian ownership. Wikipedia.

Piasecki/Vertol CH-21C Shawnee Helicopter
(Wikipedia photo)

Piasecki/Vertol CH-21 Shawnee Helicopter

The H-21 is a troop and cargo transport helicopter powered by one 1,425-hp Wright R-1820-103 Cyclone radial piston engine. It has a maximum speed of 131 mph, a service ceiling of 7,750', and a range of 400 miles. *(The Complete Encyclopedia of World Aircraft)*

The Piasecki/Vertol CH-21 "Shawnee is also known as the "Work Horse," the "Retriever," or the "Mule," but has more often been referred to as the "Flying Banana." The H-21 made its first flight in April 1952. The aircraft was originally designed by Piasecki to transport men and cargo but was later adapted for the rescue of personnel and for assault operations under combat conditions. Normally having a crew of two (pilot and copilot), the H-21 could carry either 20 fully equipped troops or 12 litter patients. In addition to serving with the USAF, the H-21 was supplied to the US Army, the French Navy, the Royal Canadian Air Force and the West German Air Force. *(Information courtesy of the National Museum of the USAF)*

The United States Air Force ordered an evaluation and service trials batch of 18 YH-21s from Piasecki Helicopter Corporation in 1949. Following successful trials with these aircraft, 32 H-21As were ordered. Production of the Workhorse continued with the UH-21B, ordered for service with Troop Carrier Command as an assault transport, and delivered from 1953. Production of the UH-21B for the USAF totaled 163. Total UH-21s was 213.

Piasecki developed the CH-21 arctic rescue helicopter from the world's first tandem rotor transport helicopter, the XHRP-1. This helicopter was first flown in March 1945. The CH-21 was equipped with an R1820-103 Wright Cyclone piston engine de-rated to 1,150 horsepower. It was first flown in April 1952. The CH-21B was equipped with a 1,425 horsepower engine developing full shaft horsepower. The CH-21 was first delivered to the United States Air Force in 1953 and immediately placed into service in the Arctic without any formal service evaluation. The CH-21 had winterization features permitting operation at temperatures as low as -65 degrees Fahrenheit and could be routinely maintenance under severe conditions. Both Canadian and USAF forces in the northern regions of Alaska, Canada, and Greenland in support of Distant

Early Warning (DEW) Line installations therefore used it. *(Information courtesy of the Strategic Air and Space Museum).*

Piper J-3 Cub
(Author photo)

Piper J-3 Cub/L4A Grasshopper

The L-4A liaison aircraft, originally designated the O-59, was the military version of the famous Piper J3 Cub. The Grasshopper was a two-seat lightplane powered by a 65-hp Continental A65 flat-four piston engine. It had a maximum speed of 92 mph, a service ceiling of 12,000', and a range of 250 miles. *The Complete Encyclopedia of World Aircraft.*

The Army ordered the first O-59s in 1941 for tests in conjunction with its growing interest in the use of light aircraft for liaison and observation duties in direct support of ground forces. Between 1941 and 1945, the Army procured almost 6,000 Piper Aircraft. During WW II, Grasshoppers performed a wide variety of functions throughout the world such as for artillery fire direction, pilot training, glider pilot instruction, courier service and front-line liaison. *(Information courtesy of the National Museum of the United States Air Force).*

Republic JB-2 Loon
(Wikipedia photo)

Republic JB-2 Loon

The JB-2 is a US made copy of the famous German V-1 surface-to-surface pilotless flying bomb first used against England on June 12-13, 1944. It is powered by one Ford PJ-31-F-1 of 900 lbs thrust (copy of German Argus-Schmidt pulse-jet) and armed with a 2,100 lb. high-explosive warhead. The Loon had an operating speed of 375-400 mph, a launching speed of 220 mph, an operating altitude of 2,000 to 4,000', and a range of 150 miles.

The airframe for the JB-2 was built by the Republic Aviation Corporation and the engine by the Ford Motor Company from drawings prepared at Wright Field, using dimensions taken from the remains of several V-1s brought from Germany.

About 1,000 JB-2s were built for the Army and Navy. Production delivery began in January 1945, but it was cancelled on VJ Day. The first one to be test flown in the US was launched at Eglin Field, Florida, in October 1944. Just before the end of the war, JB-2s were placed aboard an aircraft carrier en route to the Pacific for possible use in the proposed invasion of the Japanese home islands. Although the JB-2 was never used in combat, it provided valuable data for the design and construction of more advanced weapons. *(Information courtesy of the National Museum of the USAF).*

Republic P-47D Thunderbolt, New England Air Museum
(photo courtesy of Wikipedia)

Republic P-47D Thunderbolt

The P-47 Thunderbolt is a single-seat fighter-bomber powered by one 2,535-hp Pratt & Whitney R-2800-59W Double Wasp radial piston engine. The aircraft had a maximum speed of 697 km/h, a service ceiling of 41,000', and a range of 3058 km. The Thunderbolt was armed with eight .50 cal machine-guns and could carry a bomb-load of 2,500 lbs. The P-47N variant has a bubble canopy and a cut-down rear fuselage. *The Complete Encyclopedia of World Aircraft.*

Affectionately nicknamed Jug, the P-47 was one of the most famous AAF fighter planes of WW II. Although originally conceived as a lightweight interceptor, the P-47 developed as a heavyweight fighter and made its first flight on 6 May 1941. The first production model was delivered to the AAF in March 1942, and in April 1943 the Thunderbolt flew its first combat mission, a sweep over Western Europe.

Used as both a high-altitude escort fighter and a low-level fighter-bomber, the P-47 quickly gained a reputation for ruggedness. Its sturdy construction and air-cooled radial engine enabled the Thunderbolt to absorb severe battle damage and keep flying. During WW II, the P-47 served in almost every active war theater and in the forces of several Allied nations.

By the end of WW II, more than 15,600 Thunderbolts had been built. Production P-47B, C, early D and G series aircraft were built with metal-framed greenhouse type cockpit canopies. Late D series (dash 25 and later) aircraft and all M and N series production aircraft were given clear bubble canopies, which gave the pilot improved rearward vision. *(Information courtesy of the National Museum of the United States Air Force).*

Harold Skaarup

Republic F-84F Thunderstreak
(photo courtesy of Tom Hildreth)

Republic F-84F Thunderstreak

The swept-wing F-84F Thunderstreak evolved from the straight-wing F-84 Thunderjet. The prototype first flew on 3 June 1950 and deliveries began in 1954, primarily to the tactical Air Command as a ground support fighter-bomber. A Wright J-65W-3 turbojet powered the Thunderstreak. It was armed with six .50 cal Browning M3 machine-guns and could also carry up to 6,000 pounds of external stores. *(The Complete Encyclopedia of World Aircraft).*

Republic built 2,112 -Fs while General Motors fabricated an additional 599. Of these, 1,301 were delivered to NATO air forces. Production of a reconnaissance version, the RF-84F, totaled 718 aircraft, including 386 for allied countries. The RF-84F featured engine air intakes at the wing roots plus cameras in the nose.

F-84Fs gradually were replaced by supersonic F-100s in the late 1950s and were turned over to Air National Guard units. However, some F-84Fs were called back to temporary USAF service in the early 1960s due to the Berlin Crisis. *((Information courtesy of the National Museum of the United States Air Force).)*

Republic F-105B Thunderchief
(photo courtesy of Wikipedia)

Republic F-105B Thunderchief

The Thunderchief is a single-seat fighter-bomber powered by one 17,200-lb thrust Pratt & Whitney J75-P-19W turbojet. It has a maximum speed of 1,390 mph, a service ceiling of 41,200', and a range of 2,390 miles. It is armed with one M61 Vulcan 200mm cannon and can carry more than 14,000 lbs of mixed stores carried internally and externally. *The Complete Encyclopedia of World Aircraft.*

The F-105 evolved from a project begun in 1951 by Republic Aviation to develop a supersonic tactical fighter-bomber to replace the F-84F. The prototype first flew on October 22, 1955, but the first production aircraft, an F-105B, was not delivered to the USAF until 1958. The F-105D all-weather strike fighter and the two-place F-105F dual-purpose trainer-fighter also were built before F-105 production (833 aircraft) ended in 1964. No C or E series were produced, and the G's were modified from F-105Fs. The F-105D could carry over 14,000 pounds of ordnance, a heavier bomb load than a World War II B-17. Up to 8,000 pounds could be carried internally in the bomb bay. The F-105D was used extensively in the Viet Nam War. The last F-105D was withdrawn from USAF service on July 12, 1980.

The Thunderchief was the first supersonic fighter-bomber developed from scratch. It was operational from 1960 to 1970, and between 1965 and 1968, 75% of the USAF's assault missions over North Vietnam were carried out by Thunderchiefs. Nicknamed the Thud, this supersonic fighter-bomber carried over six tons of weaponry and cruised at Mach 2. The aircraft has a coke-bottle-shaped fuselage, narrowing toward the centre, then widening again. This shape, devised at the National Advisory Committee for Aeronautics (NACA), helped minimize drag as the plane accelerated to supersonic speed. *(Information courtesy of the National Museum of the United States Air Force).*

The Air Force Armament Museum's F-105D-1-RE, (Serial No. 58-115), is marked as F-105D-6-RE, *59-1771*, "JV" tailcode, "Foley's Folly" on the port fuselage, "Ohio Express" on the starboard fuselage, as flown by Capt. Peter Foley, 469th Tactical Fighter Squadron, Korat RTAFB, third pilot to survive 200 missions over North Vietnam. Wikipedia.

Republic RC-3 Seabee
(photo courtesy of Wikipedia)

Republic RC-3 Seabee

The RC-3 Seabee is an all-metal amphibious sports aircraft designed by Percival Spencer and manufactured by the Republic Aircraft Corporation. The RC-3 Seabee was designed by Percival Hopkins "Spence" Spencer, an aviation pioneer who built his first hang glider in April 1911. At the time he was 17 years old and constructed it from plans he found in a "Popular Mechanics" magazine. On 15 May 1914, Spencer made his first powered flight in a Curtiss Flying Boat. In 1937 he joined Sikorsky engineer Vincent A. Larsen to design their first, and only, amphibious aircraft, the Spencer-Larsen SL-12C. Development of the plane progressed slowly and in September 1940 Spencer left the partnership to form his own company. His resulting design was the Spencer S-12 Air Car Amphibian. Construction of the S-12 began on 1 March 1941 and the small, two seat S-12 prototype, registered NX29098, made its first flight on 8 August 1941. The S-12 was a fabric covered amphibian with a unique boxlike forward cabin, a high wing with a two bladed propeller in pusher configuration and a long, slender tail boom. In December 1941 Spencer put the Air Car into storage and joined the war effort as a test pilot for the Republic Aircraft Corporation. By 1943 he had flight tested 134 of the company's P-47 Thunderbolts.

In April 1943 Spencer left Republic Aircraft to join the Mills Novelty Company of Chicago, Illinois who wanted to use his Air Car to promote their company. Spencer used the company's wood forming equipment to build a new egg-shaped cabin for the Air Car and began demonstrating the aircraft to his former employers, Republic Aircraft. Seeing the potential of the Air Car as the perfect sports plane for pilots returning from the war, Republic purchased the rights to the Air Car in December 1943 and immediately began development of an all-metal version designated the Model RC-1 Thunderbolt Amphibian. On 30 November 1944 the first RC-1 Thunderbolt Amphibian, registered NX41816, made its first flight with Spencer at the controls.

The aircraft was displayed in St Louis, Missouri in December and by the end of 1944 Republic had received 1,972 civilian orders for the $3,500 airplane. The aircraft was also demonstrated to the US Navy and Army Air Corps. Both services were impressed with the design and on 19 February 1945 the Navy granted Republic Aviation the rights to use the name Seabee for the civilian version. The Army placed a large order for the aircraft, to be used for air-sea rescue operations under the designation OA-15. In September 1945, following VJ Day, both the Army and Navy canceled their orders, which by that time totaled over $20,000,000. The OA-15 Seabee was the last United States Army Air Corps aircraft to use the OA designation, which was dropped when the US Air Force was formed as a separate military branch in 1947.

Military operators included the Israeli Air Force, Paraguayan Navy, the United States Army Air Forces, and South Vietnamese Air Force. Republic sold its last new Seabee in 1948. By that time the demand for civilian aircraft had shown itself to be far less than anticipated, and the company turned its attention back to military contracts, developing the successful F-84 Thunderjet, which was built on the same assembly lines formerly used to build the Seabee. Wikipedia.

Royal Aircraft Factory F.E.8
(Wikipedia photo)

Royal Aircraft Factory F.E.8

The F.E.8 was a British single-seat fighter of the First World War designed at the Royal Aircraft Factory. Although a clean and well designed little airplane for a pusher, it could not escape the drag penalty imposed by its tail structure and was no match for the Halberstadt and Albatros fighters of late 1916. With the D.H.2, the F.E.8 was one of the first so-called "scout" aircraft designed from the outset as a single-seat fighter. In the absence of a synchronization gear to provide a forward firing machine gun for a tractor scout such as the S.E. 2, it was given a pusher layout.

On the whole the new design, produced by a team lead by John Kenworthy followed the conventional "Farman" layout, as did the competing Airco DH.2 designed by Geoffrey DeHavilland, who had also previously worked at the Royal Aircraft Factory - but it had some novel features.

The nacelle was, most unusually for the time, an all-metal structure – being framed in steel tube and covered with duralumin. The prototypes were fitted with large streamlined spinners on the propellers, although these were removed, and the production F.E.8s were built without them. The wings had a narrow chord, giving them a high aspect ratio. They featured dihedral outboard of the wide centre section, and the ailerons were of unusually long span - occupying the entire wing trailing edge outboard of the tail booms. The booms themselves were attached to the main spar of the tailplane, rather than the rudder post, giving them taper in side elevation, rather than in plan, as more usual in a "Farman" style pusher. A single 100 hp (75 kW) Gnome Monosoupape rotary engine driving a four-bladed propeller powered the aircraft.

The new aircraft made its maiden flight on 15 October 1915, flown by Frank Gooden, who was happy with the aircraft's handling. The aircraft was then armed with a single Lewis gun, which was originally fitted on a movable mount within the nose of the nacelle, with the machine gun's breech almost at the pilot's feet. This proved awkward in practice, and in production machines the gun was mounted directly in front of the pilot, in the manner of the D.H.2. Other changes required before the aircraft entered production included extra fuel to counter criticism from Hugh Trenchard, commander of the Royal Flying Corps in France, that the F.E.8's endurance was too short.

The new fighter was not a great improvement on the D.H.2 – although a little faster it did not handle quite so well. It was nonetheless ordered into production from Darracq Motors and Vickers. Neither manufacturer delivered their F.E.8s particularly quickly, so that the type ended up reaching the front in numbers six months later than the D.H.2.

After a fairly good start, the F.E.8 units quickly ran into problems with the new German fighters. On 9 March 1917 nine F.E.8 of No. 40 Squadron had a dogfight with five Albatros D.IIIs of Jagdstaffel 11, led by Manfred von Richthofen himself. Four F.E.8s were shot down, four others badly damaged, and the survivor caught fire when landing. After this disaster No. 40 Squadron was re-equipped with Nieuports but No. 41 kept their pushers until July 1917 – becoming the last single-seat pusher fighter squadron in France, using them for ground attack duties during the Battle of Messines. The only ace on the type was "Lobo" Benbow. Two F.E.8s were sent to Home Defence units in 1917, but the type was not adopted as a home defense fighter.

The Owls Head Transportation Museum in Maine has an F.E.8 reproduction in its collection, powered by a modern air-cooled, horizontally opposed engine. It was built in California, before being flown cross country and donated to the Museum upon arrival. Wikipedia.

Royal Aircraft Factory S.E.5E
(photo courtesy of the USAF)

Royal Aircraft Factory S.E.5a

The S.E. 5a was a single-seat equal-span biplane fighter. It was powered by one 200-hp Hispano-Suiza V-8 piston engine. It had a maximum speed of 138 mph, a service ceiling of 22,000' and an endurance rate of 3 hours. The aircraft was armed with one forward-firing synchronized .303in machine-gun and one Lewis gun mounted over the centre-section of the upper wing. It could also carry up to four 25-lb bombs. *The Complete Encyclopedia of World Aircraft.*

Second only to the Sopwith Camel in reputation, the S.E.5a was flown by legendary RAF aces such as Bishop, Ball, Mannock, and McCudden. The S.E.5a was admired for its stable and predictable flight characteristics, while being equal to most other fighters in speed and agility. Major W.A. (Billy) Bishop shot down 25 enemy aircraft in 12 days with this aircraft, establishing himself at the end of the war as the leading British ace with a total of 72 kills. *Information courtesy of the Canadian Forces Archives.* The S.E.5E is the American built version of the S.E.5a.

The Vermont Miitia Museum has a Royal Aircraft Factory S.E.5a 7/8-scale replica (Serial No. C1096) on display. Construction on this aircraft was begun in the UK in the 1980s by John Tetley and "Bill Sneesby. This S.E.5a replica was built using original plans, and then it was transferred to France to be completed and flown. Some parts are original, such as the engine, instruments and fuel tank. It will be finished in the colours of Lt. H. J. Hank" Burden of 56 Squadron in April 1918.

Sikorsky S-16, New England Air Museum
(Author photo)

Sikorsky S-16

The Sikorsky S-16 (named after its designer) or RBVZ S-XVI (named after its manufacturer) was a Russian equal-span single-bay two-seat biplane designed by Igor Sikorsky in 1914-15. Conceived in response to demand for an escort fighter for the Ilya Muromets bombers, it was noteworthy in that it was one of the first aircraft to possess synchronization gear for its 7.7mm machine gun. The first S-XVI was completed on 6 February 1915 with an 80 hp engine instead of the intended 100 hp because of supply problems. On 17 December 1915, the Russian government placed an order for 18 aircraft, these being delivered in early 1916. Although highly maneuverable, the S-XVI possessed a comparatively poor performance due to insufficient power. A further small batch was completed in 1917, with the aircraft being used during the Russian Revolution and staying in service until 1923. Wikipedia.

Sikorsky S-39B, New England Air Museum
(photo courtesy of Wikipedia)

Sikorsky S-39B

The S-39 amphibian was a smaller, single-engine version of the S-38 light amphibious aircraft, built in the USA by aviation firm Sikorsky Aircraft during the early 1930s. A military version was designated the C-28.

The S-39B in the New England Air Museum (Serial No. 904), Reg. No. NC 803W, first flew on 31 July 1930, and is the oldest existing Sikorsky aircraft. It was originally based in Hartford and flown by Charles W. Deeds, mainly for pleasure. During WWII, it was flown by the Civil Air Patrol out of Rehoboth, Delaware, basically on air-sea rescues. One of these missions resulted in the pilot Hugh Sharp and his observer Ed Edwards becoming the first civilians ever to be awarded the military Air Medal. It also earned Sikorsky the prestigious Collier Trophy. 904 closed out its flying days as a bush plane in Alaska. It was damaged in a forced landing in 1957 and remained where it fell until 1963 when it was recovered and brought to the museum by Phil Redden of Anchorage. Wikipedia.

Sikorsky VS-44-A Flying Boat, New England Air Museum
(Author photo)

Sikorsky VS-44-A Flying Boat

The Sikorsky VS-44 was a large four-engined flying boat built in the USA in the early 1940s. The VS-44 was designed primarily for the trans-Atlantic passenger market, with a capacity of 40+ passengers. Only three aircraft were produced: *Excalibur*, *Excambian*, and *Exeter*.

A single deck seaplane with four twin-row Pratt & Whitney Twin Wasps rated at 1,200 horsepower (895 kW) each, the new aircraft was 80 feet (24 m) in length and weighed in at 57,500 pounds (26,100 kg) for takeoff. The Boeing 314 Clipper was larger and boasted more powerful Wright Twin Cyclones of 1,600 horsepower (1,193 kW), but the VS-44 was 30 miles per hour (48 km/h) faster and could fly an average payload more than 4,000 miles (6,400 km), out distancing the big Boeing by 500 miles (800 km) and earning bragging rights with the longest full-payload range of any aircraft in the world. The VS-44 brought home several new world records after it went into operation, but, missing out on a Pan Am contract, who instead purchased the Martin M-130 and later the Boeing 314 Clipper. The VS-44's limited production would never even recoup the development costs.

The outbreak of World War II put civilian transatlantic air services on hold. Now under a Navy contract, with the Navy designation JR2S-1, AEA's three VS-44's continued flying between New York, New York and Foynes, Ireland, carrying passengers, freight and materiel.

The first VS-44, *Excalibur*, crashed on takeoff in 1942 at Botwood, Newfoundland, killing 11 of the 37 aboard.

In 1976, *Excambian* was donated to the Naval Aviation Museum at Pensacola, Florida and eventually put on permanent loan to the New England Air Museum in Connecticut. The NEAM staff restored *Excambian* to its post-World War II American Export Airlines livery with volunteer help from some of the former Sikorsky workers who had built the original VS-44. Wikipedia.

Sikorsky R-4B Hoverfly Helicopter, New England Air Museum
(photo courtesy of Wikipedia)

Sikorsky R-4B Hoverfly Helicopter

The R-4B helicopter was powered by an R550-3 engine in the main production batch of 100 aircraft. The Hoverfly Mark I was an RAF designation for the helicopter. The R-4 was the world's first production helicopter and the Air Force's first service helicopter. The original military model, the XR-4, was developed from the famous experimental VS-300 helicopter, invented by Igor Sikorsky and publicly demonstrated in 1940. The XR-4 made its initial flight on 13 January 1942 and as a result of its successful flight tests, the AAF ordered 3 YR-4As and 27 YR-4Bs for service testing and flight training. Of these 30, one went to Burma and one to Alaska, while several others were assigned to the US Navy (HNS-1), US Coast Guard and British Royal Navy. They showed such promise that the AAF ordered 100 R-4Bs.

The R-4 was first used in combat in May 1944. In a letter to a friend, Col. Philip G. Cochran, Commanding Officer (CO) of the 1st Air Commando Group, wrote Today the 'egg-beater' went into action and the damn thing acted like it had good sense. *(Information courtesy of the National Museum of the United States Air Force).*

Sikorsky R-6 Helicopter, New England Air Museum
(photo courtesy of Wikipedia)

Sikorsky R-6 Helicopter

The Sikorsky R-6 was an American-built light two-seat helicopter of the 1940s. In Royal Air Force and Royal Navy service, it was named the Hoverfly II. The R-6 Hoverfly II was developed to improve on the successful Sikorsky R-4. In order to enhance performance a completely new streamlined fuselage was designed and the boom carrying the tail rotor was lengthened and straightened. The main rotor and transmission system of the R-4 was retained. Sikorsky allotted their Model 49 designation to the new design. Later, dynamically balanced modifications to the rotor were carried out by Doman Helicopters Inc. The new aircraft could attain 100 mph compared with 82 mph by the earlier design.

Initial production was by Sikorsky, but most examples were built by Nash-Kelvinator. Some of the later aircraft were fitted with more powerful engines. The first R-6s were delivered to the United States Army Air Force (USAAF) in late 1944 and some were transferred to the United States Navy (USN). It was initially intended to pass 150 R-6s to the Royal Air Force (RAF), but delays caused by the switch of production from Sikorsky's factory at Stratford, Connecticut to Nash-Kelvinator at Detroit Michigan meant that only 27 R-6As were actually delivered to the RAF as the Hoverfly II. 15 of these were passed on to the Royal Navy's Fleet Air Arm (FAA).

The USAAF operated their R-6s in secondary roles and the survivors were redesignated H-6A in 1948. The USN examples were designated the HOS-1 and a further 64 were intended to be transferred from the USAAF, but this did not take place. Disposals of surplus military

Model 49s were made in the civil market in the late 1940s but none now remain in operation. Four are currently displayed in US museums. Wikipedia.

Sikorsky S-51 Executive Transport Helicopter
(photo courtesy of Wikipedia)

Sikorsky S-51 Dragonfly Helicopter

The S-51 Dragonfly was a four-seat helicopter used to convert pilots from fixed wing aircraft to helicopters. It was also used by some Search & Rescue units. The Army used the H-5 version for conversion training and for survey work.

The Navy accepted two three-seat Army R-5A helicopters in December 1945 for trials as HO2S-1s. Shortly thereafter, an order was placed for the development and procurement of the four-seat HO3S versions. Although intended for use in an observation role and used as such by the Marines in Korea, the Navy deployed them on aircraft carriers and other rescue ships to recover downed pilots on land as well as at sea.

The first four production HO3S-1s delivered to the Navy accompanied Admiral Richard E. Byrd's 1946-47 expedition to the Antarctic. HO3Ss also saw service with Coast Guard in a search and rescue role and were the first helicopters used in combat related duties by the British armed services.

An HO3S unofficially bettered the existing distance record when it was flown 755 miles non-stop from NAS Seattle, Washington to NAS Alameda, California. The HO3S was also the primary platform utilized in evaluating the feasibility of automatic pilot systems for helicopters. *Information courtesy of the National Museum of Naval Aviation.*

Sikorsky UH-34D Seabat Helicopter
(photo courtesy of Wikipedia)

Sikorsky LH-34D Seabat Helicopter

Sikorsky started to design the S-58 in 1951 at the request of the US Navy which was looking for a new anti-submarine helicopter to replace the Sikorsky S 55, deemed to be too small and under powered. The S-58 first flew on March 8 1954 and the US production run amounted to 1821. The US Navy version was designated HSS 1 Seabat in its anti-submarine configuration and HUS-1 Seahorse in its utility transport configuration the USN, USMC and USCG. The Army version is the H34 Choctaw. Many were exported to numerous countries (Germany, Belgium, Italy, Canada, etc.). For the war in North Africa, the French armed forces increased their rotorcraft fleets dramatically. 90 S-58's were bought from Sikorsky and 171 were built under license by Sud Aviation. The French navy operated the HSS between 1958 and 1978 for transport and anti-submarine warfare. They were replaced by the Westland Lynx in this latter mission. The French air force flew the H 34 for transport and rescue between 1958 and 1984, when they were replaced by the Aerospatiale Puma.

In North Africa, the S-58 demonstrated the helicopter gunship concept, providing firepower during the landing of the troop transport helicopters. This method was also applied by the USA in Vietnam and is now in worldwide use. The S-58 was also used to carry airline passengers between airport and city center both in the USA and Europe. Needless to say that the cabin fit was very different from the military version. Westland also bought the S-58 license from Sikorsky and built 352 Wessex helicopters, all powered by turboshafts housed in a modified nose.

The Wessex is still in use with the British armed forces. In 1970, Sikorsky did the same kind of modification to an S-58, replacing the piston engine by two PW Canada PT 6 turboshafts in a modified nose. These conversions were designated S-58 T and several are still flying worldwide, whereas the piston engined version has almost disappeared.

Sikorsky SH-34J, Sea Horse. This helicopter was manufactured by the Sikorsky Aircraft division of United Aircraft Corp. and was first produced in 1956 and flown by all US forces, eight foreign countries and commercial airlines. Used by the US Navy for anti-submarine warfare training and was used extensively for rescue work. It could carry 12 to 18 passengers, 8 litters or a payload of 4000 for 100 miles.

While the Sikorsky HO4S had been an effective anti-submarine vehicle, its limited range capability and cabin space led to the development by Sikorsky of a larger helicopter. Design features that incorporated folding rotor blades and an entire tail section with rotor that could be folded forward to facilitate shipboard storage as well as provisions to accommodate twelve passengers and a range capability of 182 miles (247 miles with a reserve tank) led the Navy to order the first prototype designated as the HSS-l Seabat in June 1952. The Marine Corps soon placed an order for a transport and utility version to be known as the HUS-1 Seahorse. Both aircraft were redesignated SH-34 and UH-34, respectively.

The SH-34s were used predominantly for anti-submarine warfare operations and were equipped with dipping sonar to locate the enemy and/or torpedoes to home in on and destroy a submarine. Some were fitted with automatic stabilization equipment for operations at night, while others were fitted with pontoon landing gear for use by the Coast Guard in search and rescue operations.

The Marine Corps Seahorses played a significant role in combat support operations during the Vietnam War and in further development of helicopter armament for attacking ground targets. Four UH-34s were modified for Antarctic operations while seven were used by the Marine Corps as part of the executive flight detachment at Quantico, Virginia to provide transportation for the President and other officials. It was a Marine Corps UH-34 that plucked astronaut CDR Alan Shepard out of the sea after he became the first American to venture into space. Information courtesy of the National Museum of Naval Aviation.

Sikorsky SH-3H Sea King Helicopter
(Wikipedia photo)

Sikorsky SH-3H Sea King Helicopter

The twin-engine, General Electric T58-10 turboshaft-powered Sea King was the first helicopter designed and equipped to conduct all-weather, night and day anti-submarine search and attack missions. The Sea Kings have been equipped with dunking sonar and anti-submarine torpedoes.

In 1954, the US Navy contracted with Sikorsky Aircraft to develop a new and larger all-weather helicopter with the ability to carry both search equipment and 840 lbs of weapons for combined hunter/killer anti-submarine operations. The end product provided was the SH-3 Sea King helicopter, a true amphibian with a water-tight hull and stabilizing floats for retractable wheels. An auto-stabilization system coupled with automatic hovering equipment and a Doppler/radar altimeter provided the SH-3 with the required all-weather capability.

Delivery to the fleet of 255 SH-3A helicopters with two 1,250 shp turbine engines began in 1961. These were soon followed by 73 SH-3D models, with 1,400-shp engines and increased fuel capacity. A number of the SH-3As were converted for a variety of missions including mine-countermeasures (RH-3A); emergency evacuation of key personnel in Washington, including the President (UH-3A); and, search and rescue operations in combat areas (HH-3A with a turret mounted 7.62 mm mini-gun). Other conversions included a Highdrink refueling system for airborne refueling from ships, a fuel dumping system and provisions for long-range fuel tanks.

Manned by a crew of four (2 pilots and 2 sonar operators), the SH-3A has a 20,500 lb maximum lift-off weight, a maximum speed of 160 mph, and a range of 625 miles. *Information courtesy of the National Museum of Naval Aviation.*

The SH-3H Sea King in the Quonset Air Museum was flown by Helicopter Anti-submarine Squadron Five (HS-5), NAS Jacksonville, Florida. On 22 December 1994 it was flown to the Quonset Air Museum and is presently on loan from the US Navy. *(Information courtesy of the Quonset Air Museum).*

Sikorsky HH-52A Sea Guard Helicopter
(Author photo)

Sikorsky HH-52A Sea Guard Helicopter

Ordered in 1962 as a replacement for the HH-34, the HH-52 Sea Guard was a variant of the Sikorsky S-62 helicopter which had proven to be highly successful in the civilian sector as the first turbine rotorcraft to ever be granted certification for commercial use.

Coast Guard squadrons operated the HH-52 as a search and rescue helicopter, a role for which it proved to be well suited because of certain design features. Chief among these was that the HH-52 was fully amphibious and that the main wheels retracted into pontoons located forward on both sides of the fuselage. The helicopter also employed a folding platform along the side of the fuselage and a winch above the door, both of which facilitated helicopter rescue. *Information courtesy of the National Museum of Naval Aviation.*

Sikorsky CH-54A Tarhe Helicopter, New England Air Museum
(Author photo)

Sikorsky CH-54A Tarhe (Skycrane) Helicopter

The Tarhe is a heavy lift crane helicopter with a three-man crew and passenger seats for two loaders. It is powered by two 9,000-shp Pratt & Whitney T73 (CH-54A) or T73-700 (CH-54B) turboshafts. It has a maximum speed of 126 mph, and a range of 230 miles. First flown on 9 May 1962, the Tarhe was built specifically as a crane helicopter. The Tarhe was used by the US Army with a special carrier pod, which could accommodate 46 troops or 24 stretchers. A few were also used as mobile command posts, communications centers, or surgical hospitals. It saw considerable service in Vietnam where it was used to lift M114 howitzers, armored vehicles, bulldozers, troops, and more than 380 damaged aircraft. A few saw service with the Army National Guard and on retirement, many have come on to the civil register. *(Information courtesy of the US Army Museum).*

Sikorsky UH-60 Blackhawk Helicopter
(photo courtesy of the USAF)

Sikorsky UH-60 Blackhawk Helicopter

The UH-60 Black Hawk is a four-bladed, twin-engine, medium-lift utility helicopter is powered by two GE T700 turboshaft engines. It has a long, low profile shape to meet the Army's requirement for transporting aboard a C-130 Hercules. It can carry 11 troops with equipment, lift 2,600 lb (1,170 kg) of cargo internally or 9,000 lb (4,050 kg) of cargo (for UH-60L/M) externally by sling. The Navy version, the SH-60 Seahawk, is the platform for the LAMPS III (Light Airborne Multi-Purpose System).

Sikorsky submitted the S-70 design for the United States Army's Utility Tactical Transport Aircraft System (UTTAS) competition in 1972. The Army designated the prototype as the YUH-60A and selected the Black Hawk as the winner of the program in 1976, after a fly-off competition with the Boeing Vertol YUH-61. The UH-60A entered service with the Army in 1979, to replace the UH-1 Iroquois as the Army's tactical transport helicopter. Wikipedia.

The Black Hawk helicopter series can perform a wide array of missions, including the tactical transport of troops, electronic warfare, and aeromedical evacuation. A VIP version known as the VH-60N is used to transport important government officials (e.g., Congress, Executive departments) with the helicopter's call sign of "Marine One" when transporting the President of the United States. In air assault operations it can move a squad of 11 combat troops or reposition a 105 mm M102 howitzer with thirty rounds ammunition, and a four-man crew in a single lift. The Black Hawk is equipped with advanced avionics and electronics for increased survivability and capability, such as the Global Positioning System.

The UH-60 can be equipped with stub wings at top of fuselage to carry fuel tanks or various armaments. The initial stub wing system is called External Stores Support System (ESSS). It has two pylons on each wing to carry two 230 US gal (870 L) and two 450 US gal (1,700 L) tanks in total. The four fuel tanks and associated lines and valves form the external extended range fuel system (ERFS). The ESSS can also carry 10,000 lb (4,500 kg) of armament such as rockets, missile and gun pods. The ESSS entered service in 1986. However it was found that with four fuel tanks it would obstruct the firing field of the door guns. To alleviate the issue, the external tank system (ETS) with unswept stub wings to carry two fuel tanks was developed.

The unit cost varies with the version due to the varying specifications, equipment and quantities. For example, the unit cost of the Army's UH-60L Black Hawk is $5.9 million while the unit cost of the Air Force MH-60G Pave Hawk is $10.2 million. Wikipedia.

The 112th Medical Company (Air Ambulance), Maine Army National Guard (MEARNG), based in Bangor, Maine, is supported with the Sikorsky UH-60 Black Hawk helicopter.

Sikorsky HH-60J Jayhawk Helicopter
(photo courtesy of Wikipedia)

Sikorsky HH-60J Jayhawk Helicopter

The HH-60J Jayhawk is a multi-mission, twin-engine, medium-range helicopter operated by the United States Coast Guard for search and rescue, law enforcement, military readiness and marine environmental protection missions. The HH-60J is designed to fly a crew of four up to 300 mi (483 km) offshore, hoist up to 6 additional people on board while remaining on-scene for up to 45 minutes and return to base while maintaining an adequate fuel reserve. Normal cruising speed of the HH-60J is 135 to 140 knots (155 to 161 mph) and the aircraft is capable of reaching 180 knots (207 mph) for short durations. The HH60J can fly at 140 kN (161 mph) for six to seven hours.

Chosen to replace the Sikorsky HH-3F Pelican, the HH-60J is a member of the Sikorsky S-70 family of helicopters and is based on the United States Navy's SH-60 Seahawk helicopter. Development began in September 1986, first flight was achieved on August 8, 1989, and the first HH-60J entered USCG service in June 1990. Production ended in 1996 after 42 helicopters were produced.

The MH-60T Medium Range Recovery Helicopter upgrade program began in 2007 and is scheduled to provide upgraded avionics and operational capabilities to all 42 existing HH-60J airframes by 2015. As each airframe upgrade is completed, the affected HH-60J will be re-designated to MH-60T. Wikipedia.

Sopwith Pup
(photo courtesy of Wikipedia)

Sopwith Pup

The Sopwith Pup was a British single seater biplane fighter aircraft built by the Sopwith Aviation Company. It entered service with the Royal Flying Corps and the Royal Naval Air Service in the autumn of 1916. With pleasant flying characteristics and good maneuverability, the aircraft proved very successful. The Pup was eventually outclassed by newer German fighters, but it was not completely replaced on the Western Front until the end of 1917. Remaining Pups were relegated to Home Defence and training units. The Pup's docile flying characteristics also made it ideal for use in aircraft carrier deck landing and takeoff experiments.

The Pup was officially named the Sopwith Scout. The "Pup" nickname arose because pilots considered it to be the "pup" of the larger two-seat Sopwith 1½ Strutter. The name never had official status as it was felt to be "undignified", but a precedent was set, and all later Sopwith types apart from the triplane acquired names of mammals or birds (Camel, Dolphin, Snipe etc.), which ended up with the Sopwith firm being said to have created a "flying zoo" during the First World War.

Development began in 1915, when Sopwith produced the SLTBP, a personal aircraft for the company's test pilot, Harry Hawker. The SLTBP was a single-seat, tractor biplane powered by a 50 hp Gnome rotary engine. Sopwith next developed a larger fighter that was heavily influenced by the SLTBP.

The resulting aircraft was a single-bay, single-seat biplane with a fabric-covered, wooden framework and staggered equal-span wings. The cross axle type main landing gear supported on V-struts attached to the lower fuselage longerons. The prototype and most production Pups were powered by the 80 hp (60 kW) Le Rhone rotary engine. Armament was a single 0.303 inch (7.7 mm) Vickers machine gun synchronized with the Sopwith-Kauper synchronizer.

A prototype was completed in February 1916 and sent to Upavon for testing in late March. The Royal Naval Air Service (RNAS) quickly ordered two more prototypes, and then placed a production order. Sopwith was heavily engaged in production of the 1½ Strutter, and produced only a small number of Pups for the RNAS. Deliveries commenced in August 1916.

The Royal Flying Corps (RFC) also placed large orders for Pups. The RFC orders were undertaken by sub-contractors Standard Motor Co. and Whitehead Aircraft. Deliveries did not commence until the beginning of 1917. A total of 1,770 Pups were built by Sopwith (96), Standard Motor Co. (850), Whitehead Aircraft (820), and William Beardmore & Co. (30).

In May 1916, the RNAS received its first Pups for operational trials with "A" Naval Squadron. The first Pups reached the Western Front in October 1916 with No. 8 Squadron RNAS, and proved successful, with the squadron's Pups claiming 20 enemy machines destroyed in operations over the Somme battlefield by the end of the year. The first RFC Squadron to re-equip with the Pup was No. 54 Squadron, which arrived in France in December. The Pup quickly proved its superiority over the early Fokker, Halberstadt and Albatros biplanes. After encountering the Pup in combat, Manfred von Richthofen said, "We saw at once that the enemy airplane was superior to ours." The Pup's light weight and generous wing area gave it a good rate of climb. Agility was enhanced by ailerons being fitted on both wings. The Pup had half the horsepower and armament of the German Albatros D.III, but was much more maneuverable, especially over 15,000 ft (4,500m) due to its light wing loading. Ace James McCudden stated that "When it came to maneuvering, the Sopwith (Pup) would turn twice to an Albatros' once ... it was a remarkably fine machine for general all-round flying. It was so extremely light and well surfaced that after a little practice one could almost land it on a tennis court." However, the Pup was also longitudinally unstable.

At the peak of its operational deployment, the Pup equipped only four RNAS squadrons (Nos. 3, 4, 8 and 9 Squadrons), and three RFC units (Nos. 54, 46 and 66 Squadrons). By spring 1917, the type was already outclassed by the newest German fighters and the RNAS had replaced theirs, first with Sopwith Triplanes, and then Sopwith Camels. The RFC Pup squadrons on the other hand had to soldier on, in spite of increasing casualties, until it was possible to replace the last frontline Pups with Camels, in December 1917. The raids on London by Gotha bombers in mid-1917 caused far more damage and casualties than the earlier airship raids. The ineffective response by British interceptor units had serious political repercussions. In response No. 66 Squadron was withdrawn to Calais for a short period, and No. 46 was transferred for several weeks to Sutton's Farm airfield near London. Two new Pup squadrons were formed specifically for Home Defence duties, No. 112 in July, and No. 61 in August.

The first Pups delivered to Home Defence units utilized the 80 hp Le Rhone, but subsequent Home Defence Pups standardized on the more powerful 100 hp Gnome Monosoupape, which provided improved rate of climb. These aircraft were distinguishable by the addition of vents in the cowling face.

Sopwith Pups were also used in many pioneering carrier experiments. On 2 August 1917, a Pup flown by Sqn Cdr Edwin Dunning became the first aircraft to land aboard a moving ship, HMS *Furious*. Dunning was killed on his third landing when the Pup fell over the side of the ship. The Pup began operations on the carriers in early 1917; the first aircraft were fitted with skid undercarriages in place of the standard landing gear. Landings utilized a system of deck wires to "trap" the aircraft. Later versions reverted to the normal undercarriage. Pups were used as ship-based fighters on three carriers: HMS *Campania, Furious* and *Manxman*. A number of other Pups were deployed to cruisers and battleships where they were launched from platforms attached to gun turrets. A Pup flown from a platform on the cruiser HMS *Yarmouth* shot down the German Zeppelin *L 23* off the Danish coast on 21 August 1917

The US Navy also employed the Sopwith Pup with famed Australian/British test pilot Edgar Percival testing the use of carrier-borne fighters. In 1926, Percival was catapulted in a Pup off the battleship USS *Idaho* at Guantanamo Bay, Cuba.

The Pup saw extensive use as a trainer. Student pilots completing basic flight training in the Avro 504k often graduated to the Pup as an intermediate trainer. The Pup was also used in Fighting School units for instruction in combat techniques. Many training Pups were in fact reserved by senior officers and instructors as their personal runabouts.

A notable, and quite accurate flying reproduction, built in the late 1960s by the late Richard King, one of the co-founders of Old Rhinebeck Aerodrome along with Cole Palen, still exists at the Owls Head Museum of Transportation in Rockland, Maine, and is still flown occasionally, with its original vintage First World War Le Rhône 9C 80 hp rotary engine, at special events during their open season. Wikipedia.

SPAD XIII, with Eddie Rickenbacker
(photo courtesy of the USAF)

Société Pour Aviation et ses Derives SPAD XIII

The SPAD XIII was designed in 1916 as a French attempt to counter the twin gun German fighters, like the Halberstadt. The SPAD XIII doubled the firepower of the earlier SPAD VII by using two Vickers 303 machine-guns with 400 rounds of ammunition for each gun. It could also carry four 25 lb. bombs. It is powered by one 200-hp. or 220-hp. Hispano-

Suiza water-cooled engine. The aircraft has a maximum speed of 135 mph, a service ceiling of 20,000' and a range of 250 miles.

The enthusiasm of the French pilots who tested the aircraft between April and September 1917 encouraged the French government to order more than 2,000. The US Air Service also began flying the SPAD XIII in March 1918 and by war's end in November 1918 the Air Service has acquired 893. Throughout 1917 and into 1918 the SPAD XIII held its own against German aircraft, but in the summer of 1918 the newly arrived Fokker D.VII outclassed it. The SPAD XIII had poor visibility and insufficient rate of climb, but it proved itself a rugged fighter with the ability to dive at high speed to escape enemy planes. *(Information courtesy of the National Museum of the USAF).*

Standard J-1
(photo courtesy of Wikipedia)

Standard J-1

The Standard J-1 is a two-seat primary trainer developed from the earlier Sloan and Standard H-series aircraft designed by Charles Healey Day. When the US entered WW I, the Army ordered the aircraft (then known as the SJ) produced as a supplement to the Curtiss Jenny then in production. The SJ was powered by one 100-hp Hall-Scott A-7 inline engine. At about the same time, Standard introduced an advanced version of the SJ called the JR. The Army bought only six of the JR-series aircraft, but some of the JR's features were incorporated into SJ production aircraft; the resulting version became known as the J-1.

Four companies, Standard, Dayton-Wright, Fisher Body and Wright-Martin, built 1,601 of the J-1s before production ended. Some 2,700 more J-1s on order were cancelled when the Armistice was signed. Hall-Scott engines were most commonly installed in the J-1, but some were equipped with Curtiss or 150-hp Wright-Hispano-Suiza engines. Similar in appearance to the JN-4, the J-1 was said to be more difficult to fly and never gained the popularity of the legendary Jenny. The E-1 variant was a smaller equal-span biplane powered by a 100-hp Gnome or 80-hp Le Rhône rotary engine, used as an advanced trainer. The M-Defense variant differed by having provision for armament. *(Information courtesy of the National Museum of the United States Air Force).*

SUD Aviation SE 210 Caravelle VIR Airliner, New England Air Museum
(Author photo)

SUD Aviation SE 210 Caravelle VIR Airliner

The Caravelle was the first short/medium-range jet airliner, produced by the French Sud Aviation firm starting in 1955 (when it was still known as SNCASE). The Caravelle would go on to be one of the more successful European first generation jetliners, selling throughout Europe and even penetrating the United States market, with an order for 20 from United Airlines. The Caravelle established the aft-mounted-engine, clean-wing design that has since been used on a wide variety of subsequent aircraft.

The first prototype of the Caravelle (F-WHHH), christened by Madame de Gaulle, was rolled out on 21 April 1955, and flew on 27 May powered by two British Rolls-Royce RA-26 Mk.522 with 4,536 kgf (44,480 N; 10,000 lbf) of unitary thrust. The flight duration was 41 minutes. The second prototype flew a year later on 6 May 1956. The first prototype had a cargo door on the lower left side of the fuselage, but this was removed in the second prototype for an all-seating arrangement. The first order was from Air France in 1956, followed by SAS in 1957. That year Sud-Est merged with Sud-Ouest to become Sud Aviation, but the original SE naming was retained. More orders followed, mainly triggered by presentations on airshows and demonstrations to potential customers. The Caravelle was certified in May 1959 and shortly afterwards entered service with SAS and Air France.

Several models were produced over the lifetime of the production run, as the power of the available engines grew and allowed for higher takeoff weights. By this time most of Sud Aviation's design department turned to a supersonic transport of the same general size and range as the Caravelle, naturally naming it the Super-Caravelle; however, this work would later be merged with similar work at the Bristol Aeroplane Company to produce the Concorde. In some configurations, aircraft had a number of rearward facing passenger seats, an uncommon seating arrangement for civil aircraft.

In total 282 Caravelles of all types were built (2 prototype or pre-production aircraft and 280 production aircraft), with Sud Aviation's break-even point at around the 200 mark. N902MW C/N 88, a former United Airlines Caravelle, in Airborne Express livery, was parked at the New England Air Museum, Windsor Locks, Connecticut, but may have been scrapped 19 August 2010. Wikipedia.

Vought-Sikorsky OS2U-3 Kingfisher
(photo courtesy of the USN)

Vought-Sikorsky OS2U-2 Kingfisher

The Kingfisher is a two-seat observation aircraft powered by one 450-hp Pratt & Whitney R-985-AN-2 radial piston engine. It has a maximum speed of 164 mph, a service ceiling of 13,000', and a range of 805 miles. It is armed with two .3in machine-guns (one forward-firing and one on a flexible mount in the rear cockpit), and can carry two 100-lb bombs on underwing racks. *The Complete Encyclopedia of World Aircraft.*

Known affectionately as the Bug and Old Slow and Ugly, the OS2U was assigned to the fleet in 1938 as a shipboard seaplane that could serve as its eyes. Kingfishers operated from land bases, battleships and cruisers. The last of 1,006 production model OS2U-3s rolled off the line in 1942. Only four OS2Us survive today, two of which are on the Gulf Coast, one in the National Museum of Naval Aviation (BuNo. 5926 obtained in 1971 from the Uruguayan Navy) and the other on the USS Alabama in Mobile, Alabama. Number three is on board the USS North Carolina and the fourth is at the National Air and Space Museum.

Several times, OS2Us engaged German U-Boats with depth bombs and machine gun fire while patrolling the Atlantic. In the Aleutians, Kingfishers often carried twice their design load to serve as dive-bombers and one shot down a Zero while serving as a naval gunfire spotter.

It was to become the Florence Nightingale of the Pacific during World War II in its air-sea rescue role. During a carrier raid on Truk in 1944, an OS2U flying from a battleship landed in choppy seas to pickup ten pilots over a period of six hours taxiing as far as 20 miles to deliver them to a submarine. A Kingfisher rescued famous World War I ace Captain Eddie Rickenbacker after the plane in which he was riding as a passenger ditched in the Pacific.

Standard procedure for recovering an OS2U at sea was to have the aircraft land in a smooth, slick sea created by a hard turn of the ship, taxi to a towed net/raft, have the engine shut down and be hoisted aboard. In one case, during a recovery in a war zone, it became necessary for the ship to leave the plane and crew when the Kingfisher came loose from the net. Attempts to restart the engine with cartridges were unsuccessful and the crew bobbed in the seas for eight hours before being rescued by a destroyer, and the plane was then sunk by the ship's guns. *Information courtesy of the National Museum of Naval Aviation.* OS2U-2 Kingfisher (Serial No. 5909), was on loan from the NASM and placed on display on the USS Massachusetts for many years until returned to the NASM in the late 1990s.

Waco YKC-S
(Author photo)

Waco YKC-S

The Waco YKC-S is one of the Waco Standard Cabin Series of American cabin biplanes built in the 1930s. The standard cabin series were Waco's first successful cabin biplane design, and was based on the F series airframe. The Model **C** series had a raised centre and rear fuselage to form a four-seat cabin which was entered through a door over the lower wing and had a rather ugly framed rear-view window dispensed with in the later standard cabins. The initial QDC model of 1931 had a 165 hp (123 kW) Continental A70 cowled engine and was fitted with a triangulated shock-cord tailwheel undercarriage.

1932 brought the OEC and UEC models which were powered respectively by the 210 hp (157 kW) Kinner C5 and the 210 hp (157 kW) Continental R-670. Continuous refinement and improvement by Waco Aircraft resulted in production of various sub-models continuing until 1939.

In 1935, Waco introduced its Custom Cabin series (which featured a sesquiplane layout without ailerons on the lower wing) and decided to differentiate between the Standard and Custom Cabin types by appending an S to the model designator. In 1936 the C-S was replaced with an 'S' signifying 'Standard'. The YKC-S was equipped with a 225 hp (168 kW) Jacobs L-4 engine, with 22 being built.

The Standard Cabin series, with its cabin comfort, proved to be popular with private pilot owners. Many were purchased by small commercial aviation firms and non-aviation businesses. Approximately 135 Standard Cabins series aircraft of several sub-models are currently registered in the USA. Wikipedia.

Wright Flyer
(photo courtesy of Wikipedia)

Wright Flyer

The original Wright Flyer built by the brothers Orville and Wilbur Wright is recognized officially as the world's first heavier-than-air craft to be flown in powered, manned, controlled and sustained flight. This was achieved at Kill Devil Hill, Kittyhawk, North Carolina, on 17 December 1903. The first of four flights was made that day piloted by Orville. The Flyer was airborne for 12 seconds and covered a distance of 120'. In its fourth and final flight, with Wilbur as the pilot, the Flyer covered a distance of 852' in 59 seconds. The initial flyer was powered by a 12-hp engine of Wright design. *(The Complete Encyclopedia of World Aircraft)*

The replicas found in New England are reproductions of the Wright 1909 Military Flyer. Upon being purchased by the Signal Corps for $30,000 on 2 August 1909, the original airplane was redesignated Signal Corps Airplane No. 1, the world's first military heavier-than-air flying machine. It was used in October 1909 for giving flight instructions to Lts. Frank P. Lahm and Frederic E. Humphreys, and in 1910 it was used by Lt. Benjamin D. Foulois to teach himself how to fly. By March 1911, the airplane was no longer fit for use and was retired. It is now on exhibit at the Smithsonian Institution, Washington D.C.

This modified version of the Wright B Flyer was the first model produced in quantity by the Wright Brothers. It is representative of Signal Corps Aeroplanes No. 3 and No. 4, purchased by the Army in 1911 and used for training pilots and in aerial experiments. At College Park, Maryland, in October 1911, a Wright B was used for the first military trials of a bombsight and bomb-dropping device. The original airplane was equipped with a four-cylinder Wright engine and the Wright's lever control system. *(Information courtesy of the National Museum of the United States Air Force).*

Wright Model B Vin Fiz
(photo courtesy of Wikipedia)

Wright Model B Vin Fiz

The Vin Fiz Flyer was an early Wright Brothers Model EX pusher biplane that in 1911 became the first to cross the North American continent by air. The publisher William Randolph Hearst had offered a US$50,000 prize to the first aviator to fly coast to coast, in either direction, in less than 30 days from start to finish. Calbraith Perry Rodgers, grandnephew of naval hero Oliver Hazard Perry and a risk-taking sort of sportsman, had taken about 90 minutes of instruction from Orville Wright in June 1911 before soloing, and had won an $11,000 air endurance prize in a contest in August.

Rodgers became the first private citizen to buy a Wright airplane; a Wright Model B modified and called the *Model EX*. Since the airplane would need a considerable support crew, Rodgers persuaded J. Ogden Armour, of meatpacking fame, to sponsor the attempt, and in return named the plane after Armour's new grape soft drink Vin Fiz.

The support team rode on a three-car train called the *Vin Fiz Special*, and included Charlie Taylor, the Wright brothers' bicycle shop and aircraft mechanic, who built their first and later engines and knew every detail of Wright airplane construction; Rodgers' wife Mabel; his mother; reporters; and employees of Armour and Vin Fiz.

The flight began at 4:30 pm, 17 September 1911, when Rodgers took off from Sheepshead Bay, New York. Although the plan called for a large number of stops along the way, in the end there were 75, at least a dozen of which were crashes, and Rodgers was injured several times. Taylor and the team of mechanics rebuilt the *Vin Fiz Flyer* when necessary, and only a few pieces of the original plane actually made the entire trip.

On 5 November, having missed the prize deadline by 19 days, Rodgers landed in Pasadena, California, in front of a crowd of 20,000. On the 12th he took off for Long Beach, California, but crashed at Compton, with a brain concussion and a spinal twist. He was hospitalized for three weeks. Finally, on 10 December he landed on the beach, and taxied the *Flyer* into the Pacific Ocean, completing the unprecedented journey of over 4,000 statute miles (6,400 km).

The original aircraft was acquired by the Smithsonian Institution in 1934, and eventually joined the collection of the National Air and Space Museum, after being fully restored for display by the Smithsonian in 1960. As of August 2009, the plane was still on display at the NASM but was undergoing further conservation. Wikipedia.

The Collings Foundation has a replica of the Wright Model B "Vin Fiz" on display at Stow.

Annex B – New England Air National Guard and USAF Units

Maine

The Maine Air National Guard consists of three units. The largest unit is the 101ˢᵗ Air Refueling Wing, which is based at **Bangor International Airport** (the former Dow Air Force Base), operating the Boeing KC-135E Stratotanker. The 101ˢᵗ ARW provides 24 hour air and ground refueling for many aircraft whose destination takes them across the Atlantic.

Additionally, the 243ʳᵈ Engineering and Installation Squadron and 265ᵗʰ Combat Communications Squadron are both based at South Portland, Maine. Maine's former military assets once included Loring Air Force Base and a number of fighter and bomber groups. Wikipedia.

New Hampshire

The New Hampshire Air National Guard consists of the 157ᵗʰ Air Refueling Wing and the 133ʳᵈ Air Refueling Squadron flying the Boeing KC-135R Stratotanker. They are based at **Pease Air National Guard Base**. Wikipedia.

Vermont

The Vermont Air National Guard and the Vermont Army National Guard are collectively known as the *Green Mountain Boys*, although women have been included in both branches since the mid-twentieth century. Both units use the original flag of the Vermont Republic as their banner. Their strength in 2010 was 2,660. The Vermont ANG operates out of **Burlington International Airport**.

The Vermont ANG's 158ᵗʰ Fighter Wing was formed in 1946. From 1989 to 1997, the wing was an Air Defense Unit, with aircraft on 5-minute alert, seven days a week, 24 hours a day.

Other components of the Vermont Air Guard include the 134th Fighter Squadron, 158th Aircraft Generation Squadron, 158th Civil Engineering Squadron, 158th Communications Flight, 158th Logistics Group, 158th Medical Squadron, 158th Operations Group, 158th Operations Support Flight, 158th Student Flight, and the 158th Support Group. The Vermont Air Guard has used the General Dynamics F-16 Fighting Falcon since the late 1980s. Wikipedia.

The Vermont Air National Guard, organized on 1 July 1946, was the fifth Air Guard unit to be formed, and was federally recognized on 14 August 1946. The Air National Guard reorganized in 1949 and the Vermont unit became part of the 101st Fighter Wing in Maine. The Vermont, New Hampshire and Maine units trained as the 101st Fighter Group at Dow Field in Bangor, Maine.

In 1953, the 134th which was operating out of the old airport administration building and the wooden hangar next to it, received its first T-33. This was the beginning of the conversion to the Lockheed F-94 Starfire, an all-weather two seat fighter. The back seat was occupied by a radar observer. The Maine, New Hampshire, and Vermont Air Guard units began holding summer camp at Otis Air Force Base after they began flying F-94s.

The 134th was reorganized as the 158th Fighter Interceptor Group in mid 1960 and was placed under the United States Air Defense Command. The Air Guard now manned alert hangars 24 hours a day, a mission which had previously belonged to the active Air Force. Summer field training was conducted at Otis Air Force Base, Cape Cod, Massachusetts, from 18 June to 2 July. When the unit returned to Burlington, the Maintenance and Operations Squadrons immediately moved into the facilities that had been vacated by the Air Force. The rest of the Group remained on the Williston Road side of the airfield. Military vehicles were allowed to cross the East end of the runway to transport personnel and materials after receiving clearance from the tower. The Vermont Air National Guard received the Operational Readiness award in October 1962, for having the greatest degree of readiness of any F-89 unit in the country.

In 1971 the 158th embarked on an intensive recruiting program that made Vermont one of the top units in the country in total strength. During this period the VT ANG began to actively recruit women into all open career fields.

The 158th Fighter Interceptor Group became the 158th Defense Systems Evaluation Group in June of 1974. The unit received 20 Martin EB-57 Canberras. These two-seat, twin-engine aircraft were equipped with electronic counter-measures and chaff emitting equipment. The new mission was to act as the "friendly enemy" to evaluate both air and ground radar systems. This mission took pilots, electronic warfare officers, and maintenance personnel all over the United States, Canada, and as far as Iceland, Korea, and Japan. The unit provided direct operational training of Air Defense aircrews in the accomplishment of their mission when their systems were severely degraded as might be expected during an attack by enemy offensive aircraft. During this nearly seven-year mission the 158th won the Flying Safety Award, the Aerospace Defense Command "A" Award, and the Outstanding Unit Award.

The 158th began a transition to the McDonnell F-4D Phantom in 1980, a powerful, two seat, two engine fighter. The Vermont Air National Guard left the Air Defense community to become part of the Tactical Air Command with a primary mission of ground attack and close air support.

In June of 1981 the Vermont Air National Guard celebrated its 35th anniversary with an air show that was capped by the final large formation flyby of EB-57s. Beginning in 1982, weekend Unit Training Assemblies often included mobility training to ready the unit for training deployments and potential overseas deployment in case of an emergency. Sorties were usually to Fort Drum, New York to drop practice bombs and strafe ground targets.

The 158th Tactical Fighter Group deployed to Gulfport, MS, in January, 1983 to prepare for the upcoming Operational Readiness Inspection. This was the unit's first large-scale deployment in 23 years. The last deployment had been for summer camp at Otis AFB, MA, in 1960.

On 1 April 1986 the flight line of the Green Mountain Boys changed with the arrival of the General Dynamics F-16 Fighting Falcon. This was the most modern state-of-the-art fighter in the Air Force inventory. The unit became the 158th Fighter Interceptor Group on 1 April 1988 when it officially""stood up" the detachment at Bangor International Airport in Maine. Two F-16s intercepted two Soviet Tupolev Tu-95D Bear bombers over the Atlantic Ocean on 1 March. This intercept brought the total of intercepted aircraft to 31 since the unit's change of mission in April 1988. The 158th hosted Exercise Maple Leaf 90 from 4 to 6 May 1990. Six other Air Guard units and the Canadian Forces (CF) McDonnell CF-188 Hornet unit from Bagotville, Quebec participated.

On 1 June 1992 the USAF Tactical Air Command (TAC) was deactivated and the USAF Air Combat Command (ACC) became the parent command for the 158th. The 158th began converting to F-16Cs in February 1994. Vermont was the first unit to receive the C models which feature more sophisticated radar and electronic components.

From 1989-1997, the Vermont Air National Guard was an Air Defense Unit, having aircraft on 5-minute alert, seven days a week, 24 hours a day. Locations of these alert aircraft included Burlington, Maine, Virginia and South Carolina. Many times Vermont F-16's were called upon to fly to a point just short of Iceland and escort Soviet bombers as they flew off the coastline of the United States. The 158th FW has also assisted with aircraft experiencing in-flight malfunctions and hijackings.

Along with the Air Defense mission, the men and women of "The Green Mountain Boys" have also been tasked seven times to deploy to different locations in Central America to help patrol the skies and intercept aircraft suspected of illegally smuggling drugs. These missions were usually flown far offshore in the middle of the night and required a high degree of proficiency. Along the way, the unit received the newer block 25 version of the F-16, and later still the advanced model of the Pratt & Whitney 220E engine and the newest in missile technology, the AIM-120 AMRAAM (advanced medium range air-to-air missile).

In the fall of 1997, the 158th Fighter Wing was evaluated by the Air Combat Command and was tasked to fight a simulated war from 2 locations, a very challenging undertaking. The 158th Wing deployed 225 personnel and ten F-16s to Canada while the rest of the Wing remained in Burlington for the comprehensive 5-day evaluation. The men and women of "The Green Mountain Boys" received the first rating of "Outstanding" (the highest possible score) ever earned by an Air Defense Unit.

1999 saw the unit convert from a 15 aircraft F-16C/D Air Defense Fighter unit to a 15 aircraft general purpose F-16C/D unit. It also saw the unit terminate its detachment at Charleston AFB, SC (though evidence suggests it might still be active). 2000 saw the 158th deploy in support of Operation Southern Watch as part of Air Expeditionary Force 9. In keeping with a changing world, the 158th Fighter Wing was tasked to convert to a General Purpose mission, which included the requirement to employ not only missiles but also to drop bombs. This conversion, required to be completed locally because of a severe shortage of available Air Force training slots, is almost complete.

In early June 2004, 50 soldiers from the 158th Fighter Wing deployed overseas for periods ranging from 15 days to four months to provide "close air support" of US troops in Iraq, but with most troops based outside of Iraq.

The federal mission of the 158th Fighter Wing is to provide the United States Air Force with combat ready personnel and equipment for utilization during times of war or national emergency. Its state mission is to provide assistance to the State of Vermont for use during local and statewide disasters or emergencies, to protect life, property, and preserve peace, and public safety.

In its 2005 BRAC Recommendations, DoD recommended to realign Atlantic City International Airport AGS, NJ. The 177th Fighter Wing's F-16s would be distributed to the 158th Fighter Wing, Burlington International Airport AGS, VT (three aircraft), and retire (12 aircraft).

Internet: http://www.globalsecurity.org/military/agency/usaf/158fw.htm.

Massachusetts

The Massachusetts Air National Guard is comprised of the 102nd Intelligence Wing, the 104th Fighter Wing flying the McDonnell Douglas F-15C Eagle from **Barnes Air National Guard Base** at Barnes Municipal Airport in Westfield, Massachusetts, and other smaller units. Prior to the Base Realignment and Closure (BRAC) of 2005, the F-15's were based at Otis ANGB located on Cape Cod, and Barnes hosted a squadron of Republic A-10A Thunderbolt II's which were reassigned as part of the restructuring.

Three other units in the state which are part of the 253rd Combat Communications Group include the 212th Engineering Installation Squadron located in Milford, the 267th Combat Communications Squadron located at **Otis Air National Guard Base**, and the Headquarters, which is the 253rd Combat Communications Group, also located at Otis Air National Guard Base. The 253rd Combat Communications Group is composed of seven geographically separated Units, over three States. Wikipedia.

Hanscom Air Force Base is located approximately 2 miles (3.2 km) south-southwest of Bedford, Massachusetts. The facility is a joint use civil airport/military base with Hanscom Field which provides general aviation and charter service. The host unit at Hanscom is the non-flying 66th Air Base Wing (66 ABW) assigned to the Air Force Materiel Command Electronic Systems Center (ESC). The 66 ABW provides services to the ESC; Air Force Reserve; National Guard and Department of Defense civilians who are assigned to the base.

Hanscom Air Force Base is named after Laurence G. Hanscom (1906–1941) in honor of the pilot, aviation enthusiast, and State House reporter for the Worcester Telegram-Gazette who was killed in a plane crash at Saugus, Massachusetts. Hanscom was active in early aviation, founding the Massachusetts Civil Air Reserve, and he had been lobbying for the establishment of an airfield in Bedford just prior to his death. The base was named in his honor on 26 June 1941. Wikipedia.

Rhode Island

The Rhode Island Air National Guard has the 143rd Airlift Wing located at **Quonset State Airport** in North Kingstown, Rhode Island. This air guard unit is the only cargo operator of the Lockheed C-130J Super Hercules in the Northeast.

The 143rd **Airlift Wing** traces its lineage back to 1915, when a group of Rhode Island residents purchased two Curtis Model "F" Flying Boats, one of which was assigned to the state national guard. From 1942 to 1975 the unit performed several varied missions including photo reconnaissance, air defense, re-supply and special operations.

The aircraft assigned included P-47 Thunderbolts, P-51 Mustangs, the SA-16A Albatross, C-47 Skytrain, C-46 Commando, the U-10 Helio Courier, the HU-16 and the C-119G/L Flying Boxcar. Finally coming into its own in 1975, the unit became the 143rd Tactical Airlift Group and was assigned the Lockheed C-130A Hercules aircraft. Wikipedia.

Connecticut

The Connecticut Air National Guard consists of approximately 1,200 airmen and officers assigned to one flying wing and one air control squadron. The 103rd Airlift Wing is based in East Granby at the **Bradley Air National Guard Base** at **Bradley International Airport**. The 103rd AW maintains and operates the Learjet C-21A military transport aircraft. Known as the "Flying Yankees", the 103rd Airlift Wing is the third-oldest Air National Guard unit in the United States with a history dating back to World War I. Until 2008, the organization was known as the 103rd Fighter Wing, operationally-gained by Air Combat Command and equipped with the A-10 Thunderbolt. As a result of Base Realignment and Closure (BRAC) actions, the wing's A-10 fighter aircraft were reassigned to other units and the 103rd re-equipped with Learjet C-21 aircraft as a "placeholder" flying mission under the Air National Guard's VANGUARD program until the 103rd's next flying mission could be determined. Following this change in mission, the unit was redesignated the 103rd Airlift Wing and placed under the operational control of Air Mobility Command (AMC).

The 103rd Air Control Squadron is based at the **Orange Air National Guard Base**. Known as "Yankee Watch", the mission of the 103rd Air Control Squadron is real-time detection, identification and surveillance of air traffic for combat operations and homeland defense. The 103rd ACS is the oldest unit of its kind in the US. Wikipedia.

Annex C – The Collings Foundation

The Collings Foundation is a non-profit, Educational Foundation (501-C3), founded in 1979. The purpose of the Foundation is to organize and support "living history" events that enable Americans to learn more about their heritage through direct participation. The original focus of the Foundation was transportation-related events such as antique car rallies, hill climbs, carriage and sleigh rides, along with a winter ice-cutting festival. During the mid-eighties, these activities were broadened to include aviation-related events such as air shows, barnstorming, historical reunions, and joint museum displays.

Since 1989, a major focus of the Foundation has been the Veterans' "Wings of Freedom Tour." This tour showcases a fully restored WWII Consolidated B-24J Liberator, originally named "All American" in tribute to a B-24J that flew in the European Theater. In 1999, it was re-painted as "Dragon and His Tail" to honor our Pacific Theater veterans. The tour also features the Boeing B-17G Flying Fortress "Nine-O-Nine", the companion of the B-24 in thousands of wartime, bombing, and reconnaissance missions. The "Wings of Freedom Tour" has two goals: to honor our veterans, letting them know they have not been forgotten; and to educate the visitors, especially younger Americans, about the planes and World War II. The Foundation encourages people to tour the planes, talk to the veterans who come to visit the aircraft, and participate in a "flight experience". In 18 years, the tour has made more than 2,172 stops at cities and towns across the lower United States and Alaska. While the exact number of visitors welcomed each year is difficult to gauge, it is estimated that between 3 and 4 million people see these warbirds annually.

The Foundation also operates additional historic aircraft that have made joint appearances with the B-24 and B-17, in addition to solo appearances. These include a 1909 Bleriot XI, Fokker DR-1 Triplane, Boeing PT-17 Stearman, North American AT-6 Texan, Grumman TBM Avenger, Fieseler FI-156 Storch, Cessna UC-78 Bobcat, Chance-Vought F4U-5NL Corsair, Douglas A-26C Invader, North American B-25J Mitchell, Lockheed T-33 Shooting Star, Bell UH-IE "Huey," Douglas TA-4JF, and a Grumman S2-F Tracker. The Foundation continually seeks projects to expand its collection of fully restored and flying aircraft.

The Foundation has restored a McDonnell F-4D Phantom II which appears at air shows and special events as the "Vietnam Memorial Flight". The recently restored Douglas TA-4J will join the F-4D in 2006. A Bell UH-IE helicopter, a veteran of Vietnam, and the Grumman S2-F, will join the F-4D and TA-4 in the future.

From our headquarters in Stow, MA, the Foundation coordinates the "Wings of Freedom" and "Vietnam Memorial" flights, acts as a clearinghouse of information on issues of both aviation and history, along with overseeing the operation of our other aircraft and projects. The Foundation also publishes a newsletter that is sent to more than 46,000 contributors.

The Stow facilities include an aviation museum and a vintage automobile collection, which are open for groups throughout the year. On average, twenty events are hosted annually, many of them fundraising events for non-profit groups. The vintage car collection includes over sixty-six American-built automobiles and vehicles from the first half of the century. Included in the collection are midget, sprint and "Indy" race cars, Frank Duesenberg's personal Duesenberg, along with a Cadillac owned by Al Capone. The aviation museum is home to a number of the Foundation's smaller aircraft, including an original Bleriot XI (1909), 1911 Wright Model B "Vin Fiz" (replica), Fokker DR-1 Triplane (replica), PT-17 Stearman (1942), AT-6 Texan (1945), UC-78 Bobcat (1943), TBM Avenger (1945), Fieseler FI-156 Storch (1943), and a T-33 Shooting Star (1948).

The Foundation also sponsors off-site educational/restoration workshops. Currently, these projects include the restoration of an A-36 Apache, and an A-26C Invader. The New Smyrna Beach, Florida location attends to the B-17's, B-24's, B-25's, and F4U's annual maintenance and has undertaken the total restoration of an A-36 dive-bomber. In Houston, TX the F-4D Phantom, TA-4J Skyhawk and UH-1E Huey are maintained. In Uvalde, Texas, an A-26 Invader is being restored. These workshops provide the Foundation with valuable services and expertise, and the volunteers and veterans provide countless hours of labor and enthusiasm.

The volunteers who support the Foundation's efforts by hosting the aircraft in their towns, maintaining and restoring the planes, educating the American public about the heritage the planes represent, and financially supporting the Foundation's efforts cannot be underestimated. The Foundation's efforts have caught the attention of people of all ages and backgrounds (the youngest volunteer started at age 12). The Foundation also relies upon the volunteer services of a number of pilots, most of whom work for major US-based airlines, who have been certified in the operation of our aircraft.

The Foundation depends solely upon private funding--receiving donations from individual members, as well as the people who visit the aircraft in each city and town. In addition, the Foundation receives on-going corporate support from Aeroquip, Aviation Propeller, Bose Corporation, Champion Spark Plug, General Electric Engine Division, Goodyear, Martin-Baker, OEA Aerospace, Texstars, Gentex, Houston Aircraft Instruments, Wheelen Engineering, and Lockheed Martin. Tax-deductible donations may be sent to the Collings Foundation, Box 248, Stow, MA 01775 and earmarked for any of the above-mentioned aircraft or for the general fund. If there are any questions you'd like answered, please call us at 978-568-8924 or email at info@collingsfoundation.org.

Epilogue

For all those who serve in the defense of North America, particularly since the terrorist attack on the World Trade Center and the Pentagon on 11 September 2001 and for my colleagues who served in Afghanistan in the ongoing war against terrorism, we thank you.

The intention of this book is to record and identify the locations of where at least some those aircraft which have been used in that defense can be found in New England.

Afterword

There is a far better way to protect our homes and our people than to fight and win a great war. The better way is to be so obviously superior in our ability to carry the war to an enemy that he will not take the risk of starting one.

Chief of Staff General Thomas D. White.

Appendix A
New England Warplanes Checklist

Alenia C-27J Spartan

Beechcraft C-45H Expeditor

Bell UH-1B/UH-1D/UH-1E/UH-1H/UH-1M Iroquois

Bell AH-1G/AH-1S Cobra

Bell OH-58D Kiowa

Benson B-8M Gyrocopter

Blanchard Balloon Basket

Blériot X1 Monoplane

Boeing-Stearman PT-17 Kaydet

Boeing B-17G Flying Fortress

Boeing B-29 Superfortress

Boeing KC-135R Stratotanker

Brooks Balloon Basket

Bunce-Curtiss Pusher

Burnelli CBY-3 Loadmaster

Cessna AT-11/T-50/UH-78 Bobcat

Chalais-Meudon Dirigible Nacelle

Chance Vought XF4U-4/Goodyear FG-1D Corsair

Chanute Herring Glider

Classic Fighters Industries Inc Me 262 replica

Consolidated B-24J Liberator

Convair F-102A Delta Dagger

Convair F-106A Delta Dart

Convair C-131D Samaritan

Curtiss Model D replica

Curtiss JN-4D Jenny

Curtiss XF15C-1

Dassault HU-25A Guardian

DeHavilland D.H.100 Vampire

DeHavilland Canada C-7A Caribou

DeHavilland Canada U-6A Beaver

Douglas DC-3-G202A

Douglas C-47 Skytrain

Douglas C-54D-1 Skymaster

Douglas A-26C/B-26B Invader

Douglas F4D-1 Skyray

Douglas A4D-1/A-4F/A-4M/TA-4J Skyhawk

Douglas F3D-2Q Skyknight

Douglas A-3D Skywarrior

Etrich Taube replica

Fairchild-Republic A-10A Thunderbolt II

Fairey Gannet AEW3 Early Warning

Fieseler Fi-156-C1 Storch

Fokker Dr.I Triplane replica

Fokker C.IVa

Fouga CM 170R Magister

Gee Bee Model A

Gee Bee R-1 Supersportster Racer, replica

General Dynamics F-16A Fighting Falcon

Goodyear ZNP-K Airship car

Great Lakes Sportster replica

Grumman TBF/General Motors TBM-3E Avenger

Grumman F6F-5 Hellcat

Grumman HU-16E Albatross

Grumman S2F-1 Tracker

Grumman C-1A Trader

Grumman E-1B Tracer

Grumman OV-1A Mohawk

Grumman A-6E Intruder

Grumman F-14A/B Tomcat

Gyrodyne QH-50 DASH

Hanson-Meyer Quickie

Heath Parasol

Hiller OH-23G Raven

Hughes OH-6A Cayuse

Kaman HH-43A Huskie

Kaman K-16B V-STOL

Kaman K-225

Laird Solution racer

Link ANT-18 Flight Trainer

Learjet C-21A

Ling-Tempco-Vought A-7D Corsair II

Lockheed L-10A Electra

Lockheed L-1649A-98 Starliner

Lockheed T-33A/TV-2 Shooting Star

Lockheed F-94A/F-94C Starfire

Lockheed F-104 Starfighter

Lockheed P2V-7 Neptune

Lockheed P-3A&C Orion

Marcoux-Bromberg Special

Lockheed Martin F-35 Lightning II

Martin RB-57A Canberra

McDonnell F-101B Voodoo

McDonnell-Douglas F-4A/F-4B/F-4D Phantom II

McDonnell Douglas F-15A Eagle

McDonnell-Douglas AV-8B Harrier

Mead Rhone Ranger replica

Mikoyan-Gurevich MiG-15 Fagot

Mikoyan-Gurevich MiG-17F Fresco C

Monerai "S"

Mosquito 166 Hang Glider

Nick's Special LR-1A

Nieuport 28 replica

Nixon Special (1918 homebuilt)

North American AT-6D/AT-6F/SNJ-5 Texan

North American A-36A Apache

North American B-25N Mitchell

North American P-51C/P-51D Mustang

North American F-86H Sabre

North American F-100A/F-100D Super Sabre

North American T-28A/T-28B/T-28D Trojan

North American AGM-28B Hound Dog Missile

Northrop F-89J Scorpion

Piasecki/Vertol H-21 Workhorse

Pioneer Flightstar Ultralight

Piper J-3C Cub/L4 Grasshopper

Pratt-Read LNE-1

Rearwin Cloudster

Republic JB-2 Loon (V-1 Buzz Bomb copy)

Republic P-47D Thunderbolt

Republic F-105B Thunderchief

Republic RC-3 Seabee amphibian

Royal Aircraft Factory F.E.8 replica

Royal Aircraft Factory S.E.5a replica

Rutan Vari-EZ

Sikorsky S-16 replica

Sikorsky S-39B Amphibian

Sikorsky VS-44-A Flying Boat

Sikorsky R-4B Hoverfly Helicopter

Sikorsky R-6 Doman conversion Helicopter

Sikorsky LH-34D Seabat Helicopter

Sikorsky S-51 Dragonfly Helicopter

Sikorsky SH-3H Sea King

Sikorsky HH-52A Sea Guard Helicopter

Sikorsky CH-54B Skycrane Helicopter

Sikorsky UH-60 Blackhawk Helicopter

Sikorsky HH-60J Jayhawk Helicopter

Sopwith Pup replica

SPAD XIII replica

Standard J-1

Stinson 10A

SUD Caravelle VIR Airliner

Viking Kittyhawk B-8

Vought OS2U-2 Kingfisher

WACO YKC-S

Wright Flyer replica

Wright Model B Vin Fiz replica

Zephyr Zal

Appendix B
New England Aviation Historical Societies

Maine

The Maine Aviation Historical Society, P.O. Box 2641, 98 Maine Avenue, Bangor, Maine 04401. Telephone: 207-941-6757. Email: les@maine.edu.

Website: http://www.maineairmuseum.org.

Aviation Archaeology in Maine. Website: http://www.mewreckchasers.com.

Between 1919 and 1989, there were 741 military aircraft involved in accidents in the State of Maine. There have been 245 American, Canadian and British Commonwealth aircrew that lost their lives in Maine forests, fields, and waters. Several hundred more were injured.

A small group of New England amateur Aviation Archaeologists, affectionately known to our peers as *wreckchasers*, are working to preserve these stories for future generations. This involves collecting written and photographic records of the incidents, interviewing witnesses, and working with landowners to preserve historic crash sites. Modern logging practices have made many remotes sites accessible and souvenir hunters have taken their toll on them. Visiting the crash site, for us, is just an important part of recording and telling the story.

History that is forgotten is not history at all. We find that many incidents have been largely forgotten by traditional historians and local historical societies. Our hope is to increase awareness of the stories of the men who died training, ferrying, and defending in the skies over the state of Maine. Pete Noddin.

New Hampshire

The New Hampshire Aviation Historical Society, PO Box 3653, Concord, NH 03302-3653. Telephone: 603-669-4820. Email: nhahs@nhahs.org.

Website: http://www.nhahs.org.

Vermont

The Vermont Historical Society, Montpelier, VT.

Massachusetts

The Massachusetts Aviation Historical Society, PO Box 457, Wakefield MA 01880-0957. Telephone: 781-662-1253. Email: info@massaerohistory.org.

Website: http://www.massaerohistory.org.

Rhode Island

The Rhode Island Aviation Hall of Fame, PO Box 845, North Kingstown, RI 02852. Aero Club of New England, Civil Air Patrol, Rhode Island Wing, EAA Chapter 1363/Ocean State Aviators, EAA Warbirds of America/Squadron 7, New England Air Museum, Ninety-Nines, New England Chapter, Quiet Birdmen, Quonset Air Museum, Rhode Island Air Guard, Rhode Island Airport Corporation, Rhode Island Army National Guard, Rhode Island Aviation and Space Education Council, Rhode Island Historical Society, Rhode Island Pilots Association, USS Saratoga Museum Foundation.

Connecticut

The Connecticut Aviation Historical Association operates the New England Air Museum. Located at Bradley International Airport in Windsor Locks, the Museum is the largest aviation museum in New England. This educational organization is dedicated to preserving and presenting historically significant aircraft and related artifacts, engaging visitors through high-quality exhibits helping them to understand aviation technology and history and inspiring students through innovative and hands-on educational programs. Website: www.neam.org.

Bibliography

BLAUGHER, Michael A. *Guide to Over 900 Aircraft Museums, USA and Canada, 25th Edition.* (Blaugher, Fort Wayne, Indiana, 2009).

BOYNE, Walter J. *Beyond the Wild Blue, A History of the United States Air Force 1947-1997.* New York, St. Martin's Press, 1997.

CRAVEN, Wesley F., and CATE, James L. *The Army Air Forces in World War II, Vol. I: Plans and Early Operations, January 1939 to August 1942; Vol. II: Europe: Torch to Pointblank, August 1942 to December 1943; Vol. III: Europe: Argument to V-E Day, January 1944 to May 1945; Vol. IV: The Pacific: Guadalcanal to Saipan, August 1942 to July 1944; Vol. V: The Pacific: Matterhorn to Nagasaki, June 1944 to August 1945; Vol VI: Men and Planes; Vol. VII: Services Around the World.* (University of Chicago Press, 1948-1958). Reprinted for the Air Force History and Museums Program, 1983.

DONALD, David, General Editor. *(The Complete Encyclopedia of World Aircraft). The development and specifications of over 2500 civil and military aircraft from 1903 to the present day.* (New York, Barnes & Noble Books, 1999).

EVINGER, William R. Editor, *Directory of US Military Bases Worldwide, Third Edition,* Oryx Press, 1998.

FREEMAN, Roger A. *The Mighty Eighth, Units, Men and Machines (A History of the US 8th Army Air Force).* (New York, Doubleday and Company, Inc., Garden City, 1970).

FUTRELL, Robert F. *The United States Air Force in Korea, 1950-1953.* (Duell, Sloan and Pearce, revised 1983, 1991).

HAGGERTY, James J. and Smith, Warren Reiland. *The US Air Force: A Pictorial History in Art.* (New York, Books, Inc., Publishers, 1966).

HALLION, Richard P. *Storm Over Iraq, Air power and the Gulf War.* (Air Force Historian, 1992).

HIGHAM, Robin, Editor. *Flying American Combat Aircraft of World War II 1939-1945.* (Mechanicsburg, Pennsylvania, Stackpole Books, 2004).

KAUFMAN, Daniel J., B.Sc., M.P.A., Ph.D. *Understanding International Relations* and *US National Security Strategy for the 1990s.*

MAURER, Maurer, (General Editor). *The US Air Service in World War 1. Vol. I: The Final Report of the Chief of Air Service AEF and a tactical History; Vol. II: Early Concepts of Military Aviation; Vol. III: The Battle of St. Mihel; Vol. IV: Postwar Review.* (Air Force History and Museums Program, 1978, 1979).

NALTY, Bernard C. *Winged Shield, Winged Sword, A History of the United States Air Force.* (Air Force History and Museums Program, USAF, Washington, D.C. 1997).

TICKNOR, Caroline, Editor; LOWELL, A. Lawrence, Introduction. *New England Aviators 1914-1918, Their Portraits and Their Records, Vol 1 & Vol 2 (1919).* (Boston, New York, Houghton Mifflin Co., 1919); reprinted by Kessinger Publishing, 2009.

PARK, Edwards. *Fighters, The World's Great Aces and Their Planes.* (New York, Barnes & Noble Books, 1990).

SKAARUP, Harold A. *Siegecraft – No Fortress Impregnable.* (Lincoln, Nebraska, iUniverse. com, 2003).

SKAARUP, Harold A. *Out of Darkness – Light, a History of Canadian Military Intelligence, Volume 1, Pre-Confederation to 1982.* (Lincoln, Nebraska, iUniverse.com, 2005).

SKAARUP, Harold A. *Out of Darkness – Light, a History of Canadian Military Intelligence, Volume 2, 1983-1997.* (Lincoln, Nebraska, iUniverse.com, 2005).

SKAARUP, Harold A. *Out of Darkness – Light, a History of Canadian Military Intelligence, Volume 3, 1998-2005.* (Lincoln, Nebraska, iUniverse.com, 2005).

SKAARUP, Harold A. *Canadian MiG Flights.* (Bloomington, Indiana, iUniverse.com, 2008).

SKAARUP, Harold A. *RCAF War Prize Flights, German and Japanese Warplane Survivors.* (Lincoln, Nebraska, iUniverse.com, 2006).

SKAARUP, Harold A. *Canadian Warbird & War Prize Survivors.* (Lincoln, Nebraska, iUniverse.com, 2005).

SKAARUP, Harold A. *Canadian Warbird Survivors.* (Lincoln, Nebraska, iUniverse.com, 2005).

SKAARUP, Harold A. *Canadian Warplanes.* ((Bloomington, Indiana, iUniverse.com, 2009).

SKAARUP, Harold A. *Canadian Warbirds of the Bi-Plane Era - Fighters, Bombers and Patrol Aircraft.* (Lincoln, Nebraska, iUniverse.com, 2001).

SKAARUP, Harold A. *Canadian Warbirds of the Bi-Plane Era - Trainers, Transports and Utility Aircraft.* (Lincoln, Nebraska, iUniverse.com, 2001).

SKAARUP, Harold A. *Canadian Warbirds of the Second World War - Fighters, Bombers and Patrol Aircraft.* (Lincoln, Nebraska, iUniverse.com, 2001).

SKAARUP, Harold A. *Canadian Warbirds of the Second World War - Trainers, Transports and Utility Aircraft.* (Lincoln, Nebraska, iUniverse.com, 2001).

SKAARUP, Harold A. *Canadian Warbirds of the Post-War Piston Era.* (Lincoln, Nebraska, iUniverse.com, 2001).

SKAARUP, Harold A. *Canadian Warbirds – Jets and Helicopters.* (Lincoln, Nebraska, iUniverse.com, 2001).

SKAARUP, Harold A. *Canadian Warplanes.* ((Bloomington, Indiana, iUniverse.com, 2009).

SKAARUP, Harold A. *Alabama Warbird Survivors 2003 - a Handbook on where to find them.* (Lincoln, Nebraska, iUniverse.com, 2002).

SKAARUP, Harold A. *Alaska Warbird Survivors 2002 - a Handbook on where to find them.* (Lincoln, Nebraska, iUniverse.com, 2002).

SKAARUP, Harold A. *Arizona Warbird Survivors 2002 - a Handbook on where to find them.* (Lincoln, Nebraska, iUniverse.com, 2002).

SKAARUP, Harold A. *Arizona Warplanes.* ((Bloomington, Indiana, iUniverse.com, 2010).

SKAARUP, Harold A. *California Warbird Survivors 2002 - a Handbook on where to find them.* (Lincoln, Nebraska, iUniverse.com, 2002).

SKAARUP, Harold A. *Colorado Warbird Survivors 2001 - a Handbook on where to find them.* (Lincoln, Nebraska, iUniverse.com, 2001).

SKAARUP, Harold A. *Colorado Warbird Survivors 2003 - a Handbook on where to find them.* (Lincoln, Nebraska, iUniverse.com, 2003).

SKAARUP, Harold A. *New England Warbird Survivors 2002 - a Handbook on where to find them.* (Lincoln, Nebraska, iUniverse.com, 2002).

SKAARUP, Harold A. *Hawaii Warbird Survivors 2002 - a Handbook on where to find them.* (Lincoln, Nebraska, iUniverse.com, 2002).

SKAARUP, Harold A. *Maryland, Virginia & Washington DC Warbird Survivors 2003 - a Handbook on where to find them.* (Lincoln, Nebraska, iUniverse.com, 2003).

SKAARUP, Harold A. *Nebraska Warbird Survivors 2002 - a Handbook on where to find them.* (Lincoln, Nebraska, iUniverse.com, 2002).

SKAARUP, Harold A. *Nevada Warbird Survivors 2002 - a Handbook on where to find them.* (Lincoln, Nebraska, iUniverse.com, 2002).

SKAARUP, Harold A. *New Mexico Warbird Survivors 2002 - a Handbook on where to find them.* (Lincoln, Nebraska, iUniverse.com, 2002).

SKAARUP, Harold A. *Ohio Warbird Survivors 2003 - a Handbook on where to find them.* (Lincoln, Nebraska, iUniverse.com, 2003).

SKAARUP, Harold A. *Oregon Warbird Survivors 2003 - a Handbook on where to find them.* (Lincoln, Nebraska, iUniverse.com, 2003).

SKAARUP, Harold A. *Texas Warbird Survivors 2003 - a Handbook on where to find them.* (Lincoln, Nebraska, iUniverse.com, 2003).

SKAARUP Harold A. *Washington Warbird Survivors 2002 - a Handbook on where to find them.* (Lincoln, Nebraska, iUniverse.com, 2002).

SKAARUP, Harold A. *Wyoming Warbird Survivors 2003 - a Handbook on where to find them.* (Lincoln, Nebraska, iUniverse.com, 2003).

SKAARUP, Harold A. *Ticonderoga Soldier – Elijah Estabrooks, 1758-1760.* (Lincoln, Nebraska, iUniverse.com, 2000).

SKAARUP, Harold A. *Whiz Bangs and Woolly Bears - Walter Ray Estabrooks and the Great War.* (Lincoln, Nebraska, iUniverse.com, 2000).

SKAARUP, Harold A. *New Brunswick Hussar.* (Lincoln, Nebraska, iUniverse.com, 2001).

SKAARUP, Harold A. *Visitors – Questions and Answers.* (Lincoln, Nebraska, iUniverse.com, 2000).

SKAARUP, Harold A. *Dream Seer – Old Wisdoms.* (Lincoln, Nebraska, iUniverse.com, 2000).

SKAARUP, Harold A. *Dream Seeker – Old Wisdoms Revisited.* (Lincoln, Nebraska, iUniverse.com, 2002).

STEMM, James, Editor. *The Pima Air & Space Museum.* Sponsored by Count Ferdinand von Galen, (Tucson, Arizona, The Aerospace Foundation, 2008).

About the Author

Major Harold (Hal) Aage Skaarup was born in Woodstock, New Brunswick, 8 August 1951. He joined the Canadian Forces Reserve Force in Feb 1971, being taken on strength with 56 Field Squadron, Royal Canadian Engineers, in St. John's, Newfoundland. In September 1971 he transferred to 723 Communications Squadron in Halifax, Nova Scotia while attending the Nova Scotia College of Art & Design (NSCAD) where he graduated with a Bachelor's degree in Fine Arts in 1974. He was enrolled as a Reserve Officer University Training Plan cadet in the fall 1972 with the HQ Militia Area Atlantic Intelligence Section. From 1977 to 1979 he was a member of the Canadian Forces Parachute Team (Skyhawks) in Edmonton. From 1979 to 1981 he was a member and Acting Officer Commanding the HQ Northern Alberta Militia District Intelligence Section, while working for an Aerial Survey firm. Between 1981 and 1983 he was on Class C Reserve service as the SO3 Intelligence at HQ CF Europe in Lahr, Germany.

In July1983, he transferred to the Regular Force and attended the Basic Intelligence Officer's Course at the Canadian Forces School of Intelligence and Security (CFSIS) at CFB Borden, Ontario, where he later served as an instructor. In March 1984 he was posted to Ottawa, where he was an Attaché trainer and Intelligence Analyst for the Director of Defence Intelligence at Tunney's Pasture. From 1986 to 1989, he served as the Regimental Intelligence Officer for the Canadian Airborne Regiment based at CFB Petawawa, Ontario, and took part in a 7-month United Nations deployment to Cyprus from August 1986 to February 1987. During his airborne service, he attended the Canadian Forces Staff School in Toronto and Army Staff College in Kingston, Ontario. He also took courses in Electronic Warfare and Psychological Operations in the UK. In June 1989 he was posted to the 4 Canadian Mechanized Brigade Group HQ and Signals Squadron based in Lahr, Germany, where he served three years as the G2 Operations. During his second tour in Germany he participated in Arms Verification Control tasks in Germany and Iceland, and took courses in Advanced Electronic Warfare in Germany, and Interrogation in the UK.

In 1992 Captain Skaarup was posted to back to CFSIS, where he served as an Instructor, and on promotion to Major in 1993, became the Officer Commanding the Intelligence Training Company, and later the Officer Commanding the Distance Learning Company. In 1994, he was posted to the Tactics School in the Combat Training Centre at CFB Gagetown, New Brunswick, where he served as the Intelligence Directing Staff Officer and Base G2. In May 1997, he was awarded his Master 's degree in War Studies at the Royal Military College (RMC) in Kingston, Ontario. From 23 June to 30 December 1997, Major Skaarup served as the CO of the Canadian

Harold Skaarup

National Intelligence Centre (CANIC) with the NATO-led Peace Stabilization Force (SFOR) in Bosnia-Herzegovina.

From 1998 to 1999 he attended the Land Forces Technical Staff Officer's Course at RMC, and following completion of the course, he was posted to the J2 Exercise Section at North American Aerospace Defence (NORAD) HQ in Colorado Springs, Colorado. In 2003, Major Skaarup was posted to Land Forces Atlantic Area (LFAA) in Halifax as the area G2. From January to July 2004, he served as the Deputy G2 and Chief Assessments on the staff of the Kabul Multinational Brigade (KMNB), International Security Assistance Force (ISAF), in Kabul, Afghanistan, returning to LFAA in August 2004. In 2006 he was posted to 3 Area Support Group, CFB Gagetown, where he serves as the Base Commander's G2 Intelligence Advisor. Hal is married to Faye and they have two sons, Jonathan and Sean. Their home is in Fredericton, New Brunswick.

Index

1

100th Bomb Wing24

101st Air Refueling Wing17, 143

101st Fighter Wing144

102nd Fighter Wing29

103rd Airlift Wing44, 45, 147

104th Fighter Wing32, 73, 146

112th Medical Company (Air Ambulance)16, 135

133rd Air Refueling Squadron143

134th Fighter Squadron143

143rd Airlift Wing147

157th Air Refueling Wing143

158th Fighter Wing25, 78, 143, 145, 146

177th Fighter Wing146

5

57th Fighter Group39, 43

6

64th Bomb Squadron26, 58

66th Air Base Wing146

A

Aero Commander 68033

Aero L-29 Delphin33

Aeronca 50 Chief40

Afghanistan14, 151, 165

Alenia C-27J Spartan45

Antonov AN-2TD Colt33

Army Historical Foundation10

Auburn-Lewiston Municipal16

B

Bangor International Airport17, 143, 145

Barnes Air National Guard Base146

Barnes Municipal Airport93, 146

Battleship Cove Heritage Park29

Beechcraft C-45H Expeditor25

Beechcraft UC-45H Expeditor45

Bell 47D Sioux40

Bell AH-1 Cobra29, 30, 32, 36

Bell AH-1G Cobra39, 40, 47

Bell AH-1S Cobra34

Bell H-13E Sioux26

Bell OH-58 Kiowa34, 47

Bell TAH-1F Cobra38

Bell UH-1 Iroquois16, 17, 18, 20, 26, 27, 29, 31, 33, 40, 46

Benson B-8M Gyrocopter40

Blériot XI6, 19, 31, 40, 48

Boeing B-17G Flying Fortress31, 49, 149

Boeing B-29 Superfortress26, 40, 50

Boeing CH-47 Chinook39

Boeing KC-135R Stratotanker17, 51, 143

Boeing-Stearman PT-17 Kaydet19, 30, 31, 40, 48

Bosnia-Herzegovina14

Bradley Air National Guard Base147

Bradley International Airport39, 44, 147, 159

Bunce-Curtiss Pusher40, 52

Bureau of Aeronautics11

Burlington International Airport143

Burnelli CBY-3 Loadmaster40, 52

C

Cessna AT-17 Bobcat31, 53

Cessna T-37B Tweet34, 53

Chance Vought F4U Corsair31, 36, 40, 54

Cole Land Transportation Museum16

Collings Foundation5, 8, 10, 31, 48, 49, 50, 53, 55, 57, 58, 69, 73, 74, 79, 80, 103, 104, 105, 106, 113, 114, 116, 142, 149, 150

Connecticut10, 13, 35, 37, 39, 44, 52, 53, 79, 90, 118, 129, 130, 139, 147, 159

Connecticut Air National Guard147

Connecticut Aviation Historical Association159

Consolidated B-24J Liberator8, 31, 57, 149

Convair C-131D Samaritan25, 60

Convair F-102A Delta Dagger25, 58

Convair F-106A Delta Dart59

Convair GF-102A Delta Dagger44

Curtis XFC15-140

Curtiss C-46A Commando25

Curtiss JN-4D Jenny19, 61

Curtiss Model D19

Curtiss Wright Jr CW118, 30

Curtiss XF15C-134, 62

Curtiss-Robertson Robin21

Cyprus14

D

Dassault HU-25A Guardian28, 63

DeHavilland Canada C7A Caribou64

DeHavilland Canada C-7A Caribou40

DeHavilland Canada DHC-2/U-6A Beaver40

DeHavilland Canada U6A Beaver64

DeHavilland D.H.100 Vampire34, 63

Douglas A-26B Invader38

Douglas A-26C Invader31, 40, 66, 149

Douglas A-3B Skywarrior40, 71

Douglas A-4C Skyhawk34

Harold Skaarup

Douglas A4D-1 Skyhawk40, 68

Douglas A-4F Skyhawk34

Douglas B-26B Invader24

Douglas C-47 Skytrain23, 25, 30, 65

Douglas C-54D Skymaster23, 65

Douglas DC-318, 23, 36, 39, 40, 43, 65

Douglas F3D-2 Skyknight34, 70

Douglas F4D-1 Skyray31, 67

Douglas F-6 Skyray40

E

Etrich Taube19, 72

F

Fairchild-Republic A-10A Thunderbolt II32, 40, 44

Fieseler Fi-156-C1 Storch31

Fokker C.IVA19, 74

Fokker Dr.I19, 31, 40, 74

Fouga CM 170R Magister27, 34, 75

G

Gee Bee Model A40, 76

Gee Bee Model E40

Gee Bee R-1 Super Sportster40

Gee Bee R1 Supersportster76

General Dynamics F-16A Fighting Falcon25, 78

General Motors TBM-3E Avenger24, 31, 34, 36, 78

Goodyear FG-1D Corsair36

Goodyear ZNP-K Airship41, 77

Great Lakes 2T-1A Sportster41

Grumman A-6B Intruder86

Grumman A-6E Intruder34

Grumman C-1A Trader22, 34, 83

Grumman E-1B Tracer41, 84

Grumman F-14A Tomcat87

Grumman F-14B Tomcat34, 41, 88

Grumman F6F-3 Hellcat80

Grumman F6F-5 Hellcat34, 41, 80, 81

Grumman HU-16E Albatross28, 41, 81, 82

Grumman OV-1A Mohawk23, 84

Grumman S2F-1 Tracker31

Grumman S2F-3 Tracker82

Grumman TBF-1 Avenger78

Gyrodyne QH-50 DASH41, 88

H

Hanscom Air Force Base146

Henri Farman III19

Hiller OH-23G Raven41, 89, 90

Hughes OH-6A Cayuse26, 27, 34, 41, 90

K

Kabul165

Kaman HH-43A Huskie41, 90

Kaman K-16B41, 91

Kaman K-22541, 92

L

Laird LC-RW300 Solution41

Learjet C-21A92, 147

Ling-Tempco-Vought A-7D Corsair II34, 41, 68, 93, 118

Link ANT-18 Flight Trainer41

Lockheed C-130J Super Hercules147

Lockheed F-104A Starfighter41, 95

Lockheed F-94A Starfire25

Lockheed F-94C Starfire41, 95

Lockheed L-10A Electra41, 93

Lockheed L-1649A-98 Starliner94

Lockheed Martin C-130J Super Hercules45, 98

Lockheed Martin F-35 Lightning II25, 99

Lockheed P-2E Neptune34

Lockheed P2V-7 Neptune18, 96, 97

Lockheed P-3A Orion18, 98

Lockheed P-3C Orion18, 97

Lockheed T-33A Shooting Star25, 29, 32, 34, 94

Lockheed TV-2 Shooting Star34, 41, 95

M

Maine10, 13, 14, 16, 20, 74, 79, 127, 135, 137, 143, 144, 158

Maine Air Museum10, 17

Maine Air National Guard143

Maine Aviation Historical Society17, 158

Manchester Army Air Base22

Marcoux-Bromberg R-3 Special41

Martin EB-57 Canberra144

Martin EB-57B Night Intruder25

Martin RB-57A Canberra41, 101

Massachusetts10, 13, 14, 28, 29, 35, 39, 58, 59, 72, 73, 76, 81, 82, 93, 140, 146, 147, 158

Massachusetts Air National Guard146

Massachusetts Aviation Historical Society159

Massachusetts Military Reservation28

McDonnell CF-101B Voodoo17

McDonnell Douglas A-4M Skyhawk34

McDonnell Douglas AV-8B Harriers107

McDonnell Douglas AV-8C Harrier34, 109

McDonnell Douglas F-15A Eagle29, 106

McDonnell Douglas F-15C Eagle146

McDonnell Douglas F-4D Phantom32

McDonnell Douglas TA-4J Skyhawk32

McDonnell F-101B Voodoo17, 102

McDonnell F-4A Phantom II34

McDonnell F-4B Phantom II34

McDonnell F-4D Phantom II25, 26, 103, 149

McDonnell-Douglas F-4D Phantom II41

Messerschmitt Me 26231, 55

Mikoyan-Gurevich MiG-15 Fagot34, 41, 109

Mikoyan-Gurevich MiG-17F Fresco C34, 110

Miller Zeta30

Monett Monerai S sailplane41

Museum of Science28

N

National Helicopter Museum38

National Museum of Naval Aviation10, 11, 47, 53, 55, 61, 62, 67, 69, 71, 72, 79, 80, 82, 83, 84, 87, 88, 89, 96, 97, 98, 105, 109, 111, 112, 120, 131, 132, 133, 140

National Museum of the Marine Corps10

National Museum of the United States Air Force10, 11, 46, 49, 51, 52, 57, 59, 60, 61, 65, 67, 73, 74, 78, 82, 86, 91, 93, 95, 96, 102, 103, 104, 107, 110, 111, 112, 113, 119, 120, 121, 123, 124, 125, 130, 138, 141

Naval Air Station Brunswick17, 18, 97, 98

New England Air Museum10, 39, 47, 48, 51, 52, 53, 54, 64, 67, 68, 71, 74, 76, 80, 82, 84, 87, 88, 89, 90, 92, 93, 94, 95, 101, 109, 114, 116, 117, 118, 123, 128, 129, 130, 134, 139, 159

New Hampshire10, 13, 20, 51, 92, 114, 143, 144, 158

New Hampshire Air National Guard143

New Hampshire Aviation Historical Society158

New Hampshire Aviation Museum21

Nicks Special LR-1A41

Nieuport 2819, 110, 111

North American A-36A Apache32, 112, 113

North American Aerospace Command11

North American AGM-28 Hound Dog Missile18, 20, 41, 120

North American AT-6 Texan27, 111, 149

North American AT-6D Texan27

North American AT-6F Texan24, 32

North American AT-6G Texan27, 37

North American B-25H Mitchell41, 114, 116

North American B-25J Mitchell114, 149

North American F-100A Super Sabre42

North American F-100D Super Sabre30, 32, 44, 118

North American F-86F Sabre41

North American F-86H Sabre27, 29, 117

North American P-51C Mustang24, 113

North American P-51D Mustang21, 23, 114

North American SNJ-5 Texan28, 30, 33, 35, 37

North American T-28 Trojan29

North American T-28B Trojan22, 24, 119

North American T-28S Fennec34

North American T-6G Texan27, 35

Northern Command3, 11

Northrop F-89D Scorpion25

Northrop F-89J Scorpion17, 42, 120

Northrop T-38A Talon34, 121

O

Orange Air National Guard Base147

Otis Air National Guard Base146

Owls Head Transportation Museum19, 72, 74, 111, 127

P

Pease Air National Guard Base143

Piasecki/Vertol CH-21C Shawnee34, 121

Piper J-3 Cub19, 122

Piper J3L-65 Cub42

Portsmouth Municipal Airport23

Q

Quonset Air Museum10, 33, 62, 64, 71, 79, 81, 84, 87, 88, 90, 93, 109, 110, 133, 159

Quonset State Airport147

R

RCAF9, 11, 49, 102, 161

Rearwin 8135 Cloudster42

Republic A-10A Thunderbolt II146

Republic F-105B Thunderchief42, 124

Republic F-84F Thunderstreak30, 32, 124

Republic JB-2 Loon42, 123

Republic P-47D Thunderbolt42, 123

Republic RC-3 Seabee42, 125

Rhode Island10, 13, 33, 35, 81, 98, 147, 159

Rhode Island Air National Guard147

Rhode Island Aviation Hall of Fame159

Rhode Island Historical Society159

Royal Aircraft Factory F.E.819, 126

Royal Aircraft Factory S.E.5a19, 26, 127, 128

Royal Canadian Air Force11, 102, 122

S

Sikorsky CH-54 Tarhe42, 79, 134

Sikorsky H-1932

Sikorsky HH-52A Sea Guard42, 133

Sikorsky HH-60J Jayhawk28, 135

Sikorsky LH-34D Seabat42

Sikorsky R-4B Hoverfly42, 129

Sikorsky R-536

Sikorsky R-642, 130

Sikorsky S-1642, 128

Sikorsky S-39B42, 128

Sikorsky S-5142

Sikorsky S-51 Dragonfly131

Sikorsky S-7639

Sikorsky SH-3H Sea King35, 132

Sikorsky UH-34D Seabat131

Sikorsky UH-60 Blackhawk134

Sikorsky VS-44-A42, 129

Sopwith Pup19, 135, 136, 137

SPAD XIII19, 110, 138

Sputnik I20

Standard J-119, 138

Stinson 10A42

Stinson L-9B Voyager35

Strategic Air Command11, 51, 102, 120

SUD Aviation SE 210 Caravelle VIR42, 139

T

Tupolev Tu-95D Bear145

Harold Skaarup

U

United States Air Force Academy10, 11

United States Army9, 45, 48, 49, 74, 111, 115, 116, 126, 134

United States Army Air Corps9, 11, 49, 116, 126

United States Army Air Force9, 11, 130

United States Coast Guard9, 11, 63, 135

United States Coast Guard Museum10

United States Marine Corps9, 11, 47, 101, 107

United States Navy9, 12, 62, 88, 101, 103, 111, 115, 130, 135

United States Space Command12

USS *Massachusetts*29

USS *Nautilus*36, 37

V

Vermont10, 13, 26, 61, 78, 99, 128, 143, 144, 145, 158

Vermont Air National Guard143

Vermont Historical Society158

Vermont Militia Museum26

Viking Kittyhawk B-842

Vought OS2U-2 Kingfisher29

Vought-Sikorsky OS2U-2 Kingfisher139

W

Waco UBF-219

Waco YKC-S42, 140

Wright Flyer19, 141

Wright Model B Vin Fiz32, 141, 142, 150

Wright Museum of WWII History24